the best of
newspaper
design

contents

	Introduction	3
	Foreword	4
1	Best of Show	5
2	Overall design	21
3	News	29
4	Features	65
5	Magazines	103
6	Special Sections	133
7	Design Portfolios	153
8	Photojournalism	175
9	Illustration	203
10	Informational Graphics	237
11	Miscellaneous	253
	Judges	265
	Index of Winners	268

fifteenth edition

The Society of Newspaper Design
The Newspaper Center • Box 4075 • Reston, VA 22090

Judging takes place at The S.I. Newhouse School of Public Communications • Syracuse University

FIRST PUBLISHED IN THE U.S.A. BY ROCKPORT PUBLISHERS, INC.

1994 SND OFFICERS

President
George Benge
Muskogee (OK) Daily Phoenix

First Vice President
Deborah Withey
Detroit Free Press

Second Vice President
Jim Jennings
Thomson Regional Newspapers (UK)

Treasurer
Neal Pattison
Albuquerque Tribune

Secretary
Lynn Staley
Boston Globe

Past President
Nancy Tobin
The (Albany, NY) Times Union

The Society of Newspaper Design
Executive Director
Ray Chattman

BOOK CREDITS

Editor
C. Marshall Matlock
S.I. Newhouse School of Public Communications
Syracuse University

Design
Michael Jantze, The Times-Picayune
Beth Aguillard, The Times-Picayune
Denise Brady, The Times-Picayune

Layout
Shamus Walker, Syracuse

Cover photos
Kim D. Johnson, The Times-Picayune

Judges' photos
Kurt Mutchler, The Times-Picayune
Scott Sines, Spokane Spokesman-Review

Reproduction photos
Bob Malish, Coppell, TX

SPECIAL THANKS

The S.I. Newhouse School of Public Communications
Syracuse University

The Times-Picayune

The Society of Newspaper Design
The Newspaper Center
Box 4075
Reston, VA 22090

First published in the United States of America by:
Rockport Publishers, Inc.
146 Granite Street
Rockport, MA 01966
Telephone: 508/546-9590
Fax: 508/546-7141
Telex: 5106019284 ROCKORT PUB

Distributed to the book trade and art trade in the U.S. and Canada by:
North Light, an imprint of F&W Publications
1507 Dana Avenue
Cincinnati, OH 45207
Telephone: 513/531-2222

Other distribution by:
Rockport Publishers, Inc.
Rockport, MA 01966

ISBN 1-56496-149-4 (Hardcover edition)
ISBN 1-878107-04-6 (Softcover edition)

10 9 8 7 6 5 4 3 2 1

Printed in Hong Kong by Regent Publishing

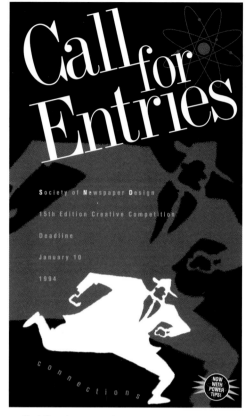

Ch-ch-ch-changes. Two years ago Randy Stano, then president of SND, called and asked if I was interested in helping with the SND judging. I told him I was. As the 15th Edition Coordinator, I was also interested in change. Not that anything was broke; I guess I just like to meddle.

Changes started by introducing the Call for Entries as a reference book instead of a poster. The contest had grown up and brought all of its baggage with it. Perhaps this change is the reason we had fewer telephone calls with less people asking questions than the two previous years. Either that or now they couldn't even find the phone numbers.

Selecting judges was another area of concern. I wanted to balance the roster with new faces from a variety of backgrounds and experiences. The competition is now an international one, and the Committee went to great pains to reflect that. I am certain next year will be an even stronger leap.

Change also surfaced in the 72 hours of judging in February. After the 16 judges had looked at nearly 9,400 entries, 987 winners were selected including four Judges' Special Recognitions and two Best of Shows which were given for work with one common thread: simplicity with perspective. As newspapers have labored in the past decade to reinvent themselves, the judges recognized these winners for their strength to make changes but not forget their readers. The two Best of Shows from The Philadelphia Inquirer Magazine and Le Devoir reflect that type of commitment. This is certainly one of the good things about the '90s.

Let's roll the credits. The judging was cosponsored by the S.I. Newhouse School of Public Communications at Syracuse University, Syracuse, NY. Marshall Matlock was again available to perform miracles throughout the process, as were the two-dozen-or-so student assistants who managed to learn a lot about newspapering while accomplishing a great deal of work.

I also wish to thank:

  • the Competition Committee members for guidance; I could not have worked in a vacuum;

  • SND Executive Director Ray Chattman;

  • Randy Stano for the forethought to bring in new blood before the Committee needed donors;

  • my bosses and co-workers at The Times-Picayune, for patience and understanding as the duties of Edition Coordinator slowly ate away at my daily work duties. Sorry and thanks.

Michael Jantze
15th Edition Coordinator

Ca-ca-ca-cambios. Hace dos años Randy Stano, entonces presidente de SND, llamó y pregunto si yo estaba interesado en colaborar con los fallos del SND. Le dije que sí. Como coordinador de la 15va. edición, también estaba interesado en un cambio. No es que algo estaba mal, sólo que me gustaba interferir, creo yo.

Los cambios comenzaron introduciendo la Llamada a Participar como un libro de referencias en lugar de un poster o afiche. El concurso había crecido y trajo todo su equipaje con él. Tal vez este cambio es la razón por la cual tuvimos menos llamadas telefónicas con menos gente haciendo preguntas que los dos años previos. O es eso, o es que ahora no han podido ni siquiera encontrar los números de teléfonos.

Seleccionar los jueces fue otra área de preocupación. Quise balancear el grupo con caras nuevas con una variedad de procedencias y experiencias. La competencia ahora es internacional, y el Comité pasó por muchas penurias para reflejar esto. Estoy seguro de que el próximo año habrá un avance aún mucho mayor.

Los cambios también ocurrieron en las 72 horas de los fallos en febrero. Después de que 16 jurados habían visto cerca de 9.400 participaciones, 987 ganadores fueron seleccionados incluyendo cuatro Dictámenes para Reconocimientos Especiales y 2 Mejores Trabajos, los cuales fueron otorgados por trabajar con una relación común: simplicidad con perspectiva. Tal como los periódicos han trabajado en la década pasada para reinventarse ellos mismos, los jueces reconocieron a estos ganadores por su esfuerzo en hacer cambios pero olvidar sus lectores.. Los dos Mejores Trabajos de la revista The Philadelphia Inquirer y Le Devoir reflejan ese tipo de promesa. Esta es verdaderamente una de las cosas buenas sobre los años 90.

Demos los créditos. El jurado fue co-auspiciado por el S.I. Newhouse School of Public Communications de la Universidad de Syracuse, Syracuse, New York. Marshall Matlock estuvo otra vez disponible para realizar milagros a través de todo el proceso, así como también las dos docenas y tantas de estudiantes asistentes que llegaron a aprender mucho sobre periódicos mientras desarrollaban gran cantidad de trabajo.

También deseo agradecer a:

  • los miembros del Comité de Competencia por su guía; yo no podría haber trabajado aisladamente;

  • Ray Chattman, Director Ejecutivo de SND;

  • a Randy Stano por su criterio y previsión por traer nueva sangre antes de que el Comité necesitase donantes;

  • a mis jefes y compañeros de trabajo en The Times-Picayune, por su paciencia y comprensión en las tareas como Coordinador de Edición que poco a poco fueron apartándome de mis obligaciones cotidianas. Pido perdón y doy las gracias.

Michael Jantze
Coordinador de la 15 va. Edición

foreword
prólogo

Nearly 9,400 entries representing thousands of tear-sheets were judged in preparation for the making of this book. Included in the following pages are more than 1,100 examples of winning entries. Although it was not possible to include every winning entry, special effort was made to include as many as possible.

The judging task started in the spring of 1993 with discussions as to the people who could best represent the Society at the 15th Edition judging. Michael Jantze, 15th Edition Coordinator, worked with the Society's Competition Committee in making the final selection of the 16 judges needed to accomplish the mammoth judging job in just three long days.

The S.I. Newhouse School of Public Communications again cosponsored the judging. Hundreds of tables were set up using a system which allows judges to vote on each entry in the 22 categories and still remain alert after a 10-to-15-hour day.

In case of a conflict, a "floating" judge was asked to judge the entry. A number of qualified "floating" judges were available on the judging floor to perform this duty. A conflict occurs when a judge comes across an entry from his or her publication, a publication he or she has done recent consulting work for (recent is defined as an 18-month period immediately prior to judging) or a publication with which he or she directly competes.

The Society presents four levels of awards:

Award of Excellence is granted for work that is truly excellent. Mere technical or aesthetic competency should not be recognized. But to receive an award these entries need not be "perfect." It is appropriate to honor entries for such things as being daring and innovative if the entry is outstanding but less than 100 percent in every respect.
Bronze Medal is granted for work that stands above the Award of Excellence. It may be granted to any entry receiving three votes in medal discussion by the judging team. The technical proficiency of the Bronze Medal should reach the limits of the medium.
Silver Medal is granted for work that goes beyond excellence. The technical proficiency of the Silver Medal should stretch the limits of the medium. These entries should shine.
Gold Medal is granted for work that defines the state of the art. Such an entry should stretch the limits of creativity. It should be impossible to find anything deficient in a Gold-winning entry.

Judges may present two additional awards

In addition to the Award of Excellence and the three medals, two special honors are possible: the Judges' Special Recognition and the Best of Show. These honors are given only when specific, special circumstances warrant the award.

Judges' Special Recognition: This honor can be awarded by a team of judges or by all judges for work that is outstanding in a particular respect not singled out by the Award of Excellence, Bronze, Silver, or Gold medal structure. This recognition has been granted for such things as use of photography, use of informational graphics and the use of typography throughout a body of work. This body of work may be a particular publication, section or sections by an individual or staff. The special recognition does not supplant any Award of Excellence, Bronze, Silver or Gold and should be seen as an adjunct. In the hierarchy of awards, it falls between the level of the Silver Medal and Gold Medal. It is clearly a step above the Silver Medal because it is normally for a body of work or for consistent excellence, but it does not earn a Gold Medal because of its narrow focus.
Best of Show: As the name implies this is the best of the Gold Medal winners. Any discussion for this award takes place at the conclusion of the judging. Judges had an opportunity to view all Silver and Gold winners at the same time. There is no limit as to the number of Best of Show awards that may be presented in one or more categories. This year two Best of Show awards were given.

C. Marshall Matlock
Competition Committee Chair

Cerca de 9.400 participaciones representando miles de hojas fueron seleccionadas en la preparación de este libro. Incluido en las páginas siguientes están más de 1.100 ejemplos de participaciones ganadoras. A pesar de que no fue posible incluir cada una de ellas, se hizo un esfuerzo especial para incluir a tantas poco fuera posible.

La tarea de selección comenzó en la primavera de 1993 con discusiones sobre la gente que pudiese representar mejor a la Sociedad en el jurado de la 15va. Edición. Michael Jantze, coordinador de la 15 va. Edición, trabajó con el Comité de Competencia de la Sociedad haciendo la selección final de los 16 jueces requeridos para cumplir el descomunal trabajo de jurado durante tres largos días solamente.

El S.I. del Newhouse School of Public Communications nuevamente co-auspició la selección. Se pusieron cientos de mesas usando un sistema que permitiese a los jurados votar en cada participación en las 22 categorías y a la vez permanecer alerta después de un día de 10 a 15 horas.

En caso de conflicto, un juez "flotante" fue requerido que juzgara la participación. Un número de jueces calificados y "flotantes" estuvieron disponibles en el lugar de la selección para realizar esta tarea. Un conflicto ocurre cuando un juez encuentra una participación de su publicación, una publicación para la cual ha realizado trabajo investigativo reciente o una publicación con la cual compite directamente. (Reciente es definido como un período de 18 meses inmediatamente anterior al juicio o selección.)

La Sociedad presenta cuatro niveles de premios:
Premio de Excelencia: es otorgado por el trabajo que es verdaderamente excelente. Algo puramente técnico o artístico no debe ser reconocido. Pero para recibir un galardón estas participaciones no requieren ser "perfectas." Es conveniente hacer honor a las participaciones por cosas buenas o novedosas, si la partipación es destacada, pero con menos de 100 por ciento en cada aspecto.
Medalla de Bronce: es otorgada al trabajo que sobresale por encima del Premio de Excelencia. Puede ser otorgado a cualquier participación recibiendo tres votos en discusiones de medallas por el grupo de jueces. La capacidad técnica de la Medalla de Bronce debe exceder los límites del médium.
Medalla de Plata: es otorgada al trabajo que va más allá de la Excelencia. La capacidad técnica de la Medalla de Plata debe exceder los límites del médium. Estas participaciones deben ser brillantes.
Medalla de Oro: es otorgada al trabajo que define un avance. Tal participación debe exceder los límites de la creatividad. Debe ser imposible encontrar algo deficiente en la participación que gane Oro.

Los jueces pueden presentar dos galardones adicionales
Además del Premio de Excelencia y las tres medallas, dos galardones especiales son posibles: el Reconocimiento Especial de los Jueces y el Mejor Trabajo. Estos galardones son otorgados únicamente cuando circunstancias específicas y especiales garantizan el premio.
Reconocimiento Especial de los Jueces: Este honor o premio es otorgado por un grupo de jueces o por todos los jueces al trabajo que sobresale en un aspecto particular no determinado por el Premio de Excelencia, o por la estructura de las medallas de Bronce, Plata y Oro. Este reconocimiento ha sido otorgado a tales aspectos como la fotografía, el uso de gráficos informativos y el uso de tipografía a través del cuerpo de trabajo. Este cuerpo de trabajo puede ser una publicación particular, sección o secciones por un individuo o grupo. Este reconocimiento especial no suplanta ninguno de los premios de Excelencia, Medalla de Bronce, Plata u Oro, y debe ser visto como un adjunto. En la jerarquía de premios, cae entre el nivel de la Medalla de Plata y la Medalla de Oro. Es claramente un paso sobre la Medalla de Plata porque es normalmente para un cuerpo de trabajo o por una excelencia con consistencia, pero no obtiene la Medalla de Oro porque tiene una focalidad estrecha.
Mejor Trabajo: Como su nombre implica, es el mejor de los ganadores de la Medalla de Oro. Cualquier discusión sobre este premio toma lugar en la final de la selección. Los jueces tienen una oportunidad para ver todos los ganadores de Plata y Oro al mismo tiempo. No hay límite para el número de premios Mejor Trabajo que pueden ser presentados en una o más categorías. Este año dos premios Mejor Trabajo fueron otorgados.

C. Marshall Matlock
Presidente del Comité de Competencia

chapter

one

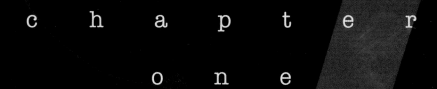

Best of Show
Le Devoir
Montreal, Canada

Art director Lucie Lacava's stunning redesign of the Le Devoir, a 37,000-circulation nationalist newspaper in Montreal, showed the power of classic typography and content-based design.

Lacava's design cues came from the origins of the newspaper. She adapted type and the grid from 1910 editions of Le Devoir. Type choices are limited: Century Oldstyle and two supplemental faces. Color is used sparingly (a press limitation): only one color, usually on section fronts or backs. The design staff is small: Lacava and two designers.

"Hopefully, this work represents a return to our roots," Judge Dale Peskin said. "Le Devoir has the look, the feel, and the emotional appeal of the golden age of newspapers. It's inviting. It's comfortable. It serves content. Everything about it is distinguished."

Judge George Benge praised Le Devoir for its simplicity and style. "This newspaper demonstrates that good design is a matter of intelligence, not resources," Benge said. "Every page showed attention to detail. Every page served readers."

Mejor Trabajo

El sorprendente rediseño del director de arte Lucie Lacava en el Le Devoir, un periódico nacionalista con circulación de 37.000 ejemplares en Montreal, demostró el poder de la tipografía clásica y el diseño basado en el contenido.

Los signos del diseño de Lacava vienen de los orígenes del periódico. Ella adaptó el tipo y las barras de Le Devoir de las ediciones de 1910. La posibilidad de tipos son limitadas. Century Antiguo y dos caras suplementarias. El color es usado frugalmente (una limitación de prensa): sólo un color, generalmente en secciones adelante o atrás. El equipo de diseño es pequeño: Lacava y dos diseñadores.

"Afortunadamente, este trabajo representa una vuelta a las raíces." El juez Dale Peskin dijo "Le Devoir tiene la apariencia, el sentido, y el atractivo emocional de un periódico de la edad de oro. Es incitante, es agradable, cómodo. Ofrece contenido. Todo sobre él es notable."

El juez George Benge elogió a Le Devoir por su simplicidad y estilo. "Este periódico demuestra que el buen diseño es cuestión de inteligencia, no de recursos" dijo Benge. "Cada página demuestra atención al detalle. Cada página al servicio de los lectores."

Lucie Lacava, Deputy Editor-in-Chief/Art Director; Bernard Descoteaux, Editor-in-Chief; Benoit Aubin, ME; Pierre Beaulieu, AME; Roch Cote, AME; Lise Bissonnette, Publisher; Jacques Grenier, Photographer; Jacques Nadeau, Photographer; Guy Taillefer, Copy Editor; Jocelin Coulon, Copy Editor; Francois Brousseau, Copy Editor; Claude Levesque, Copy Editor; Antoine Char, Copy Editor; Diane Precourt, Copy Editor; Jean-Pierre Legault, Copy Editor; Roland-Yves Carignan, Copy Editor; Michel Belair, Copy Editor; Yves D'Avignon, Copy Editor; Pierre Cagouette, Copy Editor; Aime Dallaire, Copy Editor; Benoit Munger, Copy Editor

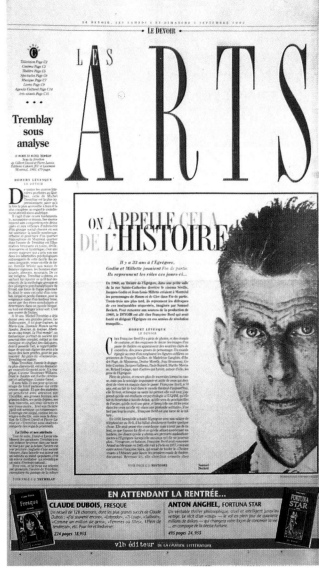

Silver & JSR
(for distinctive overall design that respects content, the traditions of typography, the principles of clear presentation, and the values of its readership)
Le Devoir
Montreal, Canada
Lucie Lacava, Deputy Editor-in-Chief/Art Director; Bernard Descoteaux, Editor-in-Chief; Benoit Aubin, ME; Pierre Beaulieu, AME; Roch Cote, AME

Silver

(Overall Redesign)
Le Devoir
Montreal, Canada
Lise Bissonnette, Publisher; Bernard Descoteaux, Editor-in-Chief; Andre Leclerc, Administrative Director; Benoit Aubin, ME; Lucie Lacava, Deputy Editor-in-Chief/Art Director

After

Before

After

KELLAMS

Before

Award of Excellence
(Section Redesign)
Le Devoir
Montreal, Canada
Bernard Descoteux, Editor-in-Chief; Lucie Lacava, Deputy Editor-in-Chief/Art Director; Odile Tremblay, Section Editor; Roland-Yves Carignan, Copy Editor & Designer

Award of Excellence
(Section Redesign)
Le Devoir
Montreal, Canada
Bernard Descoteaux, Editor in Chief; Lucie Lacava, Deputy Editor-in-Chief/Art Director; Jean-Pierre Legault, Copy Editor & Designer; Jacques Nadeau, Photographer; Claude Levesque, Copy Editor

Before

After

After

— LE DEVOIR —

À VOIR

LE DEVOIR, LE VENDREDI 17 SEPTEMBRE 1993

Théâtre

Début de saison. Rien de marquant en ce début de saison théâtrale. Mais ici et là quelques morceaux réussis: Jean-Louis Millette dans le rôle de Clov, avec son métier, sauve du désastre un *Fin de partie* bien académique au Café de la Place; Normand Canac-Marquis se donne à fond dans une interprétation nerveuse du meurtrier Gary Gilmore dans une pièce trop anecdotique sur cette histoire qui intéressa l'Amérique des années 76 et 77, Gilmore, *Que vaut la vie d'un homme?* à La Licorne. Mais le seul spectacle à recommander demeure *La Trahison orale* de Mauricio Kagel mis en scène par Denis Marleau du Théâtre Ubu, au Monument National.
Robert Lévesque

Danse

FIND. Un avant-goût du Festival International de Nouvelle Danse '93, au cinéma Parallèle, qui diffuse, à partir d'aujourd'hui, 19 heures, un cycle de vidéos de danse, présentant plusieurs des chorégraphes invités cet automne. À voir aussi, les premières représentations de la série *Émergence* de l'Espace Tangente, dédiée aux jeunes créateurs, jusqu'à dimanche.
Valérie Lehmann

Opéra

Le Vaisseau fantôme. Les chœurs, l'OSM dirigé par Spiros Argiris, la mise en scène de Bernard Uzan font du *Vaisseau fantôme*, cet opéra romantique de Richard Wagner, une production exceptionnelle. La prestation de la basse Victor von Halem en Daland est remarquable et les autres interprètes défendent fort bien leur personnage. À voir absolument à l'Opéra de Montréal, Place des Arts, samedi 20 h et aussi les 22 et 25 septembre.
Marie Laurier

Musique classique

Sons et Brioches. Pour leur premier Sons et Brioches, les Jeunesses musicales du Canada offrent un concert gratuit dimanche à 11h sur l'esplanade de la PdA, avec une initiation à l'art du taiko, ou tambour japonais avec le groupe montréalais Arashi Daiko.

75 ans en chant choral. La Société chorale de Saint-Lambert souligne dimanche à midi son 75e anniversaire sous forme d'un brunch-récital-bénéfice au 250 rue Saint-Laurent, à Saint-Lambert. Le directeur artistique David Christiani dévoilera les activités de la prochaine saison.

Sarah Chang. On connaît l'engouement de Charles Dutoit pour la violoniste Sarah Chang, engouement qu'il a communiqué au public de l'OSM. Le maestro nous la présente à la télévision radio-canadienne dimanche à 15h. Aussi un reportage sur l'IRCAM et la présentation des *Oiseaux exotiques* d'Olivier Messiaen.
Marie Laurier

Rock

Marc Cohn. On l'a bombardé James Taylor des années quatre-vingt-dix, et on n'a pas tort. Comme Taylor, Cohn est un calme, un réfléchi, un introspectif, un brillant auteur-compositeur-interprète qui chante sur un ton feutré. Mais alors que Taylor est un Nordiste de Boston, nourri de *doowop*, Cohn est un véritable Sudiste, avec le Mississippi qui lui coule dans les veines. Son étonnant amalgame de pop, de folk, de country, de blues et de gospel en fait foi. Dans le genre, *Walking In Memphis*, la chanson qui l'a lancé en 1990, vaut à elle seule le déplacement au Club Soda, ce soir à 20h30.
Sylvain Cormier

Arts visuels

Anne Deguelle. Miroir, miroir dis-moi qui est Montréal... Ce que je dis deux fois est vrai, écrit Anne Deguelle, une artiste française qui expose pour la première fois ici des œuvres *in situ*, des vues tirées sur verre qui reflètent avec des monochromes, un lieu fictif qui confronte le réel, une mouvance architecturale qui ne manque ni de piquant ni de poésie. À la Galerie Yves le Roux Art Contemporain, 5605 boulevard Saint-Laurent, espace 4136. Jusqu'au 2 octobre.
Marie-Michèle Cron

Cinéma

Trahir, de Radu Mihaileanu, dont c'est le premier long métrage. Un écrivain dissident roumain jeté en prison retrouve la liberté et la respectabilité en vendant son âme au diable, c'est-à-dire à la Securitate. L'implacable emprise d'un régime totalitaire sur ses citoyens pris en otages. Ce film, éprouvant pour les spectateurs, a d'ailleurs remporté le Grand Prix des Amériques lors de la récente édition du Festival du film de Montréal. Terrifiant.
Francine Laurendeau

Margie Gillis, la danse de la vie

«Un théâtre, c'est le lieu idéal pour le rituel et la célébration qui constituent l'essentiel de ma danse. Spirituel, intellectuel et émotionnel doivent s'y mélanger. La scène offre une opportunité unique de parler de notre condition et d'être en connection avec les choses qui nous donnent la grâce, le courage, la beauté, l'amour.» Ainsi parle Margie Gillis. Parce que sa vision de la danse ne prend pas le chemin habituel, de ses chorégraphies et de ses interprétations découlent des sensations inattendues. Lorsqu'un quelconque mortel regarde cette femme déployer ses ailes sur un plateau, une sorte de magie s'opère instantanément. Margie possède un charme qui confère à l'envoûtement. Dans chacun de ses gestes, empreints tantôt d'une lenteur extrême, tantôt d'une légèreté coquine, réside l'énergie vitale. Comme les thèmes favoris de l'artiste sont la mort, la tendresse, la vieillesse, la naissance, l'amour, la solitude... chaque danse n'est pas loin de signifier l'accord parfait, encore lorsque la chorégraphie a été composée par un œil extérieur, c'est-à-dire quand la danseuse se permet de se perdre dans les méandres de l'interprétation.

Dans le spectacle que la Margie Gillis Fondation propose ce soir et demain à la Place des Arts figurent quatre solos issus du répertoire classique de la danseuse, particulièrement représentatif du style Gillis: *Mara*, imaginé par Stéphanie Ballard, qui conte peut-être la solitude d'une sirène, *Variations* et *Slipstreams*, chorégraphiés par Margie Gillis, qui chacun à leur manière expriment liberté et fébrilité, *Vulsig Matilda*, signé de Margie également, mise en scène l'étrange passion d'une femme amoureuse.

Un cinquième solo inscrit au programme a été créé, début janvier 1993, par le danseur Christopher Gillis — le frère et l'ami aujourd'hui disparu. Il s'intitule *Landscape*, raconte la douleur d'une femme face à la maladie, la souffrance dans l'impuissance.

Mais pour célébrer dignement son retour à Montréal après deux ans d'absence, l'artiste a également choisi de présenter à la Place des Arts un nouveau duo et un quintet inédit. *Vers la Gloire*, une œuvre composée à trois, duo symbole parce qu'il a toujours été dansé par les Gillis frère et sœur, est joué par Margie et le meilleur ami de son frère, Juan, membre de la Paul Taylor Company.

A gathering, la dernière création de Stéphanie Ballard, est interprété par cinq femmes, Gioconda Barbuto, Andréa Boardman, Danielle Sturk et Suzanne Trépanier y donnent la réplique à Margie Gillis. Plus qu'une exploration du monde féminin, il s'agit, aux yeux de la créatrice canadienne, «d'un rituel d'initiation surtout, qui explique l'idée du passage et le phénomène de la transformation».

Il faut dire que depuis la mort de son complice de frère, emporté par le sida cet été, Margie Gillis n'a pas cessé de chercher comment continuer la route entamée avec ce dernier. Danser pour la cause du sida était pendant les deux dernières années une préoccupation immédiate de cette missionnaire de l'Art. À ce titre, elle a participé à de nombreux galas-bénéfices, partout dans le monde. «J'ai essayé d'aider; je ne sais pas si j'en suis capable, c'est un défi pour moi de continuer à lutter pour des choses fondamentales de la vie. Ma vision de la danse ne change pas, elle se perpétue au contraire à travers la notion de célébration. Mais... un moment précis de septembre, je ne pense qu'à la Marche pour le sida du 3 octobre organisée à Montréal, pour laquelle je suis "ambassadrice". Là est l'important pour moi.»

Valérie Lehmann

LES POMMES

La tête dans les feuilles, avec un bon chandail de laine, à ramasser tout ce qu'on a besoin pour la meilleure gelée de l'année, quel plaisir! La saison des pommes bat son plein, et c'est l'activité idéale pour la famille, puisque plusieurs producteurs encouragent le public à l'auto-cueillette. De toute façon, aller acheter des pommes sur le bord de la route peut-être le prétexte à une ballade en auto si la fin de semaine est belle. La majorité des producteurs se retrouvent dans la Montérégie, dans les secteurs de Saint-Hilaire et Rougemont, quoiqu'on peut également en trouver plusieurs dans la région de Hemmingford près de la frontière américaine, et dans la région d'Oka. Renseignements: Fédération des producteurs de pommes du Québec. 679-0530
Paul Cauchon

À LIRE

Tout Denys Arcand. À la sortie de son film *Love and Human Remains*, Denys Arcand a refusé d'accorder des entrevues à la presse. La raison en est fort simple: il a tout dit à Michel Coulombe. Les Éditions du Boréal viennent de publier ces entretiens dans un court ouvrage intitulé *Denys Arcand, La vraie nature du cinéaste*. Le cinéaste y explique largement sa vision du monde, avec une franchise qui en dérange déjà plusieurs. «Si l'anglais doit être la langue dominante au XXIe siècle, ce sera comme la lave d'un volcan. On pourra soit être enseveli, soit être enseveli en protestant», dit-il. Toute la ville en parle. À lire de toute urgence!
Pierre Cayouette

LE MARATHON

Surveillez bien vos déplacements dimanche dans les rues des villes hautes d'Outremont, Mont-Royal et Saint-Laurent. Ils pourraient être perturbés par la tenue du marathon de Montréal. Quelque 6000 coureurs sont attendus et le public est invité à applaudir ces braves en les regardant bien en toute sécurité sur les abords du parcours. Le départ se fait à 9h, face à la station de métro Édouard-Montpetit et les participants étrangers d'Europe, d'Asie et des États-Unis se mêleront aux Québécois pour lui donner ce caractère international que l'on recherche ici aussi en faire une fête de la bonne forme physique. C'est aussi télévisé. Noter que les chicanes et les barrières qui bloquent ou détournent la circulation seront levées en fin d'après-midi. Avertis d'avance, les automobilistes peuvent davantage être conciliants et s'éviter une crise d'apoplexie.
Marie Laurier

LES Z'AMOURS

Hot-dogs, bière et odeur de championnat, samedi soir, au Stade Olympique, où le Québécois Denis Boucher, le petit nouveau des Expos, sera le lanceur partant face aux redoutables Phillies de Philadelphie. Pour la chaleur de la foule, l'ambiance et un aperçu — sait-on jamais? — de la folie qui s'emparerait des amateurs si jamais l'équipe montréalaise se rendait jusqu'au bout.
Benoît Munger

À PIED

La rue Saint-Paul, entre Saint-Laurent et McGill, dans le Vieux-Montréal, est laissée au piétons durant tout le week-end. L'idée est de permettre aux familles de visiter tranquillement ce tronçon de rue historique et de flâner devant le travail des artisans installés sur les trottoirs. On peut aussi arrêter voir le Théâtre Biscuit pour enfants et l'animation d'époque du Musée Pointe-à-Callière. On propose également une exposition de voitures anciennes, des cerfs-volants, de la musique et des clowns.
Stéphane Baillargeon

CHAMPIGNONS

Cueillir ou ne pas cueillir tel ou tel champignon? Pour s'y retrouver en matière de santé, il sufit d'aller s'initier à la clinique Provigo du Jardin botanique (midi et 14h) et dimanche (midi à 17h), à la grande serre et à la salle Jacques-Rousseau. Par ailleurs, dès midi, durant les sept jours du week-end, le Pavillon Japonais offre une séance de dégustation de légumes nippons, à frais minimes.
Stéphane Baillargeon

Gold (Entertainment Section)
Le Devoir
Montreal, Canada
Lucie Lacava, Deputy Editor-in-Chief/Art Director; Michel Belair, Cultural Section Editor; Yves D'Avignon, Copy Editor; Roland-Yves Carignan, Copy Editor; Aime Dallaire, Copy Editor; Marie Lessard, Illustrator

Gold (Features Portfolio)
Le Devoir
Montreal, Canada
Lucie Lacava, Deputy Editor-in-Chief/Art Director; Michel Belair, Cultural Section Editor

Award of Excellence (Section A)
Le Devoir
Montreal, Canada
Bernard Descoteaux, Editor-in-Chief; Lucie Lacava, Deputy Editor-in-Chief/Art Direction; Pierre Beaulieu, AME; Roch Cote, AME; Benoit Aubin, ME; Claude Beauregard, Copy Editor; Diane Precourt, Copy Editor; Jacques Nadeau, Photographer; Jacques Grenier, Photographe

Silver (Features Portfolio)
Le Devoir
Montreal, Canada
Lucie Lacava, Deputy Editor-in-Chief/Art Director; Michel Belair, Cultural Section
Editor

Entre les lignes Page D2
Trufo misto Page D4
Le Bloc notes Page D5
Essais québécois Page D6

Award of Excellence (Decorative Typography)
Le Devoir
Montreal, Canada
Lucie Lacava, Deputy Editor-in-Chief/Art Director; Roland-Yves Carignan, Copy Editor & Designer; Odile Tremblay,
Book Section Editor

INSIDE: ECHOES FROM 'ROUND MIDNIGHT

INQUIRER

November 28, 1993   The Philadelphia Inquirer Magazine

AmericanDreamers

One family's struggle to reconcile traditional goals with changing realities.

PHOTOGRAPHY AND STORY BY APRIL SAUL

Gold
Inquirer magazine
Philadelphia, PA
April Saul, Photo-
grapher, Bert Fox,
Art Director &
Designer

Best of Show
Inquirer magazine
Philadelphia, Pennsylvania

The SND judges present a Best of Show to April Saul for her picture story titled "American Dreamers," edited by Bert Fox and published in the Philadelphia Inquirer magazine. With black and white pictures, tightly edited, Saul tells the story of Penny and Joe Gesualdi Jr., an ambitious middle-class family in the '90s struggling to live the American Dream defined during their childhood in the early '60s. With very candid photographs Saul reports their moments of great satisfaction and incredible difficulty in pursuing the dream.

These are the types of stories we believe newspapers should be doing. The reporting stretched over 3 years and demonstrates a solid commitment to documenatary photojournalism by April Saul, her editor Bert Fox and the Inquirer magazine.

"We all talk about showing real people and telling real stories," Judge Tim Gallagher said. "This is journalism that does it."

Mejor Trabajo

Los jueces SND otorgan el Mejor Trabajo a April Saul por su historia de fotografías tituladas "American Dreamers" (Soñadores Americanos) editada por Bert Fox y publicada en la revista Inquirer, de Philadelphia. Con fotografías en blanco y negro, editadas con premura, Saul relata la historia de Penny y Joe Gasualdi Jr., una ambiciosa familia de clase media en los años 90, luchando por vivir el sueño americano delineado durante su infancia, tempranamente en los años 60. Con verdaderas fotografías cándidas, Saul reporta sus momentos de gran satisfacción e increíble dificultad en la búsqueda del sueño.

Estas son la clase de historias que creemos que los periódicos deben estar haciendo. El reportaje abarcó 3 años y demuestra una sólida inclinación al foto-reportaje documental de April Saul, su editor Bert Fox y la revista Inquirer.

"Nosotros todos hablamos de mostrar gente real y contar historias reales." El jurado Tim Galllagher dijo. "Este es un periodismo que lo hace."

TRYING TO

PROVIDE MORE

FOR THE FAMILY

IN A WORLD

THAT YIELDS

LESS AND LESS.

RUNNING IN PLACE

PHOTOGRAPHY & STORY BY APRIL SAUL

JOE GESUALDI JR. FIRST ENTERED THE Fairless Works as an 18-year-old, when the mill took raw rock and made it into finished steel. The place was alive with the roar of furnaces, the glow of molten metal, and the bustle of 10,000 workers. "It looked like the Fourth of July all the time," he says.

Now, 20 years later, what is now known as a USX plant now does only finishing work, and employs only 800 people. And Joe, who long ago achieved his ambition of becoming an electrician, isn't the only one who checks each new schedule to make sure he's on it. "It's like living with a terrorist," Joe says.

But live with it he does, mostly because he has little choice. Like millions of other Americans, Joe Gesualdi and his wife, Penny, have pursued happiness according to the American dream: They live in a house they own, in Bristol. They started a family that now includes Joseph 3d, 6; Maricena, 5; Domenica, 2; and Jarrod, 1. They aspire to provide their children with all the comforts of home and a little more. All along, they've believed that greater security was theirs for the earning.

Now they're finding that hard work alone can't change some things, and that upward mobility has risks as well as rewards.

Joe never expected to stay at the mill this long

APRIL SAUL is an Inquirer staff photographer.

— he started feeling uneasy about the future of American steel in the early '80s. Even before he and Penny married, in 1981, he would sometimes wish he'd done something else — maybe pursued the television and radio work that was his boyhood hobby — and in 1986 he started looking for a job as an electrical or mechanical field-service rep. After investigating two dozen openings and formally applying for 12, he discovered two unnerving trends: The number of those jobs were dwindling as American corporations began downsizing, and he was either overqualified or underqualified for the jobs that were left. At the same time, Joe and Penny were growing increasingly afraid of crime and feeling squeezed by rising taxes and insurance rates. They wanted out.

So, in 1989, the Gesualdis bought two small houses in Bellefonte, four hours away in the hills northeast of State College, and an old hotel nearby. Their idea was to live in one property and rent the other two out while Joe re-established himself in another job. Penny, by her own desire, would stay home with the children.

And then they got caught in the real estate bust: Because they couldn't sell their Bristol house at a

Story and photographs continued on Page 20

Joe Gesualdi Jr. (right) tips his head back during a break with co-workers at the steel mill where he's worked for 20 years. His wife, Penny (above), doesn't let pregnancy deter her from yard work.

Decem ber 5, 1993

In late 1992, Joe's sixth layoff in 20 years sent him to the unemployment office (above) so he could file for compensation (below). The year before (right), he and Penny had to straighten out an appraiser's error before they could refinance their house.

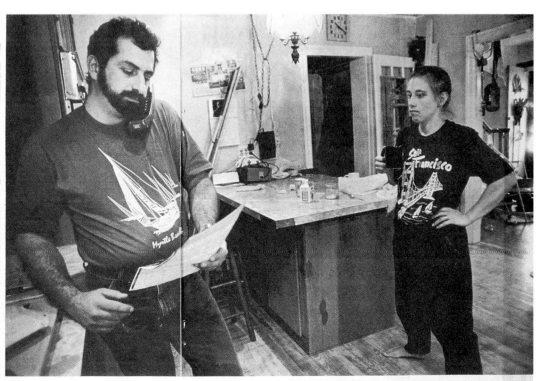

continued from Page 18
reasonable price, Joe had to pass up a business opportunity in Bellefonte. In a single year, the Gesualdis spent $10,000 just on travel and lodging so they could maintain the buildings — and repair damage their tenants inflicted in their absence.

The spring of 1992 wasn't the Gesualdis' best. Joe's fifth layoff from work lasted a few weeks. Penny was with Jarrod. They took the children to Disney World because they'd already paid for the trip. Taking stock, they surrendered their dream of moving to Bellefonte. Then they

spent the next year renovating the houses so they could sell them.

"We sustained massive real estate losses for our station in life," Joe says. "A nightmare," says Penny. Now, they're beginning to believe a second Great Depression is inevitable — but they haven't surrendered their hope of changing their lives. Meanwhile, even if Penny, at 35, wanted to trade 24-hour motherhood for a full-time job, the cost of day care would eat up whatever she could earn. So Joe, at 38, keeps reporting to the mill, always with an eye to the next work schedule.

Photographs continued on Page 22

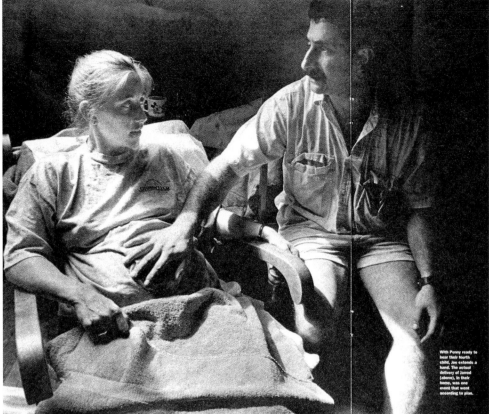

With Penny ready to bear their fourth child, Joe extends a hand. The actual delivery of Jarrod (above), in their home, was one event that went according to plan.

AMERICAN DREAMERS: THE LAST OF THREE PARTS

THE ROUTE TO FAMILY HEALTH IS PAVED WITH THE UNEXPECTED.

THE OBSTACLE COURSE

PHOTOGRAPHY & STORY BY APRIL SAUL

LAST YEAR, PENNY AND JOE GESUALDI JR. had a little health-care debate of their own. The births of their first three children, though blessed events, had left them with some unwanted expenses and a distaste for hospitals. With their fourth due in September, they wondered: Should Penny have the baby at home?

It wasn't much of an argument, although Joe was a little apprehensive. Penny had had their first three children in a hospital birthing suite with neither medication nor complications; midwives, not doctors, had delivered the younger two. By the third birth, the Gesualdis had become outraged by the bills — not just the $600 they paid out of pocket, but also the $3,200 their insurance company was billed for their eight hours in the birthing suite.

More than money was at issue here. To the Gesualdis, the health-care system had come to seem arrogant, far too complicated and devoid of compassion. They already knew uncertainty — Joe had been laid off periodically from his job as an electrician at a steel plant, and the comatose real estate market had dashed the couple's plans to move to the country. The best thing in their lives — their family — had come about as a result of planning and effort. It was only natural that they'd want some control over their lives.

So when Penny met Aaron Haseock, a Bucks County obstetrician who was enthusiastic about the home delivery even though some colleagues were warning him against it, the decision was made. "To find somebody who was more interested in making our dream come true than in protecting his professional image was absolutely incredible," says Joe.

Sure enough, on Aug. 25, 1992, Jarrod Elias Gesualdi was born at the Gesualdis' Bristol home. His birth was uncomplicated, but by no means worry-free. Ultrasounds shortly beforehand showed that Jarrod had a kidney irregularity that, doctors said, could be life-threatening. After another ultrasound when Jarrod was 3 days old, the pediatrician recommended more tests — so the Gesualdis ended up at the hospital after all, for a series of high-tech procedures that made Jarrod wail and Penny cry tears of frustration.

And for all that, the condition turned out to be harmless. Jarrod joined his siblings — Joseph 3d, now 6; Marquesa, 5; and Domenica, 2 — as another light in his parents' life. The Gesualdis even chose to skip followup tests this year ("I was not about to start stuffing isotopes into the kid again," Penny says tartly). They also chose for Joe to have a vasectomy after they conceived Jarrod, so they are through building their family.

But they are by no means through with their American dream. "The only thing that I want out of life," says Penny, "is for us to be happy, healthy, and have enough money to provide for the kids." Her

Photographs continued on next page; story continued on Page 24

APRIL SAUL is an Inquirer staff photographer.

INQUIRER **21**

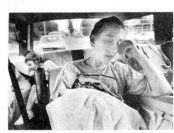

A half-hour after Jarrod was born (above), the Gesualdis were on the way to the pediatrician's office for a prearranged exam. When he was 10 days old (right), he was at the hospital for a series of tests related to a kidney irregularity that had been detected before birth. The condition eventually proved harmless, but the testing put Penny and Joe (below) through the wringer. In fact, even before the hospital appointment (bottom), their mounting anxiety led them to arrange an early christening.

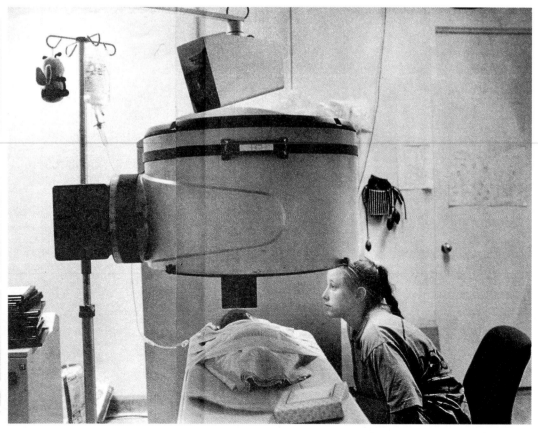

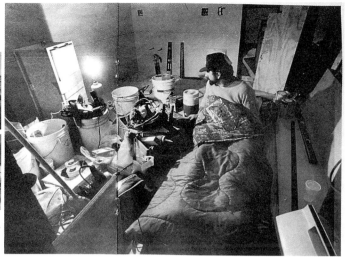

The Gonzaleses are no strangers to home improvement — Joe (above) refurbished the apartment in their Bristol home as his sister and daughter read — but a move to rural Bethlehem proved beyond their reach. When the Gonzaleses started remodeling their properties there so they could re-sell, Joe (right) would sleep with the work, or take a coffee-shop break (top) with one of his biggest helpers, his father-in-law, Dan Boffemmino. "Everything I worked for," Joe says, "was up there."

After they conceived Jarrod, Penny and Joe decided it was time for Joe to have a vasectomy. Beforehand (above), they waited together. When they were reunited afterward (right), Penny was surprised when Joe and a nurse explained why the operation took longer than expected: Doctors were looking for two ducts to snip, but Joe had been born with only one.

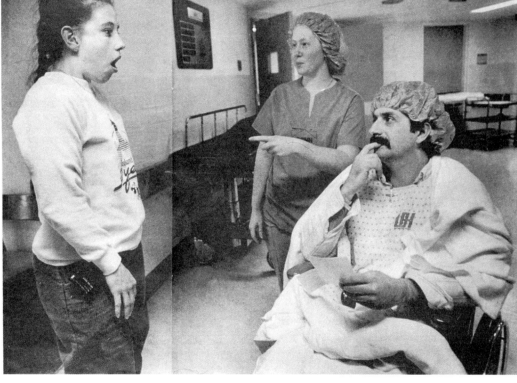

continued from Page 21

vision is both simple and grand. Happiness, she and Joe get in spades from their four "munchkins." Their ability to provide for them depends on economic forces that are indifferent to even the best-laid plans. As for their health, well, they've learned that there are some things you can't plan for.

Penny has fought anemia for three years; in 1987, a chest X-ray showed that Joe, like a number of his co-workers, has asbestosis, which may or may not lead to cancer. Penny now battles her doctors for iron injections, which they refuse because of the potential for iron toxicity. For now, she takes iron orally — at nine times the recommended dosage.

Joe, for his part, has no way of knowing what will happen, but he's certain of one thing: Even with all the problems he and Penny have faced in the last few years, they're not giving up. "We went from having a good amount of money to being broke," he says. "We went from the top of the mountain to the valley. But we've had good times, and, God willing, we'll have good times again. Just because everything is crumbling around me, I'm not going to quit."

Moments later, he's smiling. "You know at the end of those *Star Trek* movies where Mr. Spock holds up the split fingers and says, 'Live long and prosper'?" he asks. "That's the American dream to me."

Penny readily acknowledges that she sometimes has her hands full — as with an infant Jarrod in her lap and a tub full of Joe Jr. (left), Maryanne, or Maryie, and Domenica (standing). "The bad baby," she says, "really sucked the youth right out of me."

Dreamers

continued from Page 16

have pleasures right here."

After Joe Jr. was born, Penny tried returning to her job at a furniture store, but it didn't work out. The cost of day care was troubling, and at less the lack of one-on-one attention. Joe Jr. was a colicky infant, and "they just let him scream all day," Penny says. "I might as well leave him home by himself." She and Joe decided that she'd stay home, whatever the cost.

"You would not leave your new Mercedes with someone you don't know for eight hours a day, but you'll gladly give your kids to whomever for eight hours a day and think nothing of it," says Joe. "And then people wonder why they have angry children. If you do not value your children as your most prized possessions, you have a problem. And we, as a nation, have a problem."

When problems the Gonzaleses have, they want to solve themselves. They admit they're sometimes in over their heads — like the night Joe was working the graveyard shift and Penny, pregnant, was stuck with three vomiting children — but they see the challenge is part of the payoff.

Take the time they paid all four children into the museum for a drive to Florida. Although Penny daydreams about the "fun of seeing the children's faces light when they hug Mickey Mouse," Joe means, "The fun wasn't being at Disney World. The fun was in pulling off the trip — taking four kids, driving 19 hours down and 14 hours back, and living through it." We're about many things just to prove to ourselves that we could do it.

As the children grow, so will the Gonzaleses' wish list. Penny imagines herself working part-time at a Disney Store and maybe, a decade from now, pursuing a career as a teacher. Joe dreams of being a program manager for a radio station, and of taking the kids on a car trip from coast to coast when they're older. "I want my kids to have a sense that you can do and be anything you want in this world," he says. "I don't want them to say, 'Gee, I wish I had known about this or that, because I had stayed doing that.'"

Mostly, the Gonzaleses say, they are grateful — for their health and their children, for the family and friends who help out when they're needed, for the fact that they've yet to face a problem they couldn't handle. "We've been pushed to our limit," says Joe, "and we've come through in better people."

Photograph continued on next page

With four children, family milestones come often. Joe Sr. (top) got a big hug from his father (red spring when he graduated from kindergarten at St. Mark's Catholic school in Bristol. Last Christmas (above), the girls gather around with family friend Santa Schlosh while their older brother inspected a tree branch. Birthdays (bottom) are a big deal at the Gonzaleses', and after Domenica's second birthday party earlier this year, Joe Jr. takes a rest.

OVERALL DESIGN

c h a p t e r

t w o

Silver
The Sunday Tribune
Dublin, Ireland
Stephen Ryan, Design/Photo Editor; Paul Hopkins, Production Manager; Gerry Sandford, Designer; John Carlos, Photographer; Billy Stickland, Photographer; Ger Siggins, Sports Editor; Rory Godson, Business Editor; Roslyn Dee, Lifestyles Editor; Con O'Midheach, Copy Editor; Tom Vavasour, Production Manager

SPORT
World Cup
On Wednesday the Republic plays its most crucial game. A20 & 21

ACCENT
JFK myth endures
The media cranks up for the 30th anniversary. B3

PEOPLE
A paper princess
Why Diana keeps taking the tabloids. B1

THE SUNDAY
TRIBUNE

14 NOVEMBER 1993   VOL 14 NO 46   FINAL EDITION   PRICE: 98p (incl VAT), 90p in sterling area

EXCLUSIVE
CASEY

Bishop Eamonn Casey photographed last week: 'I'm sorry, please forgive me'

> **I'm sorry, please forgive me . . . God has forgiven me . . .Nobody is stopping me from going home**

BY VERONICA GUERIN

IN A series of interviews with *The Sunday Tribune* Bishop Eamonn Casey has told how he became infatuated with Annie Murphy but was told only shortly before the birth of their son that he was the father.

This conflicts with a critical element in Annie Murphy's book *Forbidden Fruit*, which deals with their relationship.

Bishop Casey has spoken of how he struggled with the "impropriety" of his sexual relationship with Annie Murphy and stated that he never said Mass, following sexual relations with her, without having had confession.

Asked what he had to say to Catholics who felt deeply ashamed by what he had done, he said "I'm sorry, please forgive me".

Repeatedly throughout the interview he expressed deep regret about what happened and the pain he brought to so many people, including Annie Murphy and Peter Murphy.

On several occasions during the course of the interviews Bishop Casey broke down in tears, notably when he reflected on the pain his actions brought to close colleagues and his friends.

He was particularly distressed on being asked how his deceased mother and father would have felt about what had happened.

Although he acknowledges his infatuation with Annie Murphy, he says he never considered leaving the priesthood to marry her. Asked if there was a possibility that they would eventually end up together he said "none".

Bishop Casey said he hoped to return to Ireland when circumstances permitted it in terms of his commitments in Ecuador, where he is now a missionary priest, and in terms of being able to return and "allowed to be myself".

He said that nobody was

Bishop Casey and reporter Veronica Guerin last week

INSIDE: THE CASEY STORY A12/A15

■ Eamonn Casey talks about his infatuation with Annie Murphy, their sexual relationship, their struggle with his conscience and his certainty of God's forgiveness.

attempting to prevent him returning — the remark was made yesterday in response to newspaper reports that the Hierarchy did not want him to return.

Bishop Casey said he had attained serenity and believed in forgiveness by God and that he felt challenged by the work he has been given in Ecuador.

The interviews arose from contacts made with Bishop Casey when he telephoned *The Sunday Tribune* on Satur-

day, 10 April, to deny that he had given an interview to *The Sunday Independent*.

He was subsequently requested by letter to give an interview and he replied saying that it was not appropriate for him to do that then, given personal commitments.

In September, this reporter went to Ecuador and delivered a letter to where Bishop Casey was staying.

The bishop subsequently made contact and several meetings and discussions took place.

Subsequently, in October there were several other meetings and discussions between this reporter and Bishop Casey, and he finally agreed to do the interviews.

The interviews took place over last weekend and there were follow up interviews on Friday and Saturday (yesterday) last week.

In accordance with undertakings given to Bishop Casey, the text of the interviews was submitted to him for him to confirm that he was being quoted correctly.

He made several changes to the text, many of them correcting misinterpretations and facts and others changing the substance of his responses.

At no stage did he insist that questions asked be withdrawn or that the scope of the interviews be restricted, although he did refuse to answer a number of questions related to his personal life and intimacies between himself and Annie Murphy.

On a number of occasions Bishop Casey was accompanied by priest friends during the interviews and pre-interview discussions.

The priest friends encouraged him to do the interviews, as did friends in Ireland including at least one senior bishop.

He asked that the location where the interviews took place not be disclosed.

Award of Excellence
(Front Page)
The Sunday Tribune
Dublin, Ireland
Stephen Ryan, Design/Photo Editor; Paul Hopkins, Production Editor

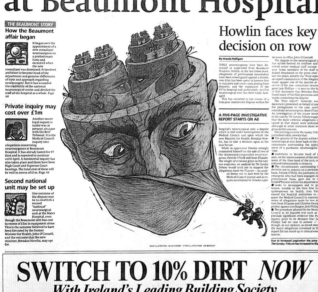

Award of Excellence
(Front Page)
The Sunday Tribune
Dublin, Ireland
Stephen Ryan, Design/Photo Editor; Paul Hopkins, Production Editor

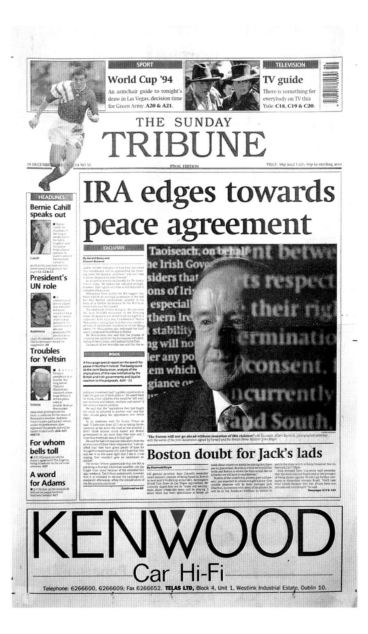

Bronze
Detroit Free Press
Detroit, MI
Deborah Withey, Design Director; Staff

Award of Excellence
(Lifestyle / Feature Page)
Detroit Free Press
Detroit, MI
James Denk, Designer

Award of Excellence
(Entertainment Page)
Detroit Free Press
Detroit, MI
Keith A. Webb, Designer

Award of Excellence
(Front Page)
Detroit Free Press
Detroit, MI
Deborah Withey, Design Director & Designer; Joe Zeff, Designer;
Keith Webb, Designer

Award of Excellence
(Typography General Use)
Detroit Free Press
Detroit, MI
James Denk, Designer

Award of Excellence
(Other Page)
Detroit Free Press
Detroit, MI
Keith A. Webb, Designer

Award of Excellence
The Detroit News
Detroit, MI
Staff

Award of Excellence
(Breaking News)
The Detroit News
Detroit, MI
Dale Peskin, AME; Joe Gray, Assistant News Editor

Award of Excellence
(Breaking News)
The Detroit News
Detroit, MI
Dale Peskin, AME; Chris Willis, Designer; Joe Gray, Assistant News Editor; Olivia Casey, Assistant News Editor

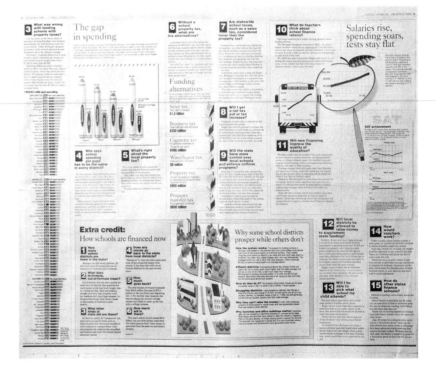

Award of Excellence
(Business Page)
The Detroit News
Detroit, MI
Don Asmussen, Designer; Wes Bausmith, Art Director

Award of Excellence
(Special News Topics)
The Detroit News
Detroit, MI
Dale Peskin, AME; Joe Gray, Assistant News Editor; Felix Grabowski, Graphics Editor; Robert Graham, Graphics Artist & Designer; Robert Richards, Graphics Artist & Designer; Mark Hass, AME/Local news; Pat McCaughan, State Editor

Award of Excellence
(Entertainment Section)
The Seattle Times
Seattle, WA
Fred Birchman, Graphics Artist & Designer; David Miller, Art Director

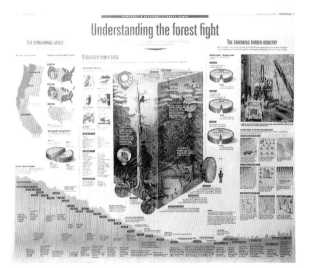

Award of Excellence
The Seattle Times
Seattle, WA
David Miller, Art Director; Staff

Award of Excellence
(Informational Graphics Two or More Colors)
The Seattle Times
Seattle, WA
Randee S. Fox, Designer, Infographics; Christine Cox, Designer, Infographics; Tom Reese, Photographer; David Miller, Art Director

Award of Excellence

The Washington Times
Washington, DC
Joseph Scopin, AME Design; Michael Keating, AME/News; Glen Stubbe, Photo Director; Gil Roschuni, Art Director; Staff

Award of Excellence

(Illustration Two or More colors)
The Washington Times
Washington, DC
John Kascht, Art Director, Designer & Illustrator

Award of Excellence

(Local News Page)
The Washington Times
Washington, DC
Don Renfroe, News Editor

chapter

three

Bronze
The Christian Science Monitor
Boston, MA
Staff

Bronze

The Detroit News
Detroit, MI
Dale Peskin, AME; Christy Bradford, ME; Jim Gatti, Deputy Managing Editor;
Sue Burzynski, AME/News; Joe Gray, Assistant News Editor; Olivia Casey,
Assistant News Editor; Craig Edwards, Designer & Copy Editor; Theresa
Badovich, Designer & Copy Editor; Bob Howard, Designer & Copy Editor

Award of Excellence
The News-Sentinel
Fort Wayne, IN
M. Daniel Suwyn, Design Editor; Denise M. Reagan, Designer;
Tom Bissett, Designer; Luisa Calderon Hayes, Designer;
Steven Austin, News Editor; Cindy Jones-Hulfachor, Graphics
& Research

Award of Excellence
Tallahassee Democrat
Tallahassee, FL
Staff

Award of Excellence
(Also winner for News Portfolio)
The San Bernardino County Sun
San Bernardino, CA
Patrick Olsen, News Editor; Marc Nurre, Wire Editor; Conrad
Wesselhoeft, Assistant News Editor

Award of Excellence
The Orange County Register
Santa Ana, CA
Bernadette Finley, Assistant News Editor/Design; Kevin
Byrne, News Editor/Design; Tia Lai, News Editor/Graphics;
Nanette Bisher, AME/Art Director; Ron Londen, News Edi-
tor/Photo; Jim Zisk, Graphic Artist; Staff

Award of Excellence
The Washington Times
Washington, DC
Staff

Bronze
The News-Sentinel
Fort Wayne, IN
William Dawson, Page Designer; Monica Denney, Section Designer; M. Daniel Suwyn, Design Director

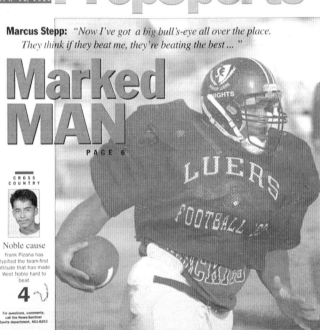

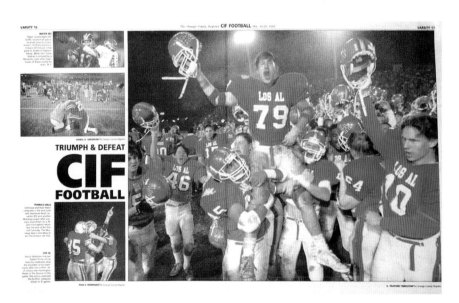

Bronze
The Orange County Register
Santa Ana, CA
Vic West, Copy Editor; David Bean, Copy Editor; Jim Rice, Copy Editor; Susan Trevarthen, Copy Editor; David Medzerian, Assistant News Editor/Design; Paul Loop, Assistant Sports Editor; Chris Carlson, Picture Editor; Mark Tomaszewski, Sports Editor; Nanette Bisher, AME/Art Director

Award of Excellence
Maine Sunday Telegram
Portland, ME
Steve Dandy, Designer; Jeff Hannon, Designer

Award of Excellence
The Times-Picayune
New Orleans, LA
Billy Turner, Deputy Sports Editor

Award of Excellence
The Detroit News
Detroit, MI
Felix Grabowski, Art Director & Designer; Nolan Finley, Section Editor; Mark Lett, AME; Don Asmussen, Graphics Artist; Robert Graham, Graphics Artist

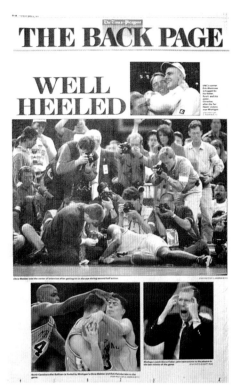

Award of Excellence
The Post-Star
Glens Falls, NY
Scott Goldman, Sunday Sports Editor

Award of Excellence
Chicago Tribune
Chicago, IL
Robb Montgomery, Art Director; Arn Arnam, Designer; Robin Johnston, Designer; Wendi Warner, Associate Editor; Stephen Cvengros, Editor

Award of Excellence
The Detroit News
Detroit, MI
Dale Peskin, AME; Luther Keith, AME/On Detroit; Felecia Henderson, Editor/On Detroit; Chris Willis, Designer; Hawke Fracassa, Designer

Close-up

THE ORANGE COUNTY REGISTER, SUNDAY, JULY 25, 1993

When Bill Seale's body let him down, he began a battle even more frightening than his tour of duty in Vietnam. In March, surgeons opened his chest and replaced his diseased heart and lungs. Yet the fight for life persists.

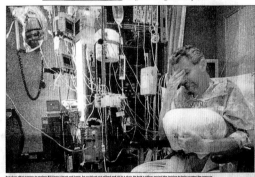

SECOND CHANCE

PROLOGUE

From pain to promise: one family's journey

Silver

The Orange County Register
Santa Ana, CA

Karen Kelso, Assistant News Editor/Design; David Medzerian, Assistant News Editor/Design; Brenda Shoun, Assistant News Editor/Design; Nadia Borowski, Photographer; Bruce Strong, Photographer; Paul Carbo, Graphics Artist; Betty Shimabukuro, Assistant Topic Editor; Kevin Byrne, News Editor/Design; Nanette Bisher, AME/Art Director

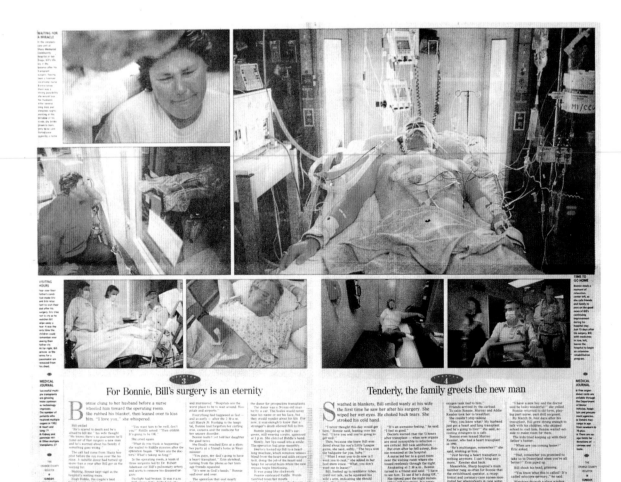

For Bonnie, Bill's surgery is an eternity

Tenderly, the family greets the new man

Bronze

Chicago Tribune
Chicago, IL
Robb Montgomery, Art Director; Arn Arnam, Designer;
Robin Johnston, Designer;
Ben Yonzon, Designer; Wendi Warner, Associate Editor;
Stephen Cvengros, Editor

Bronze

The Atlanta Journal-Constitution
Atlanta, GA
Tony DeFeria, Design Director & Design; D. W. Pine, Designer; Ellen Voss, Designer; Peggy Cozart, Photographer; Walt Stricklin, Photographer; Eric Williams, Photographer; Jeff Dickerson, Editor

Bronze

The New York Times
New York, NY
Ken McFarlin, Art Director &
Designer; Bedel Saget, De-
signer

Bronze

The San Bernardino County Sun
San Bernardino, CA
Patrick Olsen, News Editor; Conrad
Wesselhoeft, Assistant News Edi-
tor; Rosemary McClure, AME; Betts
Griffone, Art Director; John Weeks,
Assistant Features Editor

Silver
Detroit Free Press
Detroit, MI
Joe Zeff, Designer

Award of Excellence
Akron Beacon Journal
Akron, OH
Susan Mango Curtis, Designer; Debbie Van Tassel, Designer;
Art Krummel, Illustrator

Detroit Free Press

Metro Final
Partly cloudy.
High 22. Low 6.
Friday: Cloudy, cold.

Thursday
February 18, 1993
For home delivery call 222-6500
25 cents (50 cents outside 6-county metropolitan area)

On Guard For 161 Years

▶ **THE VICTIMS**
From left: LaWanda Williams, 9,
Nikia Williams, 7, Dakwan Williams, 6

Not pictured: La Quinten Lyons, 4, Venus Lyons, 2,
Anthony Lyons, 7 months, Mark Brayboy, 2

'If we do not act now,'
president says, America
can't afford consequences

7 kids die alone

CLINTON'S WARNING

BY ROBERT S. BOYD AND DAVID HESS

WASHINGTON — President Bill Clinton challenged Americans on Wednesday night to accept $340 billion in new taxes and program cuts to restore the nation's economy and halve the federal deficit over the next four years.

"Our economic plan is ambitious, but it is necessary for the continued greatness of our country," Clinton told a joint session of Congress as he unveiled a proposal for one of the most massive changes in taxing and spending policy in peacetime history.

"America has called for change, and now it is up to those of us in this room to deliver for them," the president said.

■ Tax by income level, Page 12A.
■ State firms worry, Page 1E.

"If we do not act now," he said, "we will not recognize this country 10 years from now."

The lawmakers applauded enthusiastically, but their willingness to endorse their new president's program remains very much in doubt.

Not since World War II has a president proposed such strong medicine. And not since Ronald Reagan 12 years ago called for a popular program of deep tax cuts and much more money for the Pentagon has a president recommended such a fundamental shift in how the government operates.

The extraordinary scope, cost and pain of the president's plan guarantees a major political and economic battle, lasting for months and engaging every sector of society, before it can be enacted.

Clinton foreshadowed another great battle

See CLINTON, Page 12A

▶ **ANALYSIS**

Selling the program means winning over the vast middle class

BY DAVID SHRIBMAN
Boston Globe

WASHINGTON — Now begins the most ferocious economic fight of the decade.

With Wednesday night's speech before Congress and the release of his economic game plan, President Bill Clinton has spawned a classic political debate, challenged his rivals and perhaps, even before a month has passed, put his presidency on the line.

The president's opponents will come from every quarter, region, income group and ideology. His battle will be with Republicans, conservative Democrats, and a mass of special interests, including older people, defense hawks, and the energy industry.

This is a battle about economic policy, to be sure, but it is really a gritty, cold-blooded political fight.

It is a struggle for the allegiance of the most important player in American politics, the middle class, and it will be fought and ultimately won over the most inflammatory word in American politics: taxes.

Republicans are arguing that "putting people first," the slogan that Clinton used in the fall campaign, has been distilled down to its real meaning, putting taxes first.

"Convincing the middle class on taxes is a real political mine field," said James Reichley, a

See ANALYSIS, Page 13A

▶ **IMPACT ON INDIVIDUALS**

If the president's proposals are enacted, here is how they would affect people's money.

■ **Households making less than $30,000:** Little difference. The energy tax would take some money away. Income would increase, though, by an expanded tax reimbursement for low-income workers, more food stamp aid and an energy assistance program.

■ **The middle class:** A typical family of four with income of $40,000 would lose about $200 a year. That includes about $10 a month from the energy tax.

■ **The affluent:** Single people with taxable income above $115,000 — that's after subtracting exemptions and deductions — would see their income tax rate go from 31 percent to 36 percent. So would couples with taxable income above $140,000 (meaning gross income of about $180,000).

For example, someone whose gross income is $200,000 a year would pay $3,400 more in taxes.

■ **The rich:** An additional 10 percent would be imposed on taxable incomes (not including capital gains) over $250,000. A person with $500,000 income and an $80,000 tax liability would pay an extra $8,000.

■ **Social Security recipients:** Those who now pay tax on up to half their benefits would be taxed up to 85 percent instead. This provision affects the wealthiest one-quarter of recipients.

A Detroit fire fighter carries one of seven children from a home in the 2200 block of Mack. The cause of the fire is being investigated. Educators, parents and others said Wednesday that more children left home alone are sure to perish. Story, Page 11A.

Fire sweeps east side home; security bars block escape

BY JIM SCHAEFER, L.A. JOHNSON AND ROGER CHESLEY
Free Press Staff Writers

Seven young brothers and sisters died in a locked east side home Wednesday in a fire that was marked by the very problems that have plagued the city and drawn sharp pleas from fire prevention officials.

The children were home alone.

All exits were blocked, most with security bars.

There were no smoke detectors.

"It was a tragic fire," said Chief Rodney Parnell of the community relations division of the Detroit Fire Department. "This kind of thing happens again and again and there's going to be an apathy ... for some reason, people feel it's not going to happen to them."

Killed were LaWanda Williams, 9; Nikia Williams, 7; Dakwan Williams, 6; La Quinten Lyons, 4; Venus Lyons, 2; Anthony Lyons, 7 months; and Mark Brayboy, 2.

Late Wednesday, homicide detectives questioned Shereese Williams, 30, mother of six of the children, who told police she left home to go shopping about a half hour before the 2 p.m. blaze. Detectives also questioned the children's father, Detective Sgt. of Social Services records identify him as Leroy Lyons, 38.

The pair left their home at least 30 to 45 minutes before the blaze

See FIRE, Page 11A

Two women weep outside the home where the children died Wednesday. "They can't be dead," cried one of the women, right, who was identified as a cousin of the children.

INSIDE TODAY

Ann Landers	2D
Bridge	7D
Classified Index	1F
Comics, Crossword	6D
Death Notices	4B
Editorials	14A
Entertainment	2D
Horoscope	6D
Jumble	6D
Movie Guide	2D
Obituaries	4B
Stock Markets	2E
Television	7D
Weather	2B

Vol. 162, Number 280
© 1993, Detroit Free Press

What moves the movies

Clint Eastwood, left, is among the Oscar nominees announced Wednesday. Film critic Judy Gerstel thinks he's a deserving choice for best director, but she has big questions about some other choices. Her report is in Page 1D; for a list of the nominees, see Page 4D.

AKRON BEACON JOURNAL

Sunday, February 28, 1993

Race: The great divide

A separate, but equal, focus on our differences

Blacks: They must live the daily waltz of the irritating realities of subtle and overt racism in the area

Whites: They say racism is a vital issue, but also as a riddle that leaves them grasping for solutions

Tell us what you think

INSIDE:

Traces of bomb material found at blast site

SUNDAY / INDEX

Special section	Susan Watson	Auto talks
Photos, quotes, history and more on Young	Only time could catch the man who was Detroit	Fairness a central issue as GM, UAW begin
Pages 7A-14A	Page 15A	Page 7C

Detroit Free Press

Metro Final   On Guard for 162 Years   **Wednesday**
June 23, 1993

YOUNG ENDS AN ERA

'20 years is enough'

Tired mayor won't run again, leaves an open field

BY BILL McGRAW
Free Press Staff Writer

Mayor Coleman Young makes his point during a news conference Tuesday, in which he announced he will not seek re-election but will stay active in city affairs.

Outrageous, larger than life and often contradictory, Coleman Young as mayor has been both charismatic and reclusive, progressive and paranoid, inspirational and embittered.

His 20-year reign has included epic highs and lows. Free Press Staff Writer Bill McGraw, who has covered the mayor for years, chronicles Young's extraordinary reign, starting on Page 11A.

Election '93
'I may support someone and I may not.'
COLEMAN YOUNG

Next: Detroit is in for fresh leadership, a new style

But familiar obstacles will be awaiting successor

INSIDE TODAY

Award of Excellence
Detroit Free Press
Detroit, MI
Deborah Withey, Design Director & Designer;
Lee Yarosh, Designer

Bronze
The Times-Picayune
New Orleans, LA
George Berke, Design Director; Kurt Mutchler, Photo & Graphics Editor; Staff

Award of Excellence
The Detroit News
Detroit, MI
Dale Peskin, AME; Bob Howard, Designer

Award of Excellence
New York Newsday
Melville, NY
Joanne S. Utley, Art Director & Designer; Don Forst, New York Editor; John Mancini, News Editor; Richard Lee, Photographer; Stan Wolfson, Photo Editor

Award of Excellence
The Miami Herald
Miami, FL
Daryl Kannberg, Herschel Kenner, Mel Frishman, Assistant News Editors; Steve Rice, AME Graphics; Phill Flanders, Illustrator; Randy Stano, Director of Editorial Art & Design; Juan Lopez, Graphic Arts/Intern; Dennis Copeland, Photo Director

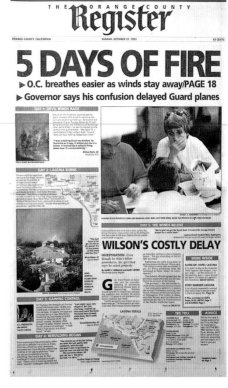

Award of Excellence
The Orange County Register
Santa Ana, CA
John Fabris, Assistant News Editor/Design; James Zisk, Graphics Artist; Daniel A. Anderson, Photographer; Bruce Chambers, Photographer; Ron Londen, News Editor/Photo; Kevin Byrne, News Editor/Design; Tia Lai, News Editor/Graphics

Award of Excellence

San Jose Mercury News
San Jose, CA

Bryan Monroe, Design Director; Jeff Thomas, Executive News Editor; Mike Mayer, Assistant News Editor; Paul Van Slambrouck, AME/News; David Yarnold, Deputy Managing Editor; Molly Swisher, Art Director; Murray Koodish, Picture Editor

Award of Excellence

The Times-Picayune
New Orleans, LA

George Berke, Design Director; Kurt Mutchler, Photo & Graphics Editor; Staff

Award of Excellence

The Times-Picayune
New Orleans, LA

George Berke, Design Director; Kurt Mutchler, Photo & Graphics Editor; Staff

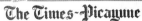
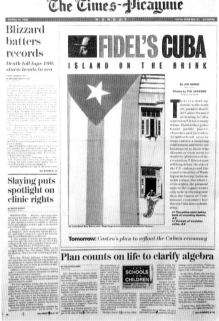

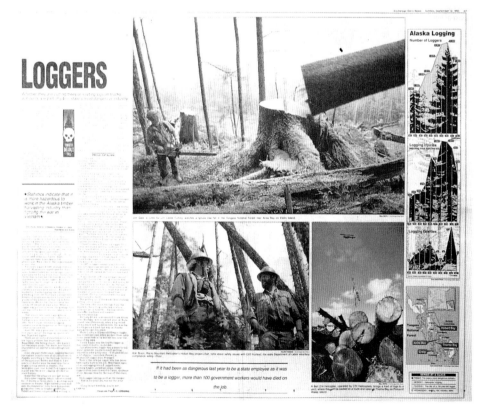

Award of Excellence

The Albuquerque Tribune
Albuquerque, NM

Tony Stewart, Designer; Joan Carlin, Picture Editor

Award of Excellence

Anchorage Daily News
Anchorage, AK

Mike Campbell, AME & Designer; Ron Engstrom, Graphics Artist; Bill Roth, Photographer

Bronze
The Citizen
Auburn, NY
Gary Piccirillo, AME Design

Bronze
The Times/Munster
Munster, IN
John Humenik, AME Design; Michael Zajakowski, Director of Photography;
Staff

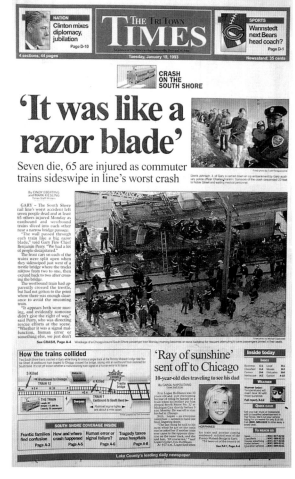

Bronze
Journal Review
Crawfordsville, IN
John Pea, ME; Dave Tomaro, News Editor

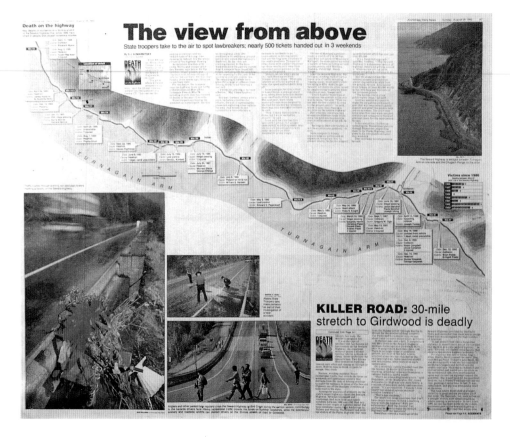

Award of Excellence
The Citizen
Auburn, NY
Gary Piccirillo, AME Design

Award of Excellence
The Citizen
Auburn, NY
Gary Piccirillo, AME Design

Award of Excellence
The Citizen
Auburn, NY
Gary Piccirillo, AME Design

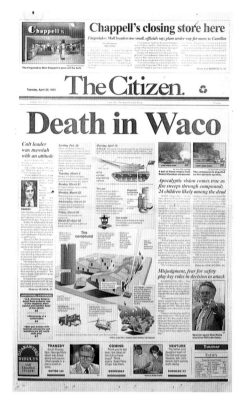

Award of Excellence
The News-Sentinel
Fort Wayne, IN
M. Daniel Suwyn, Design Editor & Designer; Luisa Calderon
Hayes, Designer; Steve Linsenmayer, Photographer; Keith
Hitchens, Photographer; Cindy Jones-Hulfachor, Graphics Il-
lustrator; Steven Austin, News Editor

Award of Excellence
The National Law Journal
New York, NY
Douglas Hunt, Design Director

Award of Excellence
El Mundo Deportivo
Barcelona, Spain
Joan Lanuza, Subdirector

Award of Excellence
Reforma
New York, NY
Roger Black, Design Consultant; Eduardo Danilo, Design Consultant; Ramon Alberto Garza, Editor; Emilio Deheza, Vice Art Director

Award of Excellence
The Times/Munster
Munster, IN
John Humenik, AME Design; Stephan Benzkofer, Designer; Sunday Staff

Award of Excellence
The Times/Munster
Munster, IN
John Humenik, AME Design; Stephan Benzkofer, Designer

Award of Excellence
(also winner for News Portfolio)
The Sun/Bremerton
Bremerton, WA
Tracy Porter, Assistant Presentation Editor

Award of Excellence
The Times/Lansing
Lansing, IL
Kara Hundley, Display Editor

Award of Excellence

The University Daily Kansan
Lawrence, KS
Ezra Wolfe, Designer; K.C. Trauer, Editor; Joe Harder, ME

Award of Excellence

The University Daily Kansan
Lawrence, KS
Ezra Wolfe, Designer; John Paul Fogel, Graphics Editor; Tom
Leininger, Photographer; K. C. Trauer, Editor; Joe Harder, M

Award of Excellence

The University Daily Kansan
Lawrence, KS
Greg Farmer, Editor; Gayle Osterberg, ME; Justin Knupp,
AME/Designer; Rachel G. Thompson, Photographer; Derek
Nolen, Graphics Artist

Award of Excellence

Los Angeles Times
Costa Mesa, CA
Dennis Lowe, Graphics Artist & Designer; Caroline Lemke,
Researcher; Marla Cone, Researcher; Tom Reinken, Deputy
Graphics Editor; Juan Thomassie, Art Director; Lily Dow,
Graphics Editor

Award of Excellence

The Virginian-Pilot
Norfolk, VA
Latane Jones, Designer & Photo Editor

Award of Excellence

The Sun/Bremerton
Bremerton, WA
Tracy Porter, Assistant Presentation Editor

Bronze
Journal Review
Crawfordsville, IN
John Pea, ME; Dave Tomaro, News Editor

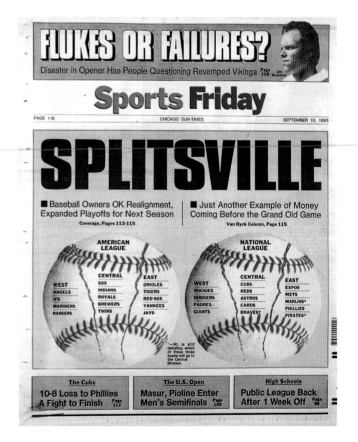

Award of Excellence
The Atlanta Journal-Constitution
Atlanta, GA
Vernon Carne, Graphics Artist & Designer; Tony DeFeria, Design Director

Award of Excellence
Chicago Sun-Times
Chicago, IL
Rick Jaffe, Deputy Managing Editor; Bill Adee, Sports Editor; Bill Linden, Designer

Award of Excellence

Detroit Free Press
Detroit, MI
Wayne Kamidoi, Design Director/Sports; Chris Magerl, Picture Editor

Award of Excellence

The New York Times
New York, NY
Fred Norgaard, Art Director

Award of Excellence

The Phoenix Gazette
Phoenix, AZ
Terry Beahm, Design Editor

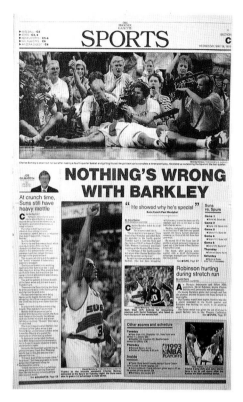

Award of Excellence

San Francisco Examiner
San Francisco, CA
Glenn Schwartz, Sports Editor; Kelly Frankeny, Art Director;
Chris Morris, Illustrator; Pete Cafone, Designer; Sports staff

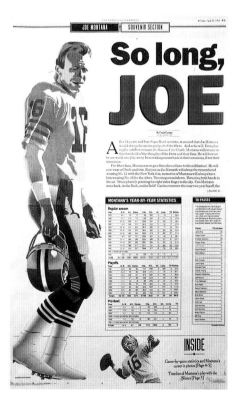

Award of Excellence

San Francisco Examiner
San Francisco, CA
Tracy Cox, Designer; Glenn Schwartz, Sports Editor; Kelly Frankeny, Art Director; Chris Morris, Illustrator

Award of Excellence

San Jose Mercury News
San Jose, CA
Albert Poon, Designer; Michael Rondou, Photographer; Paul Kitagaki, Photographer; David Tepps, Executive Sports Editor

Award of Excellence
Springfield News-Leader
Springfield, MO
Jeff Harper, Graphics Artist; John L. Dengler, Graphics Editor;
George Benge, Managing Editor

Award of Excellence
The Albuquerque Tribune
Albuquerque, NM
Randall K. Roberts, AME Graphics

Award of Excellence
The Seattle Times
Seattle, WA
Rick Lund, Designer; David Miller, Art Director; Sports Staff

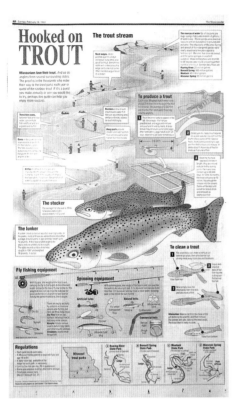

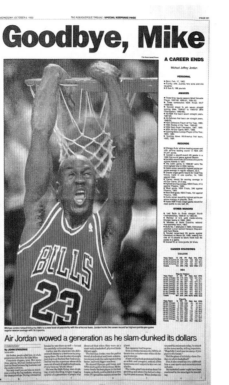

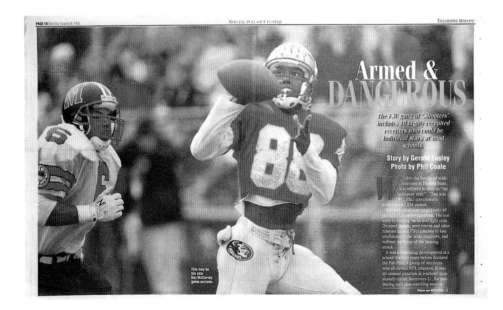

Award of Excellence
Tallahassee Democrat
Tallahassee, FL
Ron Morris, Executive Sports Editor; L. K. Mirrer, Graphics Editor

Award of Excellence
The Washington Times
Washington, DC
George Kolb, Designer

Bronze
The Ann Arbor News
Ann Arbor, MI
Alan Bliss, Editorial Art Director

Silver
The Times/Munster
Munster, IN
Aldino Gallo, Photographer; Michael McGehee, Designer

Bronze
The Sun/Lowell
Lowell, MA
Mitchell Hayes, Art Director & Designer; Allen Mudgett,
Illustrator; Dennis Whitton, Editor

Award of Excellence

Anchorage Daily News
Anchorage, AK
Mike Lewis, Designer; Erik Hill, Photographer; Lance Lekander, Graphics Artist

Award of Excellence

The Post-Star
Glens Falls, NY
Scott Goldman, Sunday Sports Editor; Joan K. Lentini, Photographer

Award of Excellence

Birmingham Post-Herald
Birmingham, AL
Don Kausler, Sports Editor & Designer; Sean Patrick Duffy, Picture Editor

Award of Excellence

The Sun/Bremerton
Bremerton, WA
Tracy Porter, Assistant Presentation Editor

Award of Excellence

Anchorage Daily News
Anchorage, AK
Mike Campbell, AME & Designer; Mark Dolan, Photographer; Jim Jager, Photo Editor

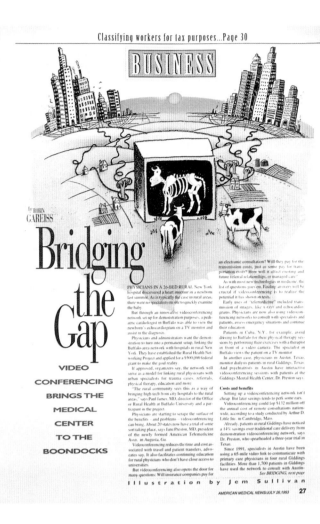

Silver

American Medical News
Chicago, IL
Barbara Dow, Art Director & Designer; Jem Sullivan, Illustrator

Bronze

The San Diego Union-Tribune
San Diego, CA
Kirk Christ, Business Graphics Editor

Bronze

American Medical News
Chicago, IL
Barbara Dow, Art Director & Designer; Jem Sullivan, Illustrator

Award of Excellence
American Medical News
Chicago, IL
Barbara Dow, Art Director & Designer; John Kascht, Illustrator

Award of Excellence
American Medical News
Chicago, IL
Jef Capaldi, Art Director & Designer; Tracy Cox, Illustrator

Award of Excellence
Dayton Daily News
Dayton, OH
David Kordalski, Designer & Illustrator; Kevin Riley, Editor;
John Thomson, AME Graphics

Award of Excellence
The New York Times
New York, NY
Greg Ryan, Art Director & Designer

Award of Excellence
Rockford Register Star
Rockford, IL
Steve Layton, Graphics Artist; Keith Grace, Graphics Editor;
John Wilson, Business Editor

Award of Excellence
San Francisco Examiner
San Francisco, CA
Tracy Cox, Designer; Katie Rabin, Business Editor; Kelly Frankeny, Art Director; Dale Henderscheid, Illustrator

Award of Excellence
The Virginian-Pilot
Norfolk, VA
Paiching Wei, Artist; Mi-ai Gaber, Editor

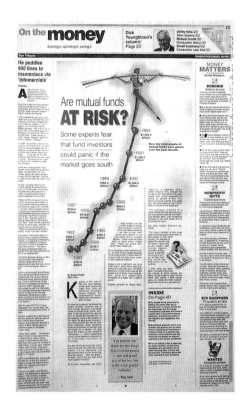

Award of Excellence
Star Tribune
Minneapolis, MN
Anders Ramberg, Art Director & Designer; Scott Gillespie, Assistant Business Editor; Susan Feyder, Writer

Award of Excellence
Star Tribune
Minneapolis, MN
Anders Rambert, Art Director & Graphic Designer; Scott Gillespie, Assistant Business Editor; Jill Hodges, Writer; Tony Kennedy, Writer

Award of Excellence
The Wall Street Journal
New York, NY
James Condon, Graphics Director; Marco Herrera, Art Director; Germaine Keller, Editorial Artist; Richard Bennett, Illustrator

Award of Excellence
The Washington Post
Washington, DC
John Anderson Jr., Art Director; Phil Foster, Illustrator

Award of Excellence
The Washington Post
Washington, DC
John Anderson Jr., Art Director; Phil Foster, Illustrator

MAY 31, 1993 — The Washington Post

Washington Business

Banks Bounce Back

*Area Lenders Recover
From Real Estate Losses*

By William F. Powers
Washington Post Staff Writer

One thing less to worry about: banks.

Just three years after it was laid low by bad real estate loans, the local banking industry—what remains of it—is bounding back to health.

Strong balance sheets, soaring profits and an invasion by vigorous out-of-town banks are dispelling the gloom that descended in 1990 with a wave of bank losses, closings and takeovers. That year, the District's oldest bank, National Bank of Washington, failed, followed by local stalwarts Madison National Bank and Perpetual Savings Bank. Other banks throughout the region also disappeared.

For consumers, the post-crisis banking landscape is an unfamiliar place, one that will take some getting used to.

The shakeout left local banking largely controlled by companies from outside greater Washington. Area business owners sometimes grouse about the loss of See **BANKS**, page 10

■ *Charts show how your bank is doing.   Page 10*

BUYER FOR VITRO CORP.	WASHTECH	WASHINGTON INVESTING
A Texas firm is expected to announce that it is buying Vitro Corp. of Silver Spring, but will not move workers from Montgomery County. **14**	CyberTalk takes a look at the PC, which is just a machine when you get right down to it. Also, safeguarding your computer server. **15**	Scott & Stringfellow, a Richmond brokerage firm, stays true to its southern roots by not straying too far from its home territory. **25**

SEPTEMBER 13, 1993 — The Washington Post

Washington Business

Associations Packing Up, Moving Out

*Low-Cost Suburbs
Lure Nonprofit Groups*

By Martha M. Hamilton
Washington Post Staff Writer

The District of Columbia, once the prestige address for nonprofit organizations and trade associations, is steadily losing ground to the suburbs as a location for this key local industry.

Associations are increasingly likely to set up shop in the suburbs because of the relatively high cost of doing business in the District and the difficulty in finding adequate facilities, according to executives at several associations.

The trend also has received a boost from active recruiting of associations by suburban jurisdictions, especially those in Northern Virginia. In contrast, the District has done little to retain associations, rarely weighing in when decisions are being made, according to association executives who said they never heard from the District during deliberations on whether to move.

"We may lose out on pure economics, but what they're saying is: We didn't get into the race," D.C. economic development chief George W. Brown said. He said he hopes to create a system that will alert D.C. officials when businesses or other employers See **ASSOCIATIONS**, page 16

REINVENTING THE REALTY MARKET	WASHTECH	WASHINGTON INVESTING
Two proposals in the administration's report on reinventing government have big implications for the area's still-struggling office market. **5**	When it comes to figuring out spreadsheets for the personal computer, sometimes it's not as easy as 1-2-3. **19**	The coming of NationsBank to Baltimore is viewed with concern by some stock brokerages as a serious competitor for financial services. **29**

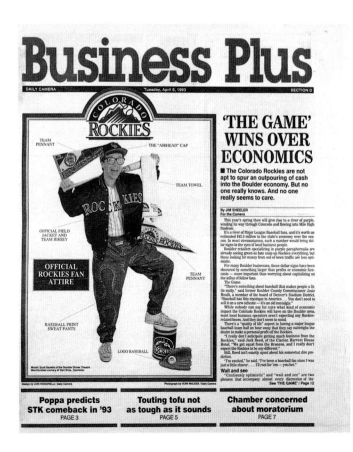

Business Plus

DAILY CAMERA   Tuesday, April 6, 1993   SECTION D

'THE GAME' WINS OVER ECONOMICS

■ The Colorado Rockies are not apt to spur an outpouring of cash into the Boulder economy. But no one really knows. And no one really seems to care.

By JIM SHEELER
For the Camera

This year's spring thaw will give rise to a river of purple, winding its way through Colorado and flowing into Mile High Stadium.

It's a river of Major League Baseball fans, and it's worth an estimated $42.5 million to the state's economy over the season. In most circumstances, such a number would bring dollar signs to the eyes of local business people.

Boulder retailers specializing in purple paraphernalia are already seeing green as fans snap up Rockies everything, but those looking for money from out-of-town traffic are less optimistic.

For many Boulder businesses, those dollar signs have been obscured by something larger than profits or economic forecasts — more important than worrying about capitalizing on the influx of fellow fans.

The Game.

"There's something about baseball that makes people a little nutty," said former Boulder County Commissioner Josie Heath, a member of the board of Denver's Stadium District. "Baseball has this mystique in America . . . You don't need to sell it on a new scheme — it's an old nostalgia."

While nobody can say for sure what kind of economic impact the Colorado Rockies will have on the Boulder area, most local business operators aren't expecting any Rockies-related boom. And they don't seem to mind.

There's a "quality of life" aspect to having a major league baseball team half an hour away that they say outweighs the desire to make a personal profit off the Rockies.

"I really don't anticipate getting much business from the Rockies," said Jack Reed, of the Clarion Harvest House Hotel. "We get squat from the Broncos, and I really don't expect the Rockies to be any different."

Still, Reed isn't exactly upset about his somewhat dire prediction.

"I'm excited," he said. "I've been a baseball fan since I was just a little shaver . . . I'll root for 'em — you bet."

Wait and see

"Cautiously optimistic" and "wait and see" are two phrases that accompany almost every discussion of the See **'THE GAME'** Page 12

TEAM PENNANT — THE "AIRHEAD" CAP — TEAM TOWEL — OFFICIAL FIELD JACKET AND TEAM JERSEY — OFFICIAL ROCKIES FAN ATTIRE — BASEBALL PRINT SWEAT PANTS — LOGO BASEBALL — TEAM PENNANT

Design by LORI RONDINELLI / Daily Camera   Photograph by VERN WALKER / Daily Camera
Model: Scott Sayette of the Boulder Dinner Theatre   Merchandise courtesy of Gart Bros., Sportsinart

Poppa predicts STK comeback in '93 PAGE 3	Touting tofu not as tough as it sounds PAGE 5	Chamber concerned about moratorium PAGE 7

Award of Excellence
Daily Camera
Franklin, WI
Lori Rondinelli, Graphics Artist

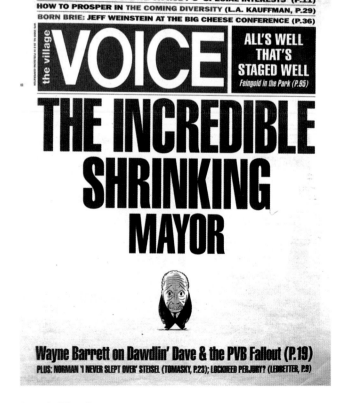

August 31, 1993•Vol. XXXVIII No. 35•The Weekly Newspaper of New York•$1.00

ANTI-GAY LITE: MINKOWITZ ON RUDY'S 'SPECIAL INTERESTS' (P.11)
HOW TO PROSPER IN THE COMING DIVERSITY (L.A. KAUFFMAN, P.29)
BORN BRIE: JEFF WEINSTEIN AT THE BIG CHEESE CONFERENCE (P.36)

the village **VOICE**

ALL'S WELL THAT'S STAGED WELL
Feingold in the Park (P.95)

THE INCREDIBLE SHRINKING MAYOR

Wayne Barrett on Dawdlin' Dave & the PVB Fallout (P.19)
PLUS: NORMAN 'I NEVER SLEPT OVER' STEISEL (TOMASKY, P.23); LOCKHEED PERJURY? (LEDBETTER, P.9)

Award of Excellence
The Village Voice
New York, NY
Robert Newman, Design Director; Eric Palma, Illustrator

Award of Excellence

(also winner for News Portfolio)
The Washington Times
Washington, DC
Joseph Scopin, AME Graphics; Paul Compton, Art Director,
Designer & Illustrator; Bert V. Goulait, Photographer; Vivian
Ronay, Photographer; Peter A. Harris, Photographer

Award of Excellence

San Jose Mercury News
San Jose, CA
Murray Koodish, Photo Editor/Designer

Award of Excellence

The Citizen
Auburn, NY
Kevin Rivoli, Photo Editor

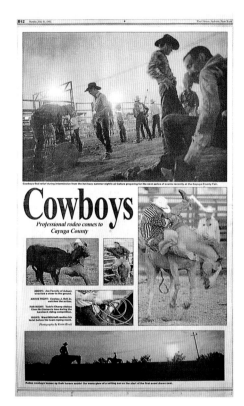

Award of Excellence

The Orange County Register
Santa Ana, CA
Brenda Shoun, Assistant News Editor/Design; Chris Carlson,
Picture Editor; Bruce Strong, Photographer; Ahn Do, Re-
porter; Betty Shimabukuro, Assistant Topic Editor

Award of Excellence

The News-Sentinel
Fort Wayne, IN
William Dawson, Designer; Steve Linsenmayer, Photograph-
er; M. Daniel Suwyn, Design Editor

Award of Excellence

The Olympian
Olympia, WA
Karen Kurtz, Sunday Editor

Silver
The Detroit News
Detroit, MI
Dale Peskin, AME; Joe Gray, Assistant News Editor; Olivia Casey, Assistant News Editor

Behind the Decision   BACK TO IRAQ

After watching Saddam Hussein flout UN cease-fire rules for months, President George Bush and his allies weighed military action. When Iraq's provocations intensified, a strike was carried out.

Bush bows out with flurry of action — and a rebuke to Hussein

WASHINGTON — In his discouragement after losing the election, he appeared. Decisions that would leave office with a whimper, instead he has chosen to go out with a bang.

"Ever as the very end of his presidency, he is using the occasion," said James Duke University professor James David Barber, author of studies of presidential character. "He's probably think-"

It is galling to Bush that Saddam Hussein still holds power in Iraq while his own power drains away in the White House. But with just seven days to act, the lame-duck president became a screaming eagle, unleashing a farewell pounding from the sky.

Military showdown was months in the making

The Detroit News

25¢
50¢ outside 6-county metropolitan area

Thursday, JANUARY 14, 1993

Can Hussein get revenge?

■ **'Wall of fire'?** He vows 'a great victory' but analysts say his weakened forces may make threat hollow.

DETROIT NEWS WIRE SERVICES

BAGHDAD — With his missile sites and military command centers damaged in Wednesday's fierce strikes by 112 allied warplanes, Saddam Hussein today was ordering his forces to turn Iraqi skies into "a wall of fire" against allied planes.

But military analysts said the Iraqi leader has no chance of mounting real opposition to the sophisticated arsenal of the allies, despite his promise of "a great victory" against the Western "criminals."

They said, however, that his 1990 invasion of Kuwait showed Hussein is capable of anything, and his actions often fly in the face of orthodox military thinking — usually with catastrophic results.

Hussein's military, partially rebuilt since the gulf war, still has about 300 warplanes, almost 2,500 tanks and an equal number of artillery pieces, but analysts said those numbers mean little against allied systems guided by lasers and radar.

The raid Wednesday on southern Iraq met only token opposition from Iraqi ground fire, which fell far short of the high-flying attack force.

The attack left a half-dozen missile and command centers smoldering.

After the strike — the bombing lasted just 30 minutes — U.S. authorities said there was no sign of new Iraqi military activity. But White House press secretary Marlin Fitzwater warned that the allies "stand ready to take additional forceful action" if Iraq tries to retaliate or continues to defy UN authority.

Please see Revenge, 14A

AT A GLANCE

■ **Casualties:** One Iraqi soldier and three civilians were killed in the U.S.-led raids on southern Iraq; 7 others were wounded.

■ **U.S. poll:** Eighty-three percent of Americans support the attack on Iraq, according to a USA Today/CNN/Gallup poll.

■ **Clinton responds:** President-elect Clinton, in a New York Times interview, said he would not rule out renewing a ground war against Iraq if necessary to force compliance with UN cease-fire resolutions but indicated he was ready for a fresh start with Iraq.

■ **More troops:** President Bush ordered a tank battalion of 1,100 troops to join 300 U.S. special operations forces in Kuwait to serve as a deterrent to further Iraqi incursions into Kuwait.

■ **Hussein defiance:** Saddam Hussein told his armed forces in a television address "fight them the way you fought God's enemies before."

■ **The attack:** U.S. officials said the 30-minute strike destroyed four fixed and several mobile anti-aircraft missile sites plus air-defense radar in Iraq's southern "no-fly" zone.

Lightning strike

112 U.S. and allied warplanes bombed anti-aircraft missile sites in southern Iraq Wednesday. The 30-minute attack involved 36 strike planes and 74 support aircraft from the United States, France and Britain. Here's a look at what happened:

SID JABLONSKI AND ROBERT GRAHAM with research by MICHELE PECHT-The Detroit News

A warplane's engine light up flight deck of the USS Kitty Hawk in the Persian Gulf Wednesday as the craft takes off and heads for targets in southern Iraq.

LAURENT REBOURS/Associated Press

6 pages of coverage

■ **The decision:** Bush consulted with allies. Page 5A
■ **Meanwhile:** Limited strike lessens risk. Page 5A
■ **Baghdad:** Iraqis worry about the future. Page 7A
■ At home: Michigan unit ready to go back. Page 8A
■ Financial markets: No one flinches. Page 13A
■ In Tempe: Nerve rattled for the raid. Page 14A

A TALK WITH BILL CLINTON

Clinton won't rule out new ground war

DETROIT NEWS STAFF AND WIRES

NEW YORK — President-elect Bill Clinton says he would not rule out renewing the ground war against Iraq if necessary to force compliance with UN resolutions, but also indicated in an interview today that he was ready for a fresh start with President Saddam Hussein.

Clinton told The New York Times he would imagine a normal relationship with Hussein provided the Iraqi leader behaved in accordance with international norms.

Clinton said he wanted to send Hussein a signal, which he summarized by saying: "I am going to judge you by your behavior. I am not going to sit around trying to figure out what is motivating you."

In an interview that the Times described as striking in its matter-of-fact, self-assured tone, Clinton repeatedly warned Hussein not to test or underestimate him.

He said that if Hussein were on the couch next to him he would say: "If you want a different future, behave differently.

Please see Interview, 14A

LOCAL IRAQIS

'No one should die, Americans or Arabs'

By Angie Cannon and Said Deep
THE DETROIT NEWS

Wednesday's bombing of Iraq was a nightmare for Ban Kado.

Two years ago, she had constantly feared that she would be killed during the U.S. bombing of Baghdad.

Wednesday afternoon, "my sister called and said, 'Did you hear the bombing?' So the bombing Iraq," said Kado, who moved to Southfield right

months ago with her family. "I was shocked. I cried.

"I said, 'How can it happen again?'"

Kado and many others in Metro Detroit's 63,000-member Chaldean-American community, many of whom still have family in northern Iraq, expressed disappointment over the decision by the United States and its Western allies to launch air raids against the Iraqi regime.

Please see Local Iraqis, 8A

■ **Sports** Pistons, Wings win; Michigan State defeats Ohio State. **1D**
■ **Metro** Greektown developers say Washington will approve casino. **1B**
■ **Business** Savings for air travelers; Delta counters Northwest's fare cuts. **1E**

INSIDE			
Classified		Horoscope	
Class/Auto		Lottery	
Comics		Movies	
Crossword		Obituaries	
Deaths		Stocks	
Editorials		TV	

The Scene   BACK TO IRAQ

The USS Kitty Hawk crackled with electricity in the aftermath of a mission accomplished. Meanwhile, in Baghdad, Iraqis appeared dispirited and occasionally panicked.

The Kitty Hawk

Thirty-five aircraft from the USS Kitty Hawk led an attack Wednesday on southern Iraq. The combat aircraft headed a force of 112 warplanes attacking command and control centers and missile sites within Iraq's no-fly zone. The Kitty Hawk, part of a 12-ship Navy task force in the Persian Gulf, carries some of the world's most sophisticated aircraft.

IN BAGHDAD

'It seems there is no way out right now'

By Nora Boustany
WASHINGTON POST

BAGHDAD, Iraq — Iraqis appeared dispirited and occasionally panicked today by their country's military showdown with the United States.

Pilots report 'beautiful, beautiful' missions

By Neil MacFarquhar
ASSOCIATED PRESS

ABOARD THE USS KITTY HAWK — The deck of this aircraft carrier swarmed with increased clamor as aircraft landed Wednesday night.

IN KUWAIT

Kuwaitis cheer air strike, but fear reprisals by Iraq

By Diana Elias
ASSOCIATED PRESS

KUWAIT CITY — Kuwaitis cheered the Western air strike on Iraq Wednesday, but are resigned to months of aggravating attacks and other provocations in the two-year feud with their neighbor.

US observer David Kim of Singapore watches relief as six missile bunkers that were reveled to Iraqi workers minutes.

Breaking News / Trade Center Bombing / King Verdict / Editor's Choice, National / Int.

news

Award of Excellence
The New York Times
New York, NY
Tom Bodkin, Design Director; Margaret O'Connor, Deputy Design Director; Rich Meislin, Graphics Director; Jean Montesino Rutter, Graphics Editor; David Montesino, Graphics Artist; Julie Shaver, Graphics Artist; Donald Parsons, Graphics Editor; Lee Frempong, Make-up Editor; Jim Mones, Make-up Editor; Peter Putrimas, Make-up Editor

Award of Excellence
St. Paul Pioneer Press
St. Paul, MN
Joe Sevick, News Editor; Don Wyatt, Executive News Editor

Award of Excellence
Dagens Nyheter
Stockholm, Sweden
Staff

Award of Excellence
Detroit Free Press
Detroit, MI
Joe Zeff, Designer

Award of Excellence
San Jose Mercury News
San Jose, CA
Bryan Monroe, Design Director; Jeff Thomas, Executive News Editor; Mike Mayer, Assistant News Editor; Paul Van Slambrouck, AME/News; David Yarnold, Deputy Managing Editor; Molly Swisher, Art Director; Scott DeMuesy, Picture Editor; Murray Koodish, Picture Editor

Award of Excellence
The Times-Picayune
New Orleans, LA
George Berke, Design Director, Staff

Gold

The Detroit News
Detroit, MI
Dale Peskin, AME; Olivia Casey, Assistant News Editor; Joe Gray, Assistant News Editor

53 days: The trial at a glance

The Detroit News

Tuesday, AUGUST 24, 1993

Juries convict cops of murder after prayers, tears and fights

EXCLUSIVE INTERVIEW

'I did not intend to kill this man,' Nevers says

Lone holdout on Budzyn jury agreed to convict under duress

Crockett's tough, past cases indicate

2 fights with group preaching protest mar peaceful gathering

'I'm happy, but it's not going to help my son any'

Verdicts are a bitter pill for officers on the force

Appeals likely, but could take years to decide

Broadcasters neared overkill

Taxpayers to foot $309,817 bill as the price of justice

Verdicts played across nation's front news pages

Judge, lawyers leave good impressions

Department probes all cases of officers using deadly force

The issue of race: Civil rights, legal experts divided on its role in the trial

Gold

The News-Sentinel
Fort Wayne, IN
M. Daniel Suwyn, Design Editor; Denise M. Reagan, Designer; Luisa Calderon Hayes, Designer; Cindy Jones-Hulfachor, Graphics Illustrator; Steve Linsenmayer, Photographer; Keith Hitchens, Photographer; Lisa Dutton, Photographer; Brian Tombaugh, Photographer; Steve Austin, News Editor

Silver

Detroit Free Press
Detroit, MI
Joe Zeff, Designer

Silver

The Times-Picayune
New Orleans, LA
Kurt Mutchler, Photo & Graphics Editor; Tom Gregory, News Editor;
Michael Jantze, Assistant Graphics Editor; Staff

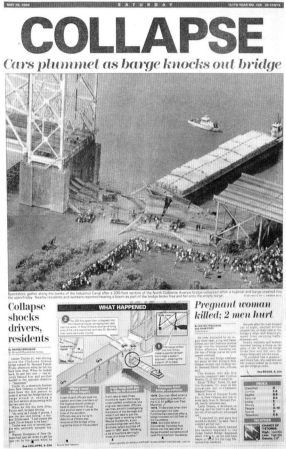

Bronze

The Detroit News
Detroit, MI
Dale Peskin, AME; Joe Gray,
Assistant News Editor; Alan
Whitt, Deputy Sports Editor;
Rob Alstetter, Assistant
Sports Editor

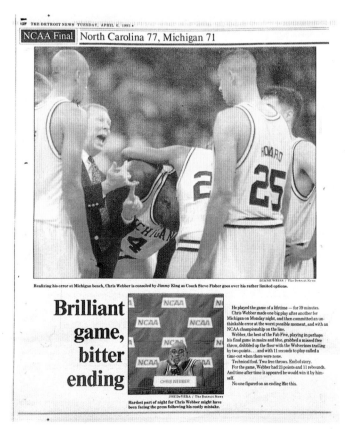

The Detroit News
Wednesday, MARCH 17, 1993

Rescued from the the waist-deep snow and icy creeks
of the Great Smoky Mountains, Cranbrook students and teachers stranded during
a wilderness adventure head home ...

Safe and sound

Does Cranbrook program put students at unnecessary risk?

Chuck Muer 3 days overdue sailing off Florida's coast

Highland closing doors after 60 years; 1,200 to lose jobs

STRANDED:
5 DAYS IN THE WILDERNESS

Weather conditions the campers faced

Globe-trotting math teacher walked into trouble this time

Price of rescue high 'but if one life is saved, it's worth every cent'

Parents sculpt hopes out of 'forgiving' clay

Ultra-modern methods used to restore blood flow

The chilling facts

Stay dry and stay alive, expert advises

Peace begins with autonomy for Gaza, Jericho

Fears run deep in an ancient land of extremes

Award of Excellence
The Detroit News
Detroit, MI
Dale Peskin, AME; Joe Gray, Assistant News Editor

SPECIAL FLOOD EDITION
83° 65°

The Des Moines Register

Floods cripple Des Moines; entire city without water

Downtown may lack electricity for a week

Volunteers fight to save W.D.M. water

Questions, answers on surviving flood crisis

To our readers and advertisers

Award of Excellence & JSR
(Driven from its home by the most devastating flood in American history, the Register produced a newspaper on that disaster that met both high standards of journalism and news presentation. It did so in the face of major obstacles and the demands of one of the biggest stories of 1993.)
The Des Moines Register
Des Moines, IA
Mike Pauly, Senior AME; Lyle Boone, AME Graphics

Bronze
The Citizen
Auburn, NY
Gary Piccirillo, AME Design

Award of Excellence
(for Front Page)

Bronze
Detroit Free Press
Detroit, MI
Deborah Withey, Design Director & Designer; Sue Parker, Designer; Lee Yarosh, Designer; Joe Zeff, Designer

Bronze
The Times-Picayune
New Orleans, LA
Kurt Mutchler, Photo & Graphics Editor; Paula Devlin, News Editor,
Michael Jantze, Assistant Graphics Editor, Staff

Bronze
The Times-Picayune
New Orleans, LA
Kurt Mutchler, Photo & Graphics Editor; Michael Jantze, Assistant
Graphics Editor; Paula Devlin, News
Editor, Dan Shea, Executive News
Editor, Staff

Award of Excellence
The Times/Munster
Munster, IN
John Humenik, AME Design

Award of Excellence
The Spokesman-Review
Spokane, WA
Scott Sines, AME/Visuals; Vince Grippi, Graphics Editor; John
Kafentzis, News Editor; Kevin Graman, Copy Editor; Richard
Miller, Copy Editor; John Sale, Photo Editor

Award of Excellence
(also winner for News Portfolio)
The Citizen
Auburn, NY
Gary Piccirillo, AME Design

Bronze
The Detroit News
Detroit, MI
Dale Peskin, AME; Joe Gray, Assistant News Editor; Felix Grabowski, Graphics Editor; Mark Lett, AME/Business and National; Alan Stamm, National Editor; Steve Kaskovich, Assistant Business Editor

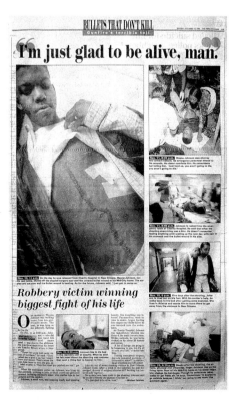

Award of Excellence
The Times-Picayune
New Orleans, LA
George Berke, Design Director; Kurt Mutchler, Photo & Graphics Editor; Tyrone Turner, Photographer

Award of Excellence
The Times-Picayune
New Orleans, LA
George Berke, Design Director; Kurt Mutchler, Photo & Graphics Editor; Tyrone Turner, Photographer

Award of Excellence
Star Tribune
Minneapolis, MN
Steve Ronald, Deputy Managing Editor; Bill Dunn, Design Director; Tim Campbell, Graphics Editor; Anders Ramberg, Art Director & Graphic Designer; Jane Friedman, Graphics Designer; Mike Healy, Photo Editor; Vicky Kettlewell, Photo Editor; Connie Nelson, Researcher; Mike Zerby, Photographer; Stormi Greener, Photographer

Bronze & JSR

(Driven from its home by the most devastating flood in American history, the Register produced a newspaper on that disaster that met both high standards of journalism and news presentation. It did so in the face of major obstacles and the demands of one of the biggest stories of 1993.)
The Des Moines Register
Des Moines, IA
Staff

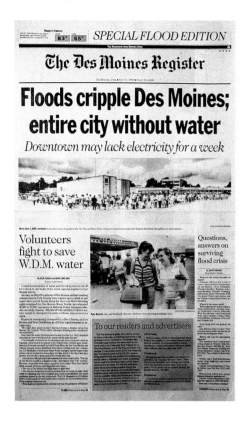

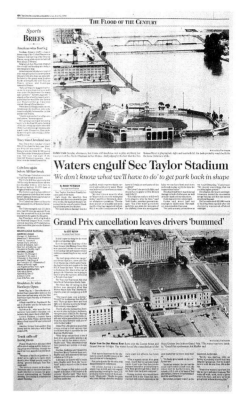

Award of Excellence
The Detroit News
Detroit, MI
Dale Peskin, AME; Joe Gray, Assistant News Editor; Felix Grabowski, Graphics Editor; Robert Graham, Graphic Artist & Designer; Charles Blow, Graphics Artist; Sean McDade, Graphics Artist; Mark Lett, AME Business; Alan Stamm, National Editor; Steve Kaskovich, Assistant Business Editor

Award of Excellence
The New York Times
New York, NY
Tom Bodkin, Design Director; Margaret O'Connor, Deputy Design Director; Rich Meislin, Graphics Director; John Papasian, Graphics Artist; Julie Shaver, Graphics Artist; David Montesino, Graphics Artist; Brent Hatcher, Graphics Editor; Jean Rutter, Graphics Editor

Award of Excellence
El Pais
Madrid, Spain
Staff

Silver
The Orange County Register
Santa Ana, CA
John Fabris, Assistant News Editor/Design; Bernadette Finley, Assistant News Editor/Design; Karen Kelso, Assistant News Editor/Design; David Medzerian, Assistant News Editor/Design;
Brenda Shoun, Assistant News Editor/Design; Kevin Byrne, News Editor/Design; Ron Londen, News Editor/Photo; Ken Brusic, Managing Editor; Tonnie Katz, Editor; Jim Zisk, Graphic Artist;
Lisa Mertins, Graphic Artist; & the Photo, Graphics, Reporting and Editing Staffs
Bronze
(for Breaking News)

chapter

four

Bronze
The Sun/Bremerton
Bremerton, WA
Tracy Porter, Assistant Presentation Editor; Gale Engelke, Illustrator; Denise Clifton, Copy Editor

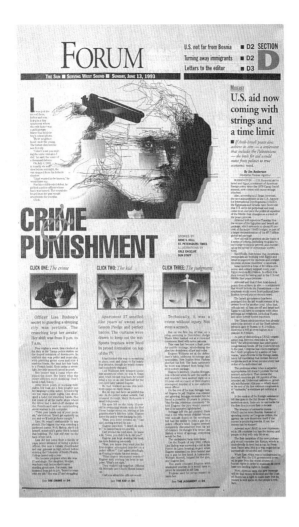

Award of Excellence
San Jose Mercury News
San Jose, CA
Ed Clendaniel, Perspective Editor; Doug Griswold, Graphics Artist; Jenny Anderson, Graphics Artist; Bryan Monroe, Design Director

Award of Excellence
(also for Illustration)
The Washington Times
Washington, DC
Joseph Scopin, Art Director; John Kascht, Designer & Illustrator; Paul Watts, Designer; Charmaine Roberts, Designer; Staff Graphics Artist

Award of Excellence
The Seattle Times
Seattle, WA
Carol Nakagawa, Designer; Fred Birchman, Designer; Scene Staff Designers; David Miller, Art Director

Silver

Scotland on Sunday
Edinburgh, Scotland
Ally Palmer, Design Editor; Richard Walker, Spectrum Assistant Editor/Design

Bronze
The Albuquerque Tribune
Albuquerque, NM
Jeff Neumann, Designer & Graphics Artist; Randall K. Roberts, AME Graphics; Kevin Hellyer, Features Editor; Scott Gullett,
Wild Life Editor

Award of Excellence
Richmond Times-Dispatch
Richmond, VA
Mary Garner-Mitchell, Assistant Flair Editor/Design

Award of Excellence
Fort Worth Star-Telegram
Fort Worth, TX
Victor Panichkul, Design Editor

Award of Excellence
The Orange County Register
Santa Ana, CA
David Medzerian, Assistant News Editor/Design; Brenda
Shoun, Assistant News Editor/Design; James Collier, Design-
er; Claudia Guerrero, Designer; Michele Cardon, Picture Edi-
tor; Lisa Lytle, Reporter

Silver
The New York Times
New York, NY
Nicki Kalish, Art Director

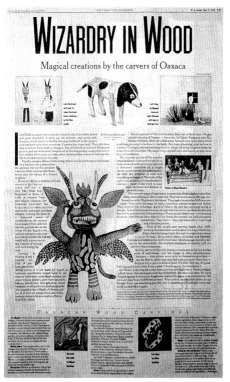

Award of Excellence
San Francisco Examiner
San Francisco, CA
Don McCartney, Designer; Kelly Frankeny, Art Director;
Bob McLeod, Director of Photography; Mignon Khargle,
Illustrator; Don George, Travel Editor

Bronze
Goteborgs-Posten
Gothenburg, Sweden
Ulf Johanson, Designer; Karin Johansson, Designer; Karin Teghammar-Arell, Designer; Eleonor Ekstrom-Frisk, Designer; Mats Widebrant, Designer; Gunilla Wernhamn, Staff; Rune Stenberg, Staff; Elisabeth Silvertsson, Designer; Karin Samuelsson, Designer

Bronze
The New York Times
New YorkNY
Steven Heller, Art Director & Designer

Award of Excellence

Financial Times
London, England
Frances Trowsedale, Designer; James Ferguson, Illustrator;
John Jensen, Illustrator; Philip Thompson, Art Editor (Weekend FT)

Award of Excellence

The Christian Science Monitor
Boston, MA
Staff

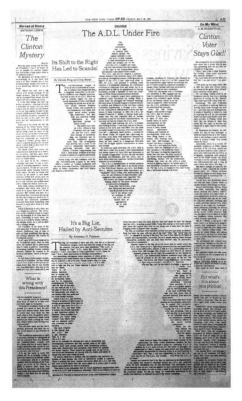

Award of Excellence

(Also for Illustration)
The Miami Herald
Miami, FL
Patterson Clark, Illustrator & Designer; Rich Bard, Viewpoint
Editor; Randy Stano, Director of Editorial Art & Design

Award of Excellence

Los Angeles Times
Los Angeles, CA
Sandra Chelist, Art Director & Designer; David Shannon, Illustrator

Award of Excellence

The New York Times
New York, NY
Mirko Ilic, Art Director & Designer

Bronze
The UCSD Guardian
La Jolla, CA
Miguel Buckenmeyer, Design Editor & Sr. Designer; Roger Kuo, Graphics Editor & Artist; Rene Bruckner, Graphics Editor & Artist

Award of Excellence
The Sun/Bremerton
Bremerton, WA
Tracy Porter, Assistant Presentation Editor

Award of Excellence
NRC Handelsblad
Rotterdam, Netherlands
Karin Mathijsen Gerst, Design Editor; Kamagurka, Illustrator; Freddy Rikken, Photographer

Award of Excellence
New Times/Miami
Miami, FL
Brian Stauffer, Art Director & Designer; Tim Archibald, Photographer

Bronze
The Indianapolis Star
Indianapolis, IN
Tom Peyton, Designer

Silver
El Norte
Monterrey, Mexico
Laura McQuade, Designer

Bronze
San Francisco Examiner
San Francisco, CA
Tracy Cox, Designer; Kelly Frankeny, Art Director; David Talbot, Arts &
Features Editor; Christine Barnes, Style Editor; Zak Trenholm, Illustrator

Bronze
The Star-Ledger
Newark, NJ
Bernadette Dashiell, Art Director; Chris Buckley, Designer; Bob Ono, Photographer

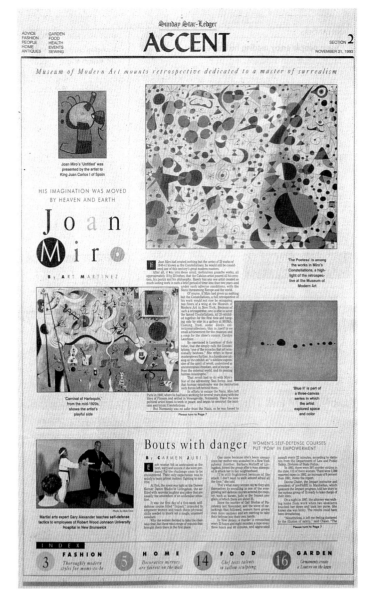

Award of Excellence
Albuquerque Journal
Albuquerque, NM
Juliette Torrez, Designer; Carolyn Flynn, Design Director; Paula Summar, YES Editor; Alexandria King, Photographer; Paul Bearce, Photo Editor

Award of Excellence
American Medical News
Chicago, IL
Barbara Dow, Art Director & Designer; Elizabeth Lada, Illustrator

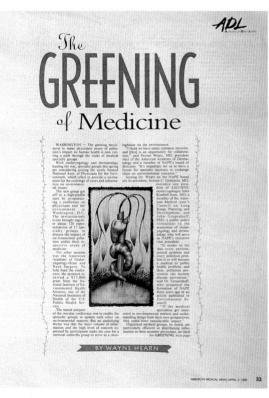

Award of Excellence
El Nuevo Herald
Miami, FL
Aurora Arrue, Illustrator & Designer; Nuri Ducassi, Art Director; Silvia Licha, Editor

Award of Excellence
El Norte
Monterrey, Mexico
Laur McQuade, Designer

Award of Excellence
El Norte
Monterrey, Mexico
Arturo Jimenez, Designer

Award of Excellence
The Palm Beach Post
West Palm Beach, FL
Sarah Franquet, Designer; Pat Crowley, Graphics Artist

Award of Excellence
NRC Handelsblad
Rotterdam, Netherlands
Kees Endenburg, Design Editor

Award of Excellence
New Times/Phoenix
Phoenix, AZ
Kim Klein, Art Director; Timothy Archibald, Photographer

Award of Excellence
The Press-Enterprise
Riverside, CA
Stephen Sedam, Graphics Artist

Award of Excellence
San Francisco Examiner
San Francisco, CA
Tracy Cox, Designer; Kelly Frankeny, Art Director; David Talbot, Arts & Features Editor; Christine Barnes, Style Editor; Zak Trenholm, Illustrator

Award of Excellence
The Spokesman-Review
Spokane, WA
John Nelson, Art Director & Designer; Anne Heitner, Graphics Artist

Award of Excellence
St Paul Pioneer Press
St Paul, MN
Larry May, Art Director & Designer; Ginger Pinson, Photographer; Mark Morson, Photographer

Award of Excellence
The Star-Ledger
Newark, NJ
Bernadette Dashiell, Art Director; Lily Lu, Designer; Jennifer A. Hulshizer, Photographer

Award of Excellence
The Albuquerque Tribune
Albuquerque, NM
Lara Edge, Designer

Bronze
The Albuquerque Tribune
Albuquerque, NM
Lara Edge, Designer; Joan Carlin, Picture Editor

Bronze
The News-Sentinel
Fort Wayne, IN
Denise M. Reagan, Art Director & Designer; Cindy Jones-Hulfachor,
Illustrator

Award of Excellence
(also for Illustration)
Anchorage Daily News
Anchorage, AK
Lance Lekander, Designer & Illustrator; Galie Jean-Louis, De-
sign Director

Award of Excellence
The Citizen
Auburn, NY
Kevin Rivoli, Photo Editor; David Tobin, Staff Reporter & Photographer

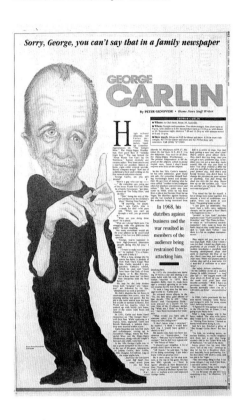

Bronze
The Philadelphia Inquirer
Philadelphia, PA
Charles Chamberlin, Graphics Artist

Award of Excellence
The Boston Globe
Boston, MA
Rena Sokolow, Art Director & Designer; Terry Allen, Illustrator

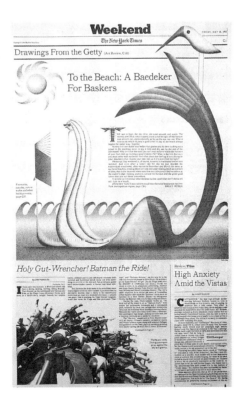

Award of Excellence
El Norte
Monterrey, Mexico
Nohemi Bernal, Designer; Emmanual Infante, Photo Design

Award of Excellence
The New York Times
New York, NY
Barbara Richer, Art Director & Designer; Terry Allen, Illustrator

Award of Excellence
The New York Times
New York, NY
Linda Brewer, Art Director & Designer;
Al Hirschfeld, Illustrator

Gold
Anchorage Daily News
Anchorage, AK
Galie Jean-Louis, Design Director & Designer

Silver
Anchorage Daily News
Anchorage, AK
Dee Boyles, Designer; Galie Jean-Louis, Design Director; Nigel Parry, Photographer

Award of Excellence
The Advocate and Greenwich Time
Stamford, CT
Jacqueline Segal, AME Design/Photography; Carlo F. Cantavero Jr., Designer

Award of Excellence
Anchorage Daily News
Anchorage, AK
Galie Jean-Louis, Design Director & Designer; Amy Guip, Photographer

Award of Excellence
Anchorage Daily News
Anchorage, AK
Dee Boyles, Designer; Galie Jean-Louis, Design Director; Tim
White, Photographer

Award of Excellence
Anchorage Daily News
Anchorage, AK
Galie Jean-Louis, Design Director & Designer; Frank Ocken-
fels, Photographer

Award of Excellence
Watertown Press
Somerville, MA
Mark Gabrenya, Art Director & Designer; Jane Tyska, Photog-
rapher

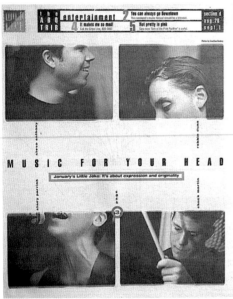

Award of Excellence
The Albuquerque Tribune
Albuquerque, NM
Jeff Neumann, Designer & Graphics Artist

Award of Excellence
El Norte
Monterrey, Mexico
Carmen Escobedo, Designer; Juan Jose Ceron, Photographer;
Sergio Aguirre, Typographer

Bronze
The Boston Globe
Boston, MA
Susan Dawson, Art Director; Mary Lynn Blasutta, Illustrator

Bronze
Los Angeles Times
Los Angeles, CA
Tracy Crowe, Art Director; Ruth Riechi, Editor; Kirk McKoy, Photographer

Award of Excellence
(also for Features Portfolio)
El Norte
Monterrey, Mexico
Carmen Escobedo, Designer; Juan Jose Ceron, Photographer;
Estudio El Norte, Photography; Emmanuel Infante, Digital
Photography

Award of Excellence
El Norte
Monterrey, Mexico
Carmen Escobedo, Designer; Juan Jose Ceron, Photographer

Award of Excellence
El Norte
Monterrey, Mexico
Carmen Escobedo, Designer; Juan Jose Ceron,
Photographer

Award of Excellence

The Miami Herald
Miami, FL
Janet Santelices, Designer & Illustrator; Felicia Gressette, Food Editor; Rhonda Prast, Design Desk Editor; Randy Stano, Director of Editorial Art & Design

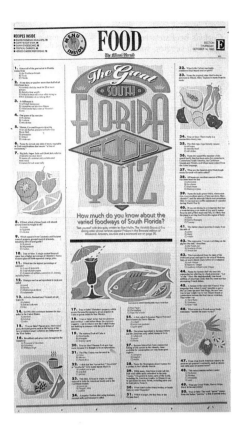

Award of Excellence

The Miami Herald
Miami, FL
Rhonda Prast, Designer; Patterson Clark, Illustrator; Felicia Gressette, Food Editor; Randy Stano, Director of Editorial Art & Design

Award of Excellence

The Orange County Register
Santa Ana, CA
James Collier, Designer; Cathy Thomas, Food Stylist; Nick Koon, Photographer; Kevin Byrne, News Editor/Design; Nanette Bisher, AME/Art Director

Award of Excellence

The Philadelphia Inquirer
Philadelphia, PA
Chrissy Dunleavy, Designer; Michael Bryant, Photographer; Marilyn Shapiro, Photo Editor

Award of Excellence

The San Diego Union-Tribune
San Diego, CA
Amy Stirnkorb, Designer; Michael Franklin, Photographer

Award of Excellence

San Francisco Examiner
San Francisco, CA
Lynn Forbes, Epicure Editor; Kelly Frankeny, Art Director; Don McCartney, Designer & Illustrator

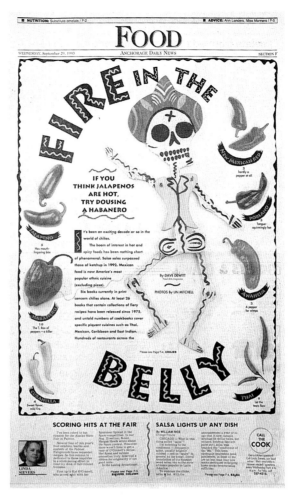

Award of Excellence

Anchorage Daily News
Anchorage, AK
Dee Boyles, Designer; Galie Jean-Louis, Design Director; Lin Mitchell, Photographer

Award of Excellence

Aberdeen American News
Detroit, MI
Deborah Withey, Art Director; Cindy Eikamp, Executive Editor; John Papendick, Designer & Copy Editor

Award of Excellence

The News-Sentinel
Fort Wayne, IN
Denise M. Reagan, Art Director & Designer; Steve Linsenmayer, Photographer; Mark Ryan, Illustrator

Award of Excellence

Financial Times
London, England
Frances Trowsdale, Designer; Kim Dalziel, Illustrator

Award of Excellence

The Columbus Dispatch
Columbus, OH
Roderick Harris, Designer; Scott Minister, Art Director

Silver
The New York Times
New York, NY
Nicki Kalish, Art Director & Designer; Terry Allen, Illustrator

Bronze
The New York Times
New York, NY
Nicki Kalish, Art Director & Designer; Simon McBride, Cover Photographer

Award of Excellence
The Boston Globe
Boston, MA
Jacqueline Berthet, Designer

Bronze
The New York Times
New York, NY
Nicki Kalish, Art Director & Designer; Douglas Peebles, Photographer

Bronze
The Boston Globe
Boston, MA
Neil C. Pinchin, Designer & Graphics Artist

Award of Excellence
The New York Times
New York, NY
Nicki Kalish, Art Director & Designer; Jonathan Player, Photographer

Award of Excellence
San Francisco Examiner
San Francisco, CA
Don George, Travel Editor; Kelly Frankeny, Art Director; Don McCartney, Designer; Jeffrey Becom, Photographer

Award of Excellence

San Francisco Examiner
San Francisco, CA
Don George, Travel Editor; Kelly Frankeny, Art Director; Mignon
Khargie, Illustrator & Designer

Award of Excellence

Horsens Folkeblad
Horsens, Denmark
Kjeld Torbjorn, Designer; Eigil Holm, Photographer; Mogens Ahrenkiel,
Editor

Award of Excellence

San Francisco Examiner
San Francisco, CA
Don George, Travel Editor; Kelly Frankeny, Art Director; Don
McCartney, Designer & Photographer

Award of Excellence

San Francisco Examiner
San Francisco, CA
Don George, Travel Editor; Kelly Frankeny, Art Director; Don
McCartney, Designer

Award of Excellence

Mesa Tribune
Mesa, AZ
Ron Dungan, Designer

Award of Excellence
American Medical News
Chicago, IL
Barbara Dow, Designer; Jef Capaldi, Art Director; Anthony Russo, Illustrator

HEALTH
Forbidden fruit

Illustration by Anthony Russo

By Flora Johnson Skelly THE PROSCRIPTION AGAINST SEXUAL RELATIONS BETWEEN DOCTOR AND PATIENT IS ONE OF THE OLDEST IN MEDICINE, ENSHRINED BY HIPPOCRATES HIMSELF IN HIS FAMOUS OATH. FOR CENTURIES, THE ATTITUDE OF THE MEDICAL PROFESSION ON THIS SUBJECT WAS SIMPLE: IT DOESN'T HAPPEN.

SEX WITH PATIENTS IS NEVER ETHICAL. AUTHORITIES IMPLORE PHYSICIANS TO HONOR THE ANCIENT TABOO.

AMERICAN MEDICAL NEWS/JUNE 28, 1993 **15**

New help with communication skills...Page 12

HEALTH
Time to Move?

Illustration by JEM SULLIVAN

By FLORA JOHNSON SKELLY

On the eve of health system reform, mid-career physicians confront the inevitability of change

AMERICAN MEDICAL NEWS SEPTEMBER 6, 1993 **11**

Award of Excellence
American Medical News
Chicago, IL
Barbara Dow, Art Director & Designer; Jem Sullivan, Illustrator

Silver
American Medical News
Chicago, IL
Barbara Dow, Art Director & Designer; Elizabeth Lada, Illustrator

Prayer can be part of cure...Page 14

HEALTH
Faith in Medicine

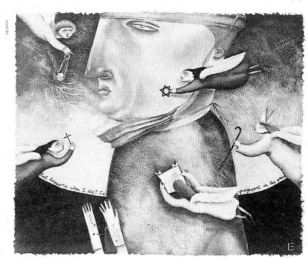

True Believers

When religion matters to patients, physicians must respond. Now, medical schools are teaching how.

Religion plays a big role in America. Coins proclaim "In God We Trust." TV stations broadcast celebrity preachers. Immigrants gather in urban storefront churches, while mosques and synagogues open their doors to the hungry homeless. And everyone celebrates Christmas as a national holiday.

Nowhere is religion more powerfully present than in the life-and-death scenarios of health care. Caught off guard by illness, church-goers and those who haven't visited a house of worship in years turn for answers and consolation to the values and rituals of their religious traditions.

Physicians inevitably come into contact – and sometimes conflict – with their patients' religious beliefs. Their own religious backgrounds also affect the way they practice medicine. Some struggle to square spiritual beliefs with science. Others turn to religion for answers to existential questions and for help with ethical decision-making. Many who describe themselves as secular humanists recognize the importance of sensitivity to patients' spiritual needs.

A new awareness of religion's role is being felt in medical education. Schools, increasingly responsive to the psychosocial dimensions of patient care, have begun to incorporate religion courses into the humanities component of their curricula.

"The substance of medical work involves the critical phases of life from birth to death," said David Barnard, PhD, chairman of the humanities department at Pennsylvania State College of Medicine.

"Religious ideas and communities of
See FAITH, next page

story by Janice Rosenberg

AMERICAN MEDICAL NEWS/DECEMBER 20, 1993 **11**

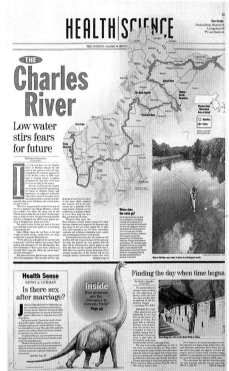

Award of Excellence

The Detroit News
Detroit, MI
Charles Blow, Graphics Artist; David Pierce, Graphics Editor;
Patricia Vegella, Researcher; John Wark, Section Editor; Felix
Grabowski, Graphics Director

Award of Excellence

The Boston Globe
Boston, MA
Cynthia Daniels, Art Director; Rico Lins, Illustrator

Award of Excellence

The San Diego Union-Tribune
San Diego, CA
Amy Stirnkorb, Designer

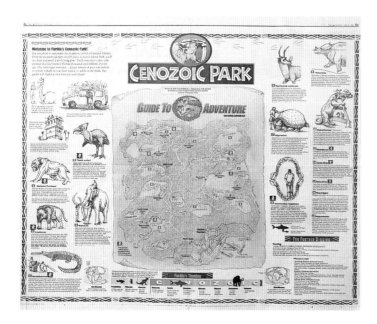

Award of Excellence

The St. Petersburg Times
St. Petersburg, FL
Don Morris, News Artist

Award of Excellence

The Chicago Reader
Chicago, IL
Nickie Sage, Production Assistant

Award of Excellence
The Asbury Park Press
Neptune, NJ
Colleen Lanchester, Designer; Andy Prendimano, Art Director; Harris Siegel, AME Design

Silver
Los Angeles Times
Los Angeles, CA
Diana Shantic, Art Director

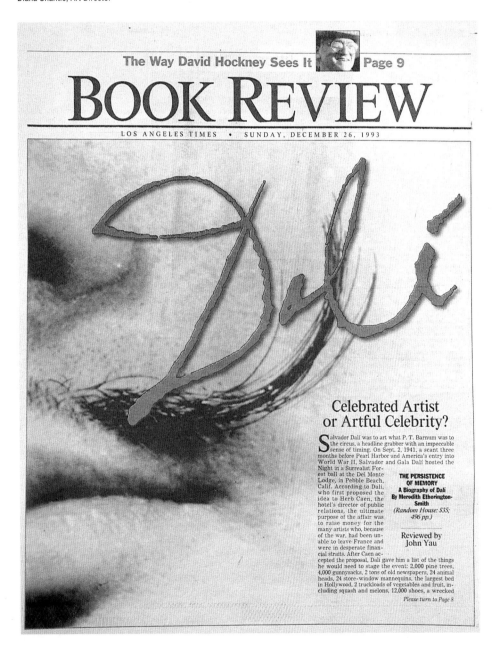

Award of Excellence
Berlingski Tidende
Copenhagen, Denmark
Gregers Jensen, Designer; Hinz/Kjaer, Photographer

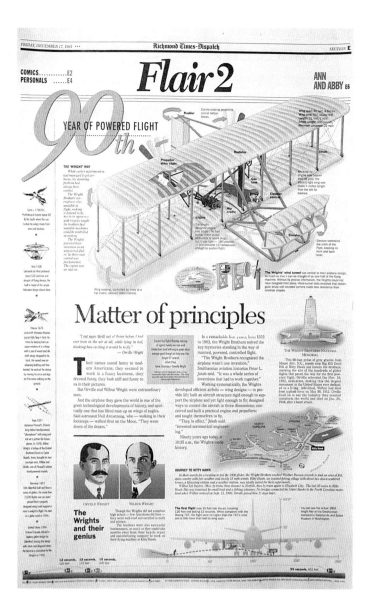

Bronze
Richmond Times-Dispatch
Richmond, VA
Mary Garner-Mitchell, Assistant Flair Editor/Design;
Stephen Rountree, Graphics Artist & Researcher; Tom
Roberts, Graphics Artist; Martin Rhodes, Graphics Artist;
John Ailor, Associate Graphics Director

Award of Excellence
The Boston Globe
Boston, MA
Jane Simon, Art Director

Award of Excellence
Dagens Nyheter
Stockholm, Sweden
Olle Enocson, Designer; Ewa Stackelberg, Photographer

Award of Excellence
Goteborgs-Posten
Gothenburg, Sweden
Mats Widebrant, Designer; Ulf Sveningson, Illustrator

Award of Excellence
Dagens Nyheter
Stockholm, Sweden
Anette Sievers, Designer

Silver
Seattle Weekly
Seattle, WA
Dan Zedek, Design Director; Melinda Beck, Illustrator

Award of Excellence
Goteborgs-Posten
Gothenburg, Sweden
Karin Samuelsson, Designer; Gunilla Wernhamn, Staff

Award of Excellence
La Vanguardia
Barcelona, Spain
Carlos Perez de Rozas, Art Director; Rosa Mundet, Art Director; Ferran Grau, Designer;
Ana Belil, Designer; Rocarols, Illustrator

Tax Revolt ■ Physio's Chest Pains ■ All-Girls Ed ■ Stegner's Redmond

Eastsideweek

APRIL 21, 1993 FREE

CYBER SKIN HEaDS

A new generation
of punks is
planning the first
electronic riot.
Their only goal:
to crash the system

© KUPER

Bronze
Eastside Week
Seattle, WA
Sandra Schneider, Art Director; Peter Kuper, Illustrator

Award of Excellence
The New York Times
New York, NY
Steven Heller, Art Director & Designer; Mark Summers, Illustrator

Why Author Photos Are So Awful / 3

EDITING NEWSPAPERS IN AFRICA CAN BE A
REMINISCENCES FROM DONALD TRELFORD,

HUMBLING EXPERIENCE, AS IS SHOWN IN THESE
FORMER EDITOR OF *The Observer*, IN LONDON

IS THAT YOU, BWANA EDITOR?

ILLUSTRATION: MICHAEL CUSTODE

Bronze
Ragged Right
Toronto, Canada
Tony Sutton, Editor & Designer; Michael Custode, Illustrator

Bronze
Goteborgs-Posten
Gothenburg, Sweden
Karin Johansson, Designer;
Gunilla Wernhamn, Staff;
Rune Stenberg, Staff

Award of Excellence
El Norte
Monterrey, Mexico
Lourdes de la Rosa, Designer / Digital Photography; Estudio El Norte, Photographer

Award of Excellence
Goteborgs-Posten
Gothenburg, Sweden
Ulf Johanson, Designer; Gunilla Wernhamn, Staff; Rune Stenberg, Staff

Award of Excellence
Goteborgs-Posten
Gothenburg, Sweden
Ulf Johanson, Designer; Gunilla Wernhamn, Staff; Rune Stenberg, Staff

chapter

five

5

Silver
El Mundo/El Mundo Magazine
Madrid, Spain
Rodrigo Sanchez, Art Director & Designer; Carmelo Caderot,
Design Director; Popa Gomez, Designer

Silver
El Pais/El Pais Semanal
Madrid, Spain
Eugenio Gonzalez, Art Director; Gustavo Sanchez, Designer; Isabel Benito, Designer; Marta Calzada, Designer

Bronze
El Pais/El Pais de las Tentaciones
Madrid, Spain
Alex Martinez Roig, Editor; Fernando Gutierrez, Art Director; Luis Magan, Picture Editor; Ignacio Rubio, Designer; Nuria Muina, Designer

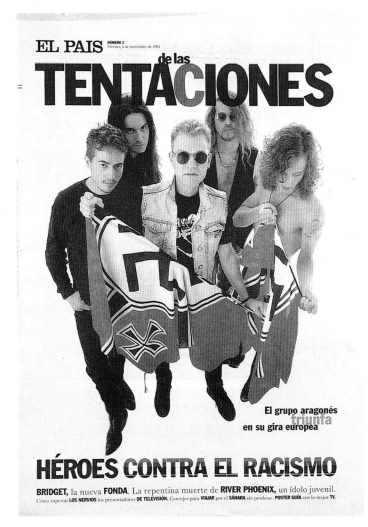

Award of Excellence
San Francisco Examiner
San Francisco, CA
Paul Wilner, AME/Features; Joey Rigg, IMAGE Art Director; Zahid Sardar, IMAGE Associate Art Director; Penni Gladstone, IMAGE Picture Editor

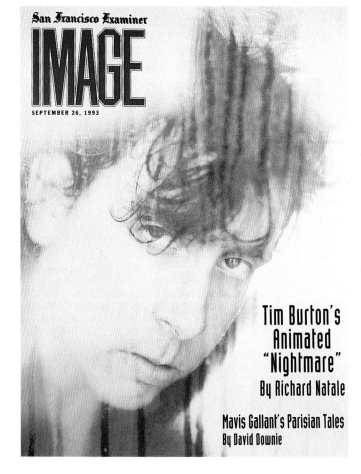

Silver
The Boston Globe Magazine
Boston, MA
Aldona Charlton, Art Director; Michael Larkin, Sunday Editor;
Robert F. Cutting, Special Sections Editor; Gail Ravgiala, Con-
tents Editor

Barn Dance
by Julie Michaels

Artist Rodney Ripps and his wife, designer
Helene Verin, like to describe their Stockbridge
home as a "rural loft." They discovered the old
carriage barn, which was an outbuilding to a
once-grand Berkshire estate, six years ago. "It
was a white elephant," says Verin, "a huge space
so overwhelming that nobody wanted it."

But the couple, who also own a loft in New
York City, were used to living in large spaces.
They saw the big rooms as both a challenge and
an opportunity, since both Ripps and his wife
require considerable elbow room to work. In addition to his painting, Ripps is a furniture designer; Verin designs shoes, wallpaper, rugs and
fashion accessories.

The barn, which was built in 1904, had
been used as a summer residence but major ren-
ovations were necessary to make the space habit-
able year round. Two heating systems were add-
ed, along with insulation; 30 new windows
opened the space to light and nature.

Julie Michaels is a member of the Globe staff.

PHOTOGRAPHS BY NANCY HILL

A ONE—TIME WHITE ELEPHANT EXPLODES WITH COLOR, WIT AND STYLE

Room for all
by Janice Byrd

A basement becomes a place where the
whole family can play

A toddler stands at the top of the stairs
leading to the family room and rattles
the gate with excitement. He can't
wait to head down and play, and
neither can his parents.

Having a playroom in the cellar isn't
always successful. Children, especially
younger boys and girls, don't like to be
isolated from the adults, but the grown-
ups usually prefer the more comfortable
parts of the house. Keeping that in mind,
the raw cellar Continued on page 82

Janice Byrd is a free-lance writer.

POOL TABLE
CHILDREN'S AREA
WALL MURAL
SITTING AREA
AUDIO VISUAL UNIT
BAR AREA
EXERCISE ROOM

FOR CHILDREN, A FANTASY
CASTLE, LEFT, AND AN
ACTIVITY NOOK, ABOVE.
FOR ADULTS, A HANDSOME
ENTERTAINMENT AREA,
ABOVE RIGHT.

photographs by Anton Grassl / graphics by Neil C. Pinchin

Silver
Los Angeles Times Magazine
Los Angeles, CA
Staff

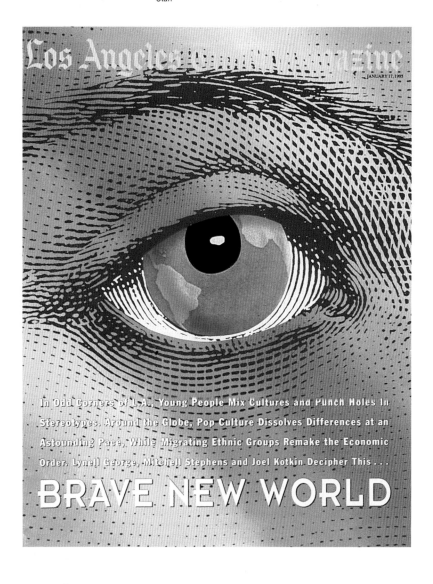

In Odd Corners of L.A., Young People Mix Cultures and Punch Holes In Stereotypes. Around the Globe, Pop Culture Dissolves Differences at an Astounding Pace, While Migrating Ethnic Groups Remake the Economic Order. Lynell George, Mitchell Stephens and Joel Kotkin Decipher This . . .

BRAVE NEW WORLD

BRAVE NEW WORLD

FAMILY TIES IN THE NEW GLOBAL ECONOMY

ETHNIC TRIBES—FROM THE JEWS TO THE JAPANESE, CHINESE AND INDIANS—ARE RESHAPING INTERNATIONAL COMMERCE

HE 20TH CENTURY IS ENDING WITH HARBINGERS OF A FUTURE ROOTED DEEPLY, EVEN terrifyingly, in the past. Rather than the triumph of a rational and universal world order, we are witnessing a resurgence of popular interest in ethnic identities, religious roots and ancient affiliations that is shaking societies from the remnants of the former Soviet Empire to the streets of Los Angeles. In the words of sociologist Harold Isaacs: "Science advanced, knowledge grew, nature was mastered, but Reason did not conquer and tribalism did not go away." • This resurgence contrasts with widespread hopes, sparked by the end of the Cold War, of the dawn of a new age liberated from national, religious and tribal constraints. Indeed, in much of Africa, South Asia and Eastern Europe, this renewal of ethnic and religious sentiments has been devastating, breaking apart many long-established nation states and triggering hideous outbreaks of intolerance and barbarity. • At the same time, and less noticed, we have seen the continued flowering of transnational ethnic groups—or global tribes—that increas-

BY JOEL KOTKIN

Silver
The New York Times Magazine
New York, NY
Janet Froelich, Art Director; Gina Davis, Art Director; Hal Ruberstein, Editor; Lois Greenfield, Photographer

WAITING FOR A BREEZE

There are days in summer when it doesn't pay to budge. Once heat

rules, stillness is required. Move when the air does.

Until then, staying cool is all.

PHOTOGRAPHS BY RANDALL MESDON

44 MEN'S FASHIONS OF THE TIMES

The New York Times Magazine
PART 2 / MARCH 28, 1993

MEN'S
FASHIONS OF THE TIMES

Turn Me
Loose

BY HAL RUBENSTEIN

Who Lives in a Shoe?

TOP LEFT: CUSTOM-MADE LEATHER "FRANCISCAN SLIP-IN" SANDAL, $165 A PAIR, AT BARBARA SHAUM LEATHER, 69 EAST FOURTH STREET.

TOP RIGHT: LEATHER SANDAL WITH RUBBER SOLE FROM BARNEYS NEW YORK COLLECTION, $115 A PAIR, AT BARNEYS NEW YORK, NEW YORK CITY; CHICAGO; DALLAS; HOUSTON, AND SEATTLE.

FAR LEFT: LEATHER FISHERMAN SANDAL WITH RUBBER SOLE FROM

BARNEYS NEW YORK COLLECTION, $115 A PAIR, AT BARNEYS NEW YORK, NEW YORK CITY AND SEATTLE.

CENTER LEFT: LEATHER CRISS-CROSS SANDAL FROM SIGERSON MORRISON, $300 A PAIR, AT SIGERSON MORRISON SHOES, 431 BROADWAY, BY SPECIAL ORDER.

CENTER: LEATHER FISHERMAN SANDAL WITH LEATHER SOLE

FROM BARNEYS NEW YORK COLLECTION, $135 A PAIR, AT BARNEYS NEW YORK, NEW YORK CITY AND DALLAS.

CENTER RIGHT: LEATHER GLADIATOR SANDAL BY GIANNI VERSACE, $525 A PAIR, AT GIANNI VERSACE, 816 MADISON AVENUE.

FAR RIGHT: LEATHER FISHERMAN SANDAL, FROM GAP SHOES, $68 A PAIR, AT GAP SHOE STORES, NATIONWIDE.

Why should your feet be cooped up inside in summer? They want to get out and have fun just as much as you do. Sandals should be a part of their lives.

THE NEW YORK TIMES MAGAZINE / MARCH 28, 1993   23

Award of Excellence
The Boston Globe Magazine
Boston, MA
Lucy Bartholomay, Art Director & Designer; Tom Herde, Photographer; Richard Sanchez, Graphics Artist

Award of Excellence
The Detroit News
Detroit, MI
Don Asmussen, Graphics Artist; Robert Graham, Art Director
& Designer; Felix Grabowski, Graphics Editor & Designer; Ray
Jeskey, Auto Editor; Nolan Finley, Business Editor; Mark Lett,
AME

Award of Excellence
El Periodico de Catalunya
Barcelona, Spain
Juan Vorela, Editor-in-Chief

Award of Excellence
El Mundo/El Mundo Magazine
Madrid, Spain
Rodrigo Sanchez, Art Director & Designer; Carmelo Caderot, Design Director; Popa Gomez, Designer

Award of Excellence
Los Angeles Times Magazine
Los Angeles, CA
Staff

Award of Excellence
The New York Times Magazine
New York, NY
Janet Froelich, Art Director; Gina Davis, Art Director; Hugh Hales-Tooke, Cover photographer; Hal Ruberstein, Editor

Award of Excellence
The New York Times Magazine
New York, NY
Michael Valenti, Art Director & Designer; Seymour Chwast, Illustrator/Cover; Nancy Newhouse, Editor

Award of Excellence
The New York Times Magazine
New York, NY
Tuan Dao, Art Director & Designer; Carrie Donovan, Editor; John Huba, Cover photographer

Award of Excellence
The New York Times Magazine
New York, NY
Tuan Dao, Art Director & Designer; Carrie Donovan, Editor; Ruven Afanador, Cover Photographer

Award of Excellence
The New York Times Magazine
New York, NY
Nicki Kalish, Art Director & Designer; Teresa Fasolino, Illustrator

Award of Excellence
San Francisco Examiner
San Francisco, CA
Paul Wilner, AME Features; Joey Rigg, IMAGE Art Director;
Zahid Sardar, IMAGE Associate Art Director; Penni Gladstone,
IMAGE Picture Editor

Award of Excellence
Anchorage Daily News
Anchorage, AK
Pamela Dunlap-Shohl, Designer; Galie Jean-Louis, Design Director; Art Wolfe, Photographer

Award of Excellence
Los Angeles Times Magazine
Los Angeles, CA
Nancy Duckworth, Art Director & Designer; Dan Winters, Photographer

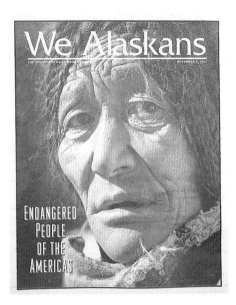

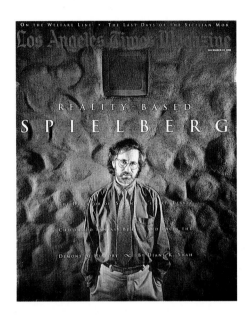

Award of Excellence
The Philadelphia Inquirer Magazine
Philadelphia, PA
Bert Fox, Art Director; Jessica Helfand, Art Director, Designer
& Illustrator

Award of Excellence
Baltimore Jewish Times
Baltimore, MD
Robyn Katz, Art Director

Award of Excellence
The Boston Globe Magazine
Boston, MA
Lucy Bartholomay, Art Director & Designer; Tom Herde, Photographer; Sanjay Kothari, Electronic Imaging

Gold & JSR

(To recognize the courage in American journalism exemplified by this work, as well
as the sensitivity and taste with which it was executed.)
The New York Times Magazine
New York, NY
Janet Froelich, Art Director; Kathy Ryan, Photo Editor; Matuschka, Photographer

Silver
The Boston Globe Magazine
Boston, MA
Lucy Bartholomay, Art Director & Designer; Peter Vanderwarker, Photographer

Silver
El Mundo/El Mundo Magazine
Madrid, Spain
Carmelo Caderot, Design Director; Manuel de Miguel, Assistant Art Director; Gorka Sampedro, Illustrator

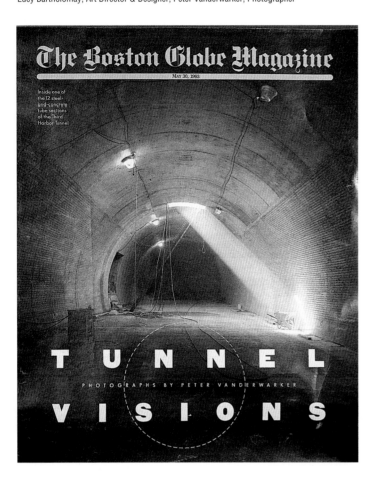

Award of Excellence
The Boston Globe Magazine
Boston, MA
Lucy Bartholomay, Art Director & Designer; Everhard Williams, Photographer

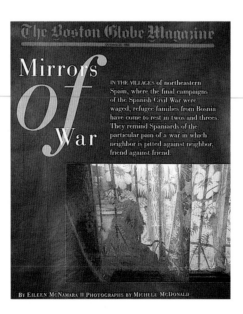

Award of Excellence
The Boston Globe Magazine
Boston, MA
Lucy Bartholomay, Art Director & Designer; Michele McDonald, Photographer

Award of Excellence
Dallas Morning News/Dallas Life Magazine
Dallas, TX
Lesley Becker, Art Director & Designer; Cindy Yamanaka, Photographer

Silver
The New York Times Magazine
New York, NY
Janet Froelich, Art Director; Gina Davis, Art Director; Hugh Hales-Tooke, Photographer; Hal Ruberstein, Editor

Silver
The New York Times Magazine
New York, NY
Linda Brewer, Art Director & Designer; John Dugdale, Photographer

Award of Excellence
El Mundo/El Mundo Magazine
Madrid, Spain
Rodrigo Sanchez, Art Director & Designer; Carmelo Caderot, Design Director

Award of Excellence
Detroit Free Press Magazine
Detroit, MI
Claire C. Innes, Art Director & Designer; Mike Benny, Illustrator

Award of Excellence
Detroit Free Press Magazine
Detroit, MI
Claire C. Innes, Art Director & Designer; Christopher Zakarov, Illustrator

Bronze
The New York Times Magazine
New York, NY
Janet Froelich, Art Director; Kathi Rota, Designer; Kathy Ryan, Photo Editor; Michael O'Brien, Photographer

Bronze
The Hartford Courant/Northeast Magazine
Hartford, CT
Patti Nelson, Design Director; Richard Thompson, Illustrator

Award of Excellence
El Nuevo Dia
San Juan, PR
Jose L. Diaz de Villegas Jr, Art Director, Designer & Illustrator

Award of Excellence
The Hartford Courant/Northeast Magazine
Hartford, CT
Patti Nelson, Design Director; Laura Uram, Illustrator

Award of Excellence
El Mundo/Metropoli
Madrid, Spain
Carmelo Caderot, Design Director; Manuel de Miguel, Assistant Art Director

Bronze
El Pais/El Pais Semanal
Madrid, Spain
Eugenio Gonzalez, Art Director; Gustavo Sanchez, Designer; Isabel Benito, Designer; Marta Calzada, Designer; Tim O'Sullivan, Photographer

Bronze
El Pais/El Pais Semanal
Madrid, Spain
Eugenio Gonzalez, Art Director; Gustavo Sanchez, Designer; Isabel Benito, Designer; Marta Calzada, Designer

Award of Excellence
Los Angeles Times
Los Angeles, CA
Carol Kaufman, Art Director

Award of Excellence
La Vanguardia Magazine
Barcelona, Spain
Carlos Perez de Rozas, Art Director; Emili Alvarez, Photographer; Pedro Madueno, Photographer

Award of Excellence
The Hartford Courant/Northeast Magazine
Hartford, CT
Patti Nelson, Design Director

Award of Excellence
Los Angeles Times Magazine
Los Angeles, CA
Steven Banks, Designer; Philip Burke, Illustrator

Award of Excellence
Los Angeles Times Magazine
Los Angeles, CA
Nancy Duckworth, Art Director & Designer; Eric Tucker, Illustrator

Award of Excellence
Los Angeles Times Magazine
Los Angeles, CA
Nancy Duckworth, Art Director & Designer; Matt Mahurin, Illustrator

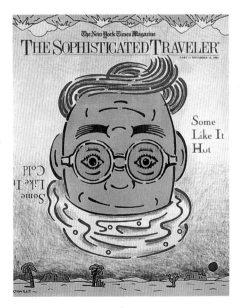

Award of Excellence
The New York Times Magazine
New York, NY
Nicki Kalish, Art Director & Designer; Joan Landis, Illustrator

Award of Excellence
The New York Times Magazine
New York, NY
Michael Valenti, Art Director & Designer; Seymour Chwast, Illustrator

Award of Excellence
The New York Times Magazine
New York, NY
Nicki Kalish, Art Director & Designer; Milton Glaser, Illustrator

Award of Excellence
The New York Times Magazine
New York, NY
Janet Froelich, Art Director; Nancy Harris, Designer; Blair Drawson, Illustrator

Award of Excellence
The Phoenix Gazette/Marquee
Phoenix, AZ
Jennifer Ignaszewski, Designer; Tony Bustos, Illustrator

Award of Excellence
San Francisco Examiner/Image Magazine
San Francisco, CA
Paul Wilner, AME/Features; Joey Rigg, Art Director; Zahid Sardar, Associate Art Director; Penni Gladstone, Picture Editor

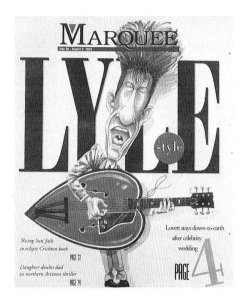

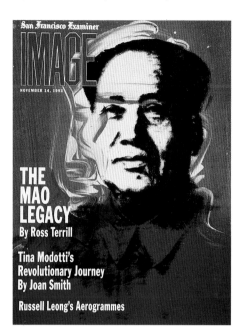

Award of Excellence
San Jose Mercury News/West Magazine
San Jose, CA
Sandra Eisert, Art Director & Designer; Jason M. Grow, Photographer

Award of Excellence
San Jose Mercury News/West Magazine
San Jose, CA
Sandra Eisert, Art Director & Designer; Steve Lyons, Graphics Artist

Award of Excellence
The Washington Post Magazine
Washington, DC
Kelly Doe, Art Director & Designer; Torkil Gludnason, Photographer

Award of Excellence
The Washington Post Magazine
Washington, DC
Richard Baker, Art Director & Designer; Torkil Gudnason,
Photographer

Award of Excellence
The Baltimore Sun
Baltimore, MD
Joseph Hutchinson, Graphics Director & Designer; John Goecke, AME Graphics/Photography; Cotton Coulson, Photo Director;
Patrick Sandor, Photographer

Award of Excellence
The Boston Globe
Boston, MA
Rena Sokolow, Art Director; Sharon
Roberts, Photographer

Award of Excellence
The Boston Globe Magazine
Boston, MA
Catherine Aldrich, Art Director;
Philip Porcella, Photographer; Mari
Quirk, Stylist

Gold
El Mundo
Madrid, Spain
Rodrigo Sanchez, Art Director & Designer; Carmelo
Caderot, Design Director; Popa Gomez, Designer

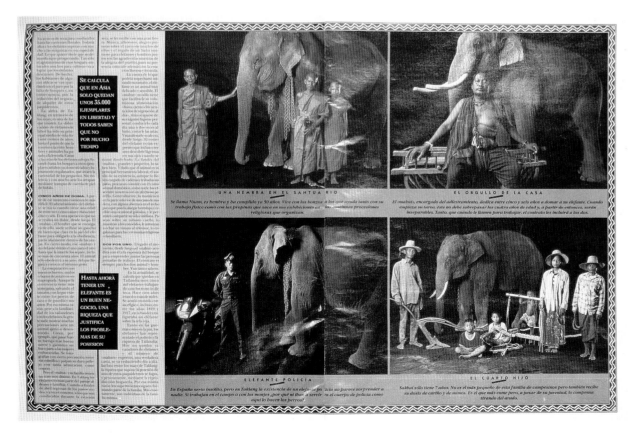

Gold
El Mundo/El Mundo Magazine
Madrid, Spain
Rodrigo Sanchez, Art Director & Designer; Carmelo
Caderot, Design Director; Popa Gomez, Designer

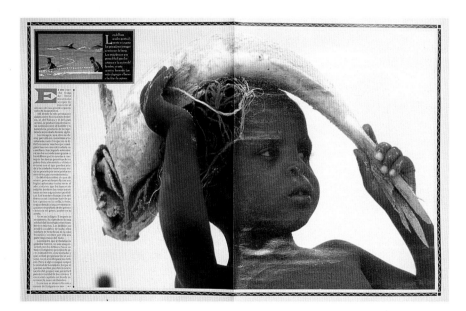

Nothing distracts from the mood of the face, the line of the body, the expression

of who you are. When artifice and adornment are lacking, the impulse is to

polish, refine and enhance your look with what should appear as little effort as possible.

Going natural can be the height of sophistication. For example, the hair style at right,
known in Haiti as "papillote," or "butterfly cocoon," is as free of Western influence as it is of chemicals and as
playful as a soft sculpture. The scalp is parted in diamonds and the hair within divided in two
and twisted, with a result that can be liberating in more ways than one. Having gone natural after years of
processing her hair, Alice Walker once exulted: "The ceiling at the top of my brain lifted."

48   THE NEW YORK TIMES MAGAZINE / MAY 16, 1993   PHOTOGRAPHS BY KURT MARCUS FOR THE NEW YORK TIM

Silver
The New York Times Magazine
New York, NY
Janet Froelich, Art Director; Gina Davis, Designer; Kurt
Markus, Photographer; Polly Hamilton, Stylist

BEAUTY
BY RONA BERG

A Time for Revealing

The look this summer is muted: no hard edges, no sharp angles. Rigid notions of beauty

are as out of place as knife-edged tailoring. As the body loses its

exaggerated musculature and becomes more lissome, the face takes on a more natural allure.

Beauty takes two directions this summer — the bare, almost overexposed face and the one that's softly stylized.
Both are artfully natural, or as one makeup artist put it, "real enhancing," cleaned up and gently polished with makeup.
The face above is a delicate cameo of 1920's style. The brow has lost its exaggerated thinness; cheeks are softly
flushed; lips are strong but sweetened with gloss; hair is sculpted into a marcel wave. For women of color, the thin knots
and spaghetti braids, right, are a throwback to childhood, when everything felt natural and free.

Photographs by Kurt Marcus

42   THE NEW YORK TIMES MAGAZINE / MAY 16, 1993

The biggest change in makeup is texture, not color. The new blushes and tinted moisturizers are so sheer,
and applied so subtly, they look like color from within. New blushes from Estée Lauder are slightly iridescent. Tinted
moisturizers with a strong pigment, like Yves Saint Laurent and M.A.C.'s, have just enough red to warm
the skin. Lipsticks are more like a glossy stain. And eyes look naked but they're not. The lid is rubbed with one of the
newer shades of pale, like Chanel's vanilla, a pastel wash or a fleshy brown.

PHOTOGRAPHS BY KURT MARCUS FOR THE NEW YORK TIMES   THE NEW YORK TIMES MAGAZINE / MAY 16, 1993

Silver
The New York Times Magazine
New York, NY
Janet Froelich, Art Director; Petra Mercker, Designer; Kurt Markus, Photographer; Polly Hamilton, Stylist

Silver
Los Angeles Times Magazine
Los Angeles, CA
Nancy Duckworth, Art Director; Steven Banks, Designer; Tim Gabor, Illustrator

jus' what kind of good ole boy is president billy? by florence king

Silver
El Mundo/El Mundo Magazine
Madrid, Spain
Rodrigo Sanchez, Art Director & Designer; Carmelo Caderot, Design Director; Angel Baltasar, Illustrator; Popa Gomez, Designer

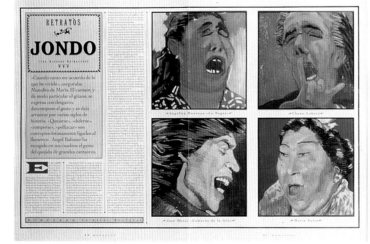

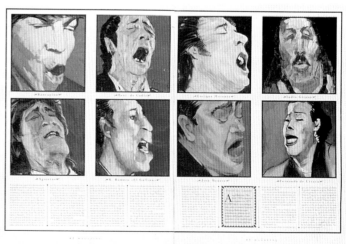

Bronze
El Pais/El Pais Semanal
Madrid, Spain
Eugenio Gonzalez, Art Director; Gustavo Sanchez, Designer; Isabel
Benito, Designer; Marta Calzada, Designer; Roman Gubern, Writer;
Francis Giacobetti, Photographer

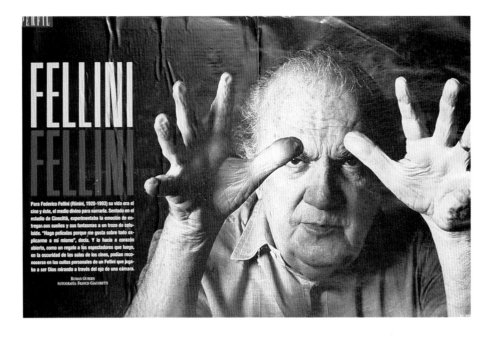

Award of Excellence
El Mundo/El Mundo Magazine
Madrid, Spain
Rodrigo Sanchez, Art Director & Designer; Carmelo Caderot, Design Director; Popa Gomez, De-
signer

Award of Excellence
Diario 16
Madrid, Spain
Carlos Perez Diaz, Art Director & Designer; Staff

Bronze
El Pais/El Pais Semanal
Madrid, Spain
Eugenio Gonzalez, Art Director; Gustavo Sanchez, Designer; Isabel Benito, Designer; Marta Calzada, Designer; Fietta Jarque, Writer

Award of Excellence
Los Angeles Times Magazine
Los Angeles, CA
Nancy Duckworth, Art Director; Carol Wakano, Designer; Joseph Astor, Photographer

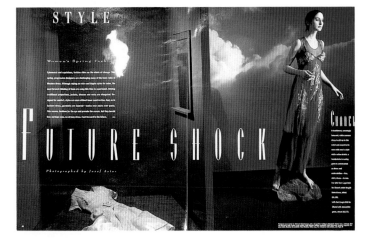

Award of Excellence
Los Angeles Times Magazine
Los Angeles, CA
Nancy Duckworth, Art Director; Steven Banks, Designer; Alastair Thain, Photographer; Nancy Ogami, Typography

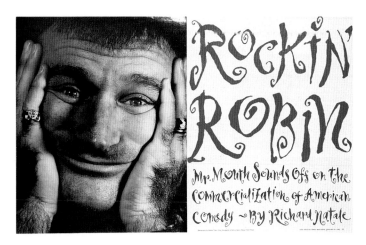

Bronze
Silver (for Illustration)
The New York Times Magazine
New York, NY
Janet Froelich, Art Director; Kathi Rota, Designer; Sue Coe, Illustrator

The New York Times Magazine / OCTOBER 3, 1993

CHINA IN THE YEAR 2000

Repressive? Expressive? Anarchic?

BY NICHOLAS D. KRISTOF

The emperor appears to be dying.

Deng Xiaoping is a fighter, and it is possible he will hang on for months or even years. But each time China's 89-year-old paramount leader hobbles a few steps in one of his rare television appearances, his trembling hands and blank stares invite a fundamental question: what next?

When an emperor last died in China, in 1976, the country changed course. Mao Zedong's death led to basic changes in the way people lived: black miniskirts replaced Mao jackets; angry rock music succeeded tunes like "The Party Is My Mommy"; living standards surged so that many peasants could enjoy a measure of prosperity for the first time in thousands of years.

The death of Emperor Deng may be just as significant, for the Communist Party today faces a fundamental crisis of legitimacy. The expression in Chinese for crisis is *wei ji*. It is made up of the term for danger, "wei," and the word for opportunity, "ji." So a crisis, in Chinese, holds both danger and opportunity. That is precisely the situation now for a country with a fifth of the world's population. Imagine the possibilities: the Balkans, but with 1.1 billion people and nuclear weapons. Or Japan, but with 25 times the territory and nine times the population.

What will China be like in the year 2000? Predicting its course even a year from now is like forecasting next year's weather. Nonetheless, while a return to radical Maoism seems unlikely, three scenarios — based on actual characters and settings — may best reflect the immense promise and perils of China in the 1990's.

WHO'S WHO

Chen Ziming, 41, a democracy campaigner serving a 13-year prison sentence for helping to organize the 1989 Tiananmen demonstrations. A short and pudgy man, he became a think tank in the 1980's by running a hugely successful correspondence school.

Chi Haotian, 63, a sober and stolid soldier since he was a teen-ager, now the Defense Minister commanding strong loyalties throughout the military.

Jiang Zemin, 66, Communist Party leader nicknamed Weathervane for his tendency to shift with the political winds.

Li Peng, 64, Prime Minister and a hard-line Politburo member, perhaps the most hated man in China. Even his mother, on her deathbed in Beijing Hospital in 1985, complained about him to anyone who would listen.

Liu Yanwen, 25, a peasant living in Tongzhi Village in Hunan Province. An ambitious woman brimming with self-confidence, Liu worked in a factory making stuffed toys for export and then tried, unsuccessfully, to start a cottage industry in her own village.

Xue Fei, 35, an earnest and soft-spoken television anchor fired in 1989 for announcing the establishment of martial law — part of the Tiananmen crackdown — in a dull and obviously disapproving monotone. Since then he has gone into business selling consumer products to Eastern Europe.

Zhu Rongji, 64, a thin man with an even thinner face, who is Deputy Prime Minister and economic czar. He is sometimes called China's Gorbachev because of his willingness to accept political and economic change.

ILLUSTRATIONS BY SUE COE

THE AUTHORITARIAN STATE

May 4, 2000. Paoju Detention Center, one of Beijing's oldest jails. Rats and roaches scurry along its dank hallways, and generations of prisoners have left their graffiti on the stone walls. Torture has long been common in prisons throughout China.

LIU YANWEN COUGHS quietly from a corner in Interrogation Room No. 4.

She never imagined pain and humiliation of this kind. When it began, she didn't think she would last another minute, and yet the minutes, and days, have passed. She never knew there was such a thing as a shackleboard — an old door, the knob still attached, with a set of handcuffs in each corner. Yet here she is, fastened by her wrists and ankles to a shackleboard propped against a wall. A hole in the door functions as her toilet. Twice a day, a guard hoses her off.

"We want to help you," says an Army officer — the chief interrogator — from his chair several feet away. He pulls out a Marlboro, lights it with a gold lighter and inhales twice. Like the two other men in the room, he wears a neatly pressed Army uniform.

"Little Liu, you must realize that you're just an egg attacking a rock," the Army man continues. "On May Day, when you threw the paint at the great portrait of the Generalissimo at Tiananmen, you only hit the frame. We washed it off in 10 minutes. You accomplished nothing."

Liu grits her teeth. "You should never have taken down the portrait of Mao and replaced it with one of Chi Haotian."

"Chi Haotian is the great Generalissimo who keeps our country

Nicholas D. Kristof, who recently completed nearly five years as chief of the Beijing bureau of The Times, is now writing a book about China with Sheryl WuDunn.

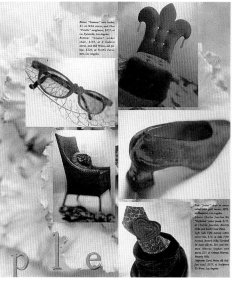

THE DEMOCRATIC STATE

strong," responds the chief interrogator. "China is rich now. It's the envy of the world."

"Chi Haotian is a fascist *tuzaizi*" — a little rabbit — "and this is a Government for the rich. Aaaaah!" She screams as a cigarette sizzles against her left cheek. She wriggles violently, aggravating the raw sores on her ankles. The youngest of the interrogators laughs shrilly; he isn't used to seeing naked women being burned with cigarettes. The others watch obsequiously as the chief interrogator relights his cigarette.

Liu Yanwen closes her eyes, remembering how it all began with Old Meng, hating him, hating them all. She wonders if they will kill her.

She never thought it would end like this. Like most Chinese, she welcomed the coup of '95. In her new brick home in Tongzhi Village, she watched as Chi Haotian, then the Defense Minister, appeared on television to announce the overthrow of the Gang of Three. Chi explained that corruption and inflation had eaten away at the country. Yet the Gang of Three lived lavishly, even spending $7,000 each to buy American-made whirlpool baths, skimming off the cream of the nation's profits and harming the war effort. The war could have been won

months earlier if it hadn't been for their mismanagement. The People's Army had not wanted to intervene, but there was no alternative.

Even after the war, with the South China Sea secured and the Vietnamese aggressors defeated, the Gang of Three had squabbled among themselves as prices soared and social order collapsed. "Corruption and crime are attacking China today, and they are just as dangerous as any invading army," Chi Haotian said. "It is time for the People's Army to defend the motherland."

When she heard that, Liu Yanwen whooped in delight. Since Deng Xiaoping's death in early 1994, corruption, chaos and inflation had increased tenfold. After the Vietnamese attack on the Chinese Spratly Islands in '95, inflation soared. Now, at last, someone was taking charge again and talking about order.

The Generalissimo's decision to dismantle the Communist Party and create a new umbrella organization, the Patriotic Association to Save China, was welcomed at home and abroad. President Clinton, narrowly winning re-election, characterized the fall of the Chinese Communist Party as an achievement of his tough foreign policy. The new British Prime Minister, John Smith, said it would be inappropriate to impose sanctions against military leaders who had deposed "an odious Communist dinosaur."

There was, of course, some diplomatic unpleasantness when the Patriotic Association showed the executions of the Gang of Three on national television. Hardly anyone in China, however, felt the least bit sorry for Li Peng, Jiang Zemin or Zhu Rongji.

Through this mist of memories, Liu hears the chief interrogator speaking.

"So, tell us," he is saying, "when did you form this underground clique to overthrow the Patriotic Association?"

She closes her eyes, trying to remember. Fire sears her other cheek. She screams again and as she writhes the handcuffs bite into her flesh, bringing on a pain so great she feels on the verge of blacking out.

The chief interrogator looks at his watch. Almost 11:30 — time to hurry things up a bit if he's to make it to lunch on time. He lights another cigarette.

"Two years ago," she whispers. "October '98. I was working at a shoe factory. Worked 14 hours a day, seven days a week. The factory manager — Old Meng — rode around in a Mercedes-Benz."

She pauses but quickly struggles on. She doesn't want to be burned again.

"It was a little factory along the coast, in Wenzhou. My sister and I worked there. Old Meng wanted me. Said he had hired me; said he owned me. I kept saying no. Finally, he put me and my sister on the sole-making machine. It's a huge machine. We couldn't manage it. My sister got caught in the gears. She was 16."

"So you've been a bandit since '98?"

"A freedom fighter!"

He raises his cigarette and Liu screams: "You're right, a bandit! A bandit! After I heard about the Beijing University uprising at the beginning of last year, I came to Beijing. After Beijing University was closed down——."

"Suspended," the chief interrogator interrupts.

"Suspended. After the university was suspended, lots of students formed underground groups. I joined a cell in the underground Communist Party. A fair society — that's all we

---

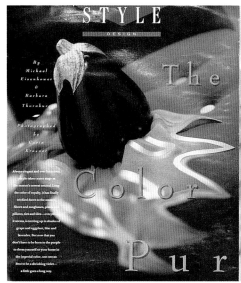

S · T · Y · L · E
DESIGN

By Michael Eisenhower & Barbara Thornburg

Photographed by Carin Krasner

The Color Purple

Award of Excellence
Los Angeles Times Magazine
Los Angeles, CA
Nancy Duckworth, Art Director & Designer; Carin Krasner, Photographer

THE AUTHORITARIAN STATE

Bronze
San Francisco Examiner/Image Magazine
San Francisco, CA
Paul Wilner, AME/Features; Joey Rigg, Art Director,
Zahid Sardar, Associate Art Director; Penni Gladstone,
Picture Editor; Richard Barnes, Photographer

The Living and the Dead

THE SOUND OF COSSACK THUNDER

The fearsome horsemen of a violent Russian past are back, teaching a new gene ration to fight for God and country.

Award of Excellence
The New York Times Magazine
New York, NY
Janet Froelich, Art Director; Gina Davis, Designer; Kathy Ryan, Photo Editor; Ellen Binder, Photographer

FOUR FUTURES FOR RUSSIA
New Coup? ■ Civil War? ■ Muddling Through? ■ Happy Ending?

Award of Excellence
The New York Times Magazine
New York, NY
Janet Froelich, Art Director & Designer; Kayo der Serkissian, Designer; Owen Smith, Illustrator

Award of Excellence
The Seattle Times
Seattle, WA
Robin Avni, Art Director & Designer & Picture Ed.; Gary
Settle, Picture Editor; Benjamin Benschneider, Photo-
grapher

Award of Excellence
San Francisco Examiner
San Francisco, CA
Paul Wilner, AME/Features; Joey Rigg, IMAGE Art Di-
rector; Zahid Sardar, IMAGE Associate Art Director;
Penni Gladstone, IMAGE Picture Editor

Award of Excellence
The Rhode Islander Magazine
Providence, RI
Susan Huntemann, Designer & Creative Director; Mick
Cochran, Art Director; Bob Thayer, Photographer;
Anestis Diakopoulos, Photo Editor

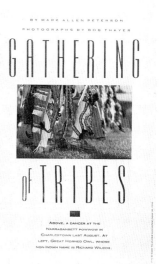

Award of Excellence
The Philadelphia Inquirer Magazine
Philadelphia, PA
Bert Fox, Art Director; Jessica Helfand,
Design Director & Designer; Michael S.
Wirtz, Photographer

Award of Excellence
El Mundo/El Mundo Magazine
Madrid, Spain
Rodrigo Sanchez, Art Director; Carmelo
Caderot, Design Director; Popa Gomez, De-
signer

Award of Excellence
The Boston Globe Magazine
Boston, MA
Catherine Aldrich, Art Director; Hornick Rivlin, Photographer; Louise Roche, Stylist

SPECIAL SECTIONS

chapter

six

Bronze
El Mundo
Madrid, Spain
Carmelo Caderot, Design Director; Manuel de Miguel, Assistant Art Director

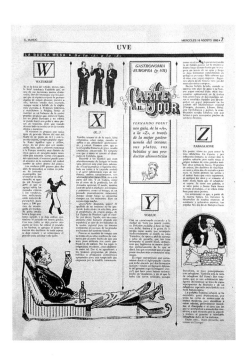

Award of Excellence
The Christian Science Monitor
Boston, MA
Photo Staff; John Van Pelt, Design Director; Karen T. Everbeck, Designer; Tom Brown, Designer

Award of Excellence
Chicago Tribune
Chicago, IL
Stacy Sweat, Graphics Editor; Stephen Ravenscraft, Graphics Artist; Rick Tuma, Graphics Artist; Martin Fischer, Graphics Researcher; Jim Prisching, Photographer

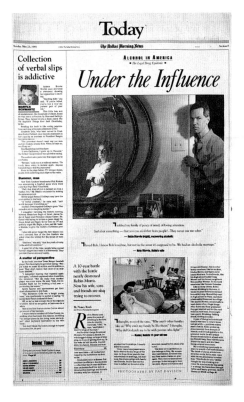

Award of Excellence
The Dallas Morning News
Dallas, TX
Marilyn Glaser, Designer & Assistant Art Director; Pat Davison, Photographer; Clif Bosler, Illustrator; Lisa Thatcher, Assistant Today Editor

Award of Excellence
The Providence Journal-Bulletin
Providence, RI
Thea Breite, Chief Picture Editor; Tim Barmann, Photographer;
Mike Duval, Graphics Artist; Bill Ostendorf, Photo Director

Award of Excellence
The Times-Picayune
New Orleans, LA
George Berke, Design Director; Doug Parker, Assistant Photo
Editor; John McCusker, Photographer

Award of Excellence
The Times-Picayune
New Orleans, LA
George Berke, Design Director; Kurt Mutchler, Photo & Graphics Editor; Tyrone Turner, Photographer

Award of Excellence
The Houston Post
Houston, TX
Susan Barber, Art Director & Designer; Jim Preston, Photo Editor & Designer; Marla Cloud,
News Artist; Nuri Vallbona, Photographer

Award of Excellence
The Times-Picayune
New Orleans, LA
George Berke, Design Director; Kurt Mutchler, Photo & Graphics Editor; Staff

Gold

Detroit Free Press

Detroit, MI

(also won a Silver Medal for Special Section Cover Page; a Silver Medal for Photojournalism Photo/Design; an Award of Excellence for Photojournalism Photo Story)

Deborah Withey, Design Director; Tim Oliver, Designer; David C. Turnley, Photographer; Mike Smith, Photo Director; Marcia Prouse, Deputy Photo Director; Bob Cronin, Copy Editor; Andy Countryman, Copy Editor; W. Kim Heron, Copy Editor

Sunday, November 28, 1993 | **Detroit Free Press** | Section **H**

COMMENT

IMMIGRATION

HATE & HOPE

ROY BRANDT – BETTER KNOWN AS BOMBER, ONE OF THE MOST FEARED NEO–NAZI SKINHEAD LEADERS IN BERLIN – HAS A LESSON FOR HIS 3-YEAR-OLD SON, PAUL. "YOU WANT TO KNOW WHAT I THINK ABOUT FOREIGNERS?" HE BARKS. "THEY HAVE TO GET OUT OF GERMANY. THEY HAVE TO GET OUT OF EUROPE. ... EUROPE MUST BE A FORTRESS."

EUROPE

As borders close, ugliness is laid bare

BY CHARLES MITCHELL
Free Press Foreign Editor

BERLIN, Germany — The doors to Western Europe have been slammed shut. The countries that once offered freedom and opportunity to those trapped in the communist east have hung out a new sign: Immigrants stay out.

Meanwhile, the millions of African, Asian, Turkish and Caribbean black immigrants already in Western Europe are facing a new and brutal wave of intolerance. Crimes of racial hatred are rampant, and their viciousness is intensifying.

In Solingen, a manufacturing city in northwestern Germany, neo-Nazi skinheads torched a house in May, killing five Turkish women and girls. At least 30 people, most of them immigrants from non-European countries, have died in Germany in the past 20 months in right-wing violence.

In Britain, Indian and Bangladeshi immigrants claim police have lost control of the streets, so they are forming vigilante street gangs to protect families. They fear marauding neo-Nazi thugs, and their other white neighbors as well.

See **EUROPE**, Page **7H**

A young woman who lives part of the year in California enjoys a carnival in Tanaquillo, her Mexican hometown, where most families get checks from relatives in the United States.

One of the largest immigration tides in history is sweeping across the United States and Western Europe. But on both sides of the Atlantic, refugees from war, oppression and poverty face intolerance and a sometimes violent backlash. In the United States, there are calls for tougher laws and tighter borders. In Europe, immigrants have been harassed and attacked. This four-part special report chronicles the rising hate and the indomitable hope of the immigrants.

UNITED STATES

Fearful clamor arises: Stop the tide

BY GERALD VOLGENAU
Free Press Staff Writer

TANAQUILLO, Mexico — Evaristo Duarte doesn't realize he's headed for serious, and growing, hostility.

Wearing designer jeans and a Polo shirt that give him a definite California look, the sapling-thin Mexican is headed back to the USA.

Here's his plan: He'll drop his waiter's job popping caps off Corona bottles in a dirt-floor cantina in Tanaquillo, an adobe village southeast of Guadalajara. Then he'll hop a northbound bus to Tijuana, wait for the 10:30 p.m. shift change by the U.S. Border Patrol, wade across the pollution-poisoned Tijuana River and scoot toward I-5 and a ride to east Los Angeles.

Mexicans such as Duarte know America too well to believe the streets are paved with gold. But they do know *El Norte* means opportunity, a chance to makes five times as much money as can be made at home.

This 34-year-old man with a wispy moustache has gone north scores of times, each time leaving his wife and two children for several months. It is a way of life. His father did it before him; so have his neighbors.

See **U.S.**, Page **4H**

A   S P E C I A L   S E C T I O N

PHOTOGRAPHY BY DAVID C. TURNLEY

Doors slam on asylum in Europe

ROME

GYPSIES FIND NO WELCOME, NO PEACE

A 1993 STUDY FOUND 90 PERCENT OF ROMANIA'S ADULT GYPSIES LIVE IN POVERTY.

CZECH-GERMAN BORDER

NOWHERE TO TURN: FAMILY'S DREAM ENDS WITH A NUMBER, CELL

In Europe, far right adds clout

IN 1992, IMMIGRANTS IN GERMANY PAID $56 BILLION IN TAXES AND SOCIAL INSURANCE.

Many find newcomers a net gain

U.S.–MEXICO BORDER

THE CROSSING: EVERY NIGHT, THE WAVE RETURNS

PRICE OF A FORGED GREEN CARD IN DOWNTOWN LOS ANGELES: $50.

ABOUT THIS SERIES

ITALY

STARTING OVER IN SQUALOR

COMING UP

SHARE YOUR STORY

WORLDWIDE, IMMIGRANTS SEND $66 BILLION HOME.

Silver

(also winner of an Award of Excellence for Special Section Cover Page)
Detroit Free Press
Detroit, MI
Deborah Withey, Designer/Illustrator; Steve Anderson, Art Director & Designer; Cathy Collison, Editor; Jon Buechel, Illustrator; Phil Marden, Illustrator; Tom Close, Graphics; Hank Szerlag, Graphics; Ted Williamson, Graphics

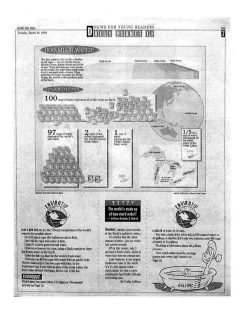

Award of Excellence
The Arizona Republic/Phoenix Gazette
Phoenix, AZ
Reuben Munoz, Design Editor; Diana Shantic, Design Editor; Mark Henle, Photographer; Michael Ging, Photographer

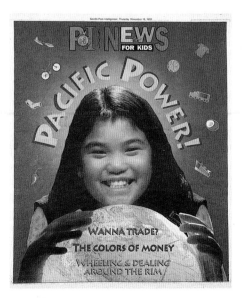

Award of Excellence
Seattle Post-Intelligencer
Seattle, WA
Ben Garrison, Staff Artist; Duane Hoffmann, Staff Artist; Kim Carney, Staff Artist; Steve Greenberg, Staff Artist; David Horsey, Staff Artist

Silver
The Detroit News
Detroit, MI
Robert Graham, Graphics Artist & Designer; Felix Grabowski, Graphics Editor & Designer; Charles Blow, Graphics Artist; Anthony Miller, Graphics Artist; Steve Kaskovich, Section Editor; Susan Tompor, Reporter; James P. Gannon, Reporter; Michele Fecht, Research; Mark Lett, AME

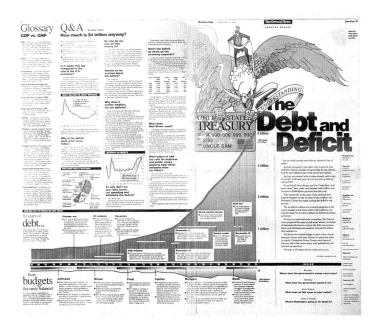

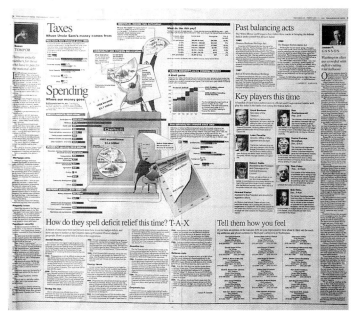

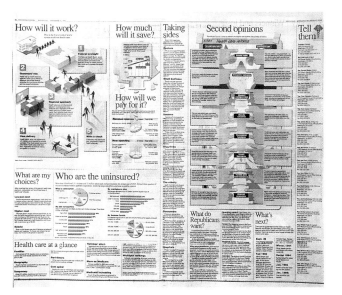

Award of Excellence
The Detroit News
Detroit, MI
Robert Graham, Graphics Artist & Designer; Felix Grabowski, Graphics Director & Designer; Charles Blow, Graphics Artist; Sean McDade, Graphics Artist; Alan Stamm, Section Editor; Steve Kaskovich, Section Editor; Mark Lett, Section Editor; Michele Fecht, Researcher; Carol Stevens, Researcher

Award of Excellence
The Hartford Courant
Hartford, CT
Toni Finch Kellar, Picture Editor; Cecilia Prestamo, Photographer

Award of Excellence
Los Angeles Times/Orange County Edition
Costa Mesa, CA
Lily Dow, Designer; Chuck Nigash, Designer; David Puckett, Designer

Silver

The Detroit News
Detroit, MI

Robert Graham, Graphics Artist & Designer; Bob Richards, Graphics Artist; Felix Grabowski, Graphics Editor & Designer; Mark Hornbeck, Reporter; Michele Fecht, Researcher; Pat McCaughan, Section Editor; James V. Higgins, Section Editor; Dale Peskin, AME; Mark Hass, AME

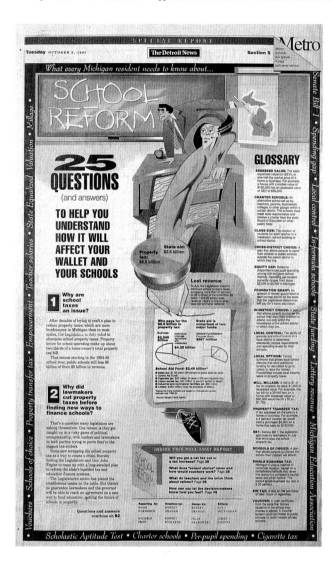

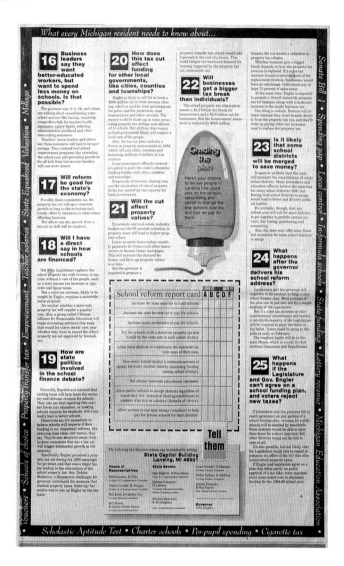

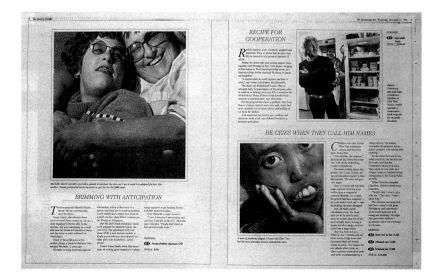

Bronze

The Sacramento Bee
Sacramento, CA

Lisa Roberts, Photo Editor & Designer; Jose Luis Villegas, Photographer

Silver
The Orange County Register
Santa Ana, CA
Bruce Strong, Photographer; Brenda Shoun, Assistant News Editor/Design; Ron Londen, News Editor/Photo; Betty Shimabukuro, Assistant Topic Editor

ALZHEIMER'S: THE QUIRKY SIDE

MOMENTS OF HOPE IN THE EARLY DAYS AT HOME

Once Opa arrived home from the hospital, his physical condition improved, although his mental state fluctuated in ways that could be alarming – or amusing. Some days, such as this one, he was not only "normal" but mischievous. He could surprise us: One morning he suddenly began speaking fluent French, a language no one in the family realized he understood. He conversed with his daughter, Elizabeth, who had studied French. As the year progressed, though, he was more likely to awaken confused and combative.

A LAST KISS: MY MOM'S FAREWELL

GREATEST CONCERN IS FOR OMA'S LIFE WITHOUT OPA

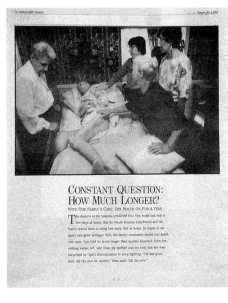

CONSTANT QUESTION: HOW MUCH LONGER?

WITH THE FAMILY'S CARE, OPA HOLDS ON FOR A YEAR

Award of Excellence
La Vanguardia
Barcelona, Spain
Carlos Perez de Rozas, Art Director; Rosa Mundet, Art Director; Ferran Grau, Designer; Joan Corbera, Designer

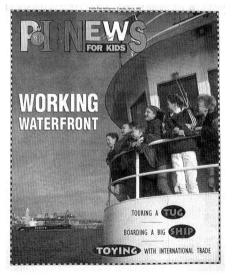

Award of Excellence
Seattle Post-Intelligencer
Seattle, WA
Ben Garrison, Staff Artist; Duane Hoffmann, Staff Artist; Steve Greenberg, Staff Artist; Dave Gray, Staff Artist; Kim Horsey, Staff Artist

Silver

The Orange County Register
Santa Ana, CA

Brenda Shoun, Assistant News Editor/Design; Jay Bryant, Picture Editor; Paul Carbo, Graphics Artist; Richard Cheverton, Graphics Artist; Betty Shimabukuro, Assistant Topic Editor; Nanette Bisher, AME/Art Director; Tia Lai, News Editor/Graphics

Award of Excellence

La Vanguardia
Barcelona, Spain

Carlos Perez de Rozas, Art Director; Rosa Mundet, Art Director; Ferran Grau, Designer; Joan Corbera, Designer

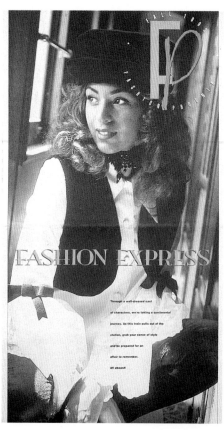

Award of Excellence

The Phoenix Gazette
Phoenix, AZ

Jennifer Ignaszewski, Designer; Jacques Barbey, Photographer

Silver
The Times-Picayune
New Orleans, LA
Michael Jantze, Assistant Graphics Editor; Susan Shoaff, Graphics Artist; Angela Everhart-Hill, Graphics Artist; Mark Schleif-stein, Reporter

Award of Excellence
(also a Bronze Medal winner for
Special News Topics)
The Press Democrat
Santa Rosa, CA
Kent Porter, Photographer; John
Metzger, Director of photography;
Ron Makabe, Section editor; Sharon
Roberts, Designer/AME/Design;
Mark Aronoff, Photographer; John
Burgess, Photographer; Jeff Kan
Lee, Photographer; Chad Surmick,
Photographer; Annie Wells, Photog-
rapher

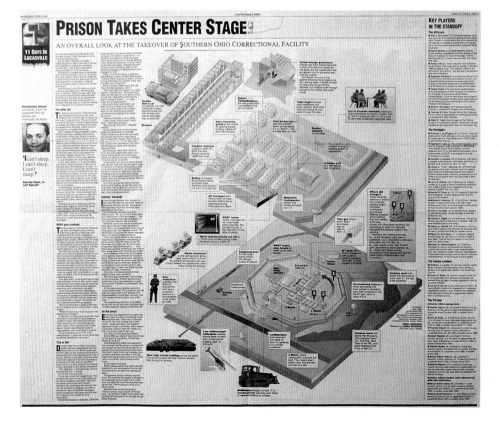

Bronze
Dayton Daily News
Dayton, OH
David Kordalski, Art Director & Designer; Ted Pitts, Illustrator; Ron Rollins, Editor; John Hancock, Graphics Artist; John Thomson, AME Graphics; Linda Monroe, Graphic Research; Photo Staff

Silver
(also a Silver Medal for Inside Page)
The Wall Street Journal Reports
New York, NY
Greg Leeds, Designer & Design Director; Randall Enos, Illustrator; Nick Klein, Art Director & Designer

Award of Excellence
The Miami Herald
Miami, FL
Janet Santelices, Illustrator & Designer;
Kendall Hamersly, Editor; Rhonda Prast,
Design Desk Editor; Randy Stano, Director of Editorial Art & Design

Award of Excellence

The Miami Herald

Miami, FL

Mel Frishman, Assistant News Editor; Daryl Kannberg, Assistant News Editor; Mary Behne, Assistant News Editor; Herschel Kenner, Assistant News Editor; Tim Burke, Assistant Sports Editor; Marty Pantages, Assistant Sports Editor; Bonnie Snyder, Sports Design Editor; Ana Lense-Larrauri, Designer; Hiram Henriquez, Graphics Artist; Derek Hembd, Graphics Artist Intern; Ilena Oroza, AME; Steve Rice, AME; Paul Anger, Executive Sports Editor; Dennis Copeland, Director of Photography; Randy Stano, Director of Editorial Art & Design

Award of Excellence

(Breaking News, Editor's Choice / Local)

Award of Excellence (Sports Page)

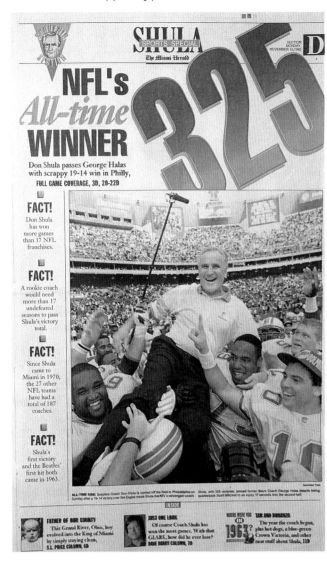

Silver

(also Award of Excellence for Special Section With Ads)
La Vanguardia
Barcelona, Spain
Carlos Perez de Rozas, Art Director; Rosa Mundet, Art Director; Ferran Grau, Designer; Joan Corbera, Designer

Silver

Diario de Noticias
Lisbon, Portugal
Jose Sapinho, Designer; Jose Pires, Editor; Maria Jose Lima, Deputy Art Director; Jose Maria Ribeironho, Art Director; Mario Resendes, Editor in Chief

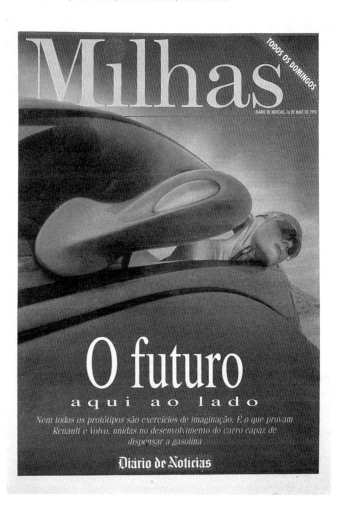

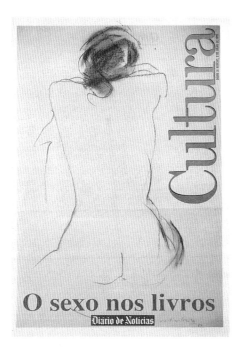

Award of Excellence

Diario de Noticias
Lisbon, Portugal
Jose Saphino, Designer; Maria Jose Lima, Deputy Art Director; Jose Maria Ribeironho, Art Director; Mario Resendes, Editor in chief

Award of Excellence

Diario 16
Madrid, Spain
Carlos Perez Diaz, Art Director & Designer; Staff

Award of Excellence

Computer Reseller News
Manhasset, NY
Gene Fedele, Sr. Art Director; Peter Siu, Illustrator; Camille DeMarzo, Editor

Award of Excellence
Contra Costa Times
Walnut Creek, CA
Sharon Henry, Designer; Meri Simon, Photographer

Award of Excellence
The Detroit News
Detroit, MI
Dale Peskin, AME

Award of Excellence
The Detroit News
Detroit, MI
Dale Peskin, AME

Award of Excellence
Fort Worth Star-Telegram
Fort Worth, TX
Brenda Leferink, Designer; Ralph Lauer, Photographer

Award of Excellence
The Augusta Chronicle
Augusta, GA
Rick McKee, Chief Artist; Dan Doughtie, Director, Photo &
Graphics

Award of Excellence
The Charlotte Observer
Charlotte, NC
Michael Persinger, Designer

Award of Excellence
The Globe and Mail
Toronto, Canada
Eric Nelson, Art Director & Designer; Jack McHale, Editor;
Mark Stegel, Photographer

Award of Excellence
Houston Chronicle
Houston, TX
Michael Dean, Illustrator; Joseph Markman, Designer

Award of Excellence
News-Press
Fort Myers, FL
Paul Fresty, Graphics Editor; Randy Lovely, AME Design;
Cathy Riddick, Special Projects Editor; John Severson, Photographer; Ken Riddick, Photo Editor

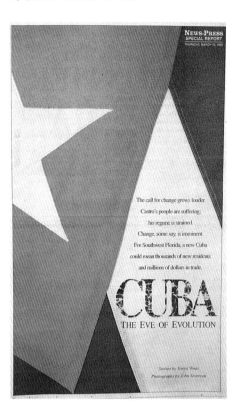

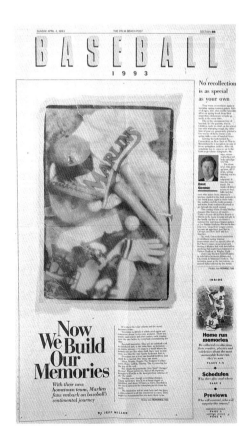

Award of Excellence
The Palm Beach Post
West Palm Beach, FL
Mark Buzek, Design Editor; Sherman Zent, Photographer; Pat
McManamon, Sports Editor

Award of Excellence
The San Diego Union-Tribune
San Diego, CA
Bill Gaspard, Art Director & Designer; Barry Fitzgerald,
Illustrator

Award of Excellence
The Wall Street Journal Reports
New York, NY
Greg Leeds, Designer & Design Director; Christopher Bing,
Illustrator

Bronze
El Mundo Deportivo
Barcelona, Spain
Quique Belil, Senior Writer

Award of Excellence
The Florida Times-Union
Jacksonville, FL
D. Tom Patterson, AME Graphics; Vasin Douglas, Art Director;
Bob Mack, Photo Director; Al Vieira, Design Director; Lisa
Young, Artist

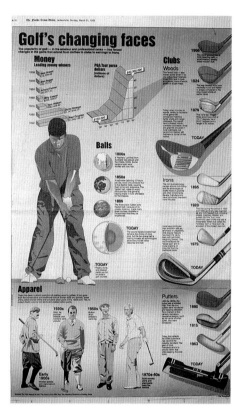

Award of Excellence
El Mundo Deportivo
Barcelona, Spain
Quique Belil, Senior Writer

Award of Excellence
El Mundo
Madrid, Spain
Carmelo Caderot, Design Director; Manuel de Miguel,
Assistant Art Director; Raul
Arias, Illustrator

Award of Excellence
The Dallas Morning News
Dallas, TX
Alison Cocks Hamilton, Illustrator & Designer; Kathleen Vincent, Art Director

Award of Excellence
Springfield News-Leader
Springfield, MO
Gregory A. Branson, Graphics Artist & Researcher; John L. Dengler, Graphics Editor

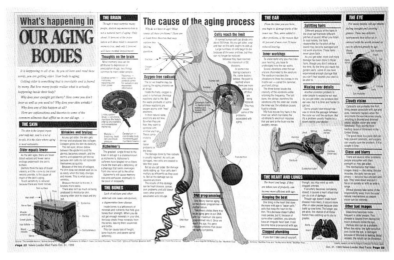

Award of Excellence
The Kansas City Star
Kansas City, MO
Jean Moxam, AME Graphics/Design; Bill Kempin, Designer;
Vic Winter, Photo Editor; Mark Blackwell, Graphics Artist;
Dave Eames, Graphics Artist; Jesse Barker, Designer; Lance
Thomas, Designer

Award of Excellence
El Pais/El Pais de las Tentaciones
Madrid, Spain
Alex Martinez Roig, Editor; Fernando Gutierrez, Art Director &
Designer; Luis Magan, Picture
Editor

Award of Excellence
The Phoenix Gazette
Phoenix, AZ
Tony Bustos, Illustrator & Designer; Rob Weideman, Illustrator & Designer

Award of Excellence
St. Louis Post-Dispatch
St. Louis, MO
Tom Borgman, Graphics Editor

Silver

San Francisco Examiner
San Francisco, CA

Steve Cook, AME/Enterprise; Marge Rice, Graphics Coordinator; Tracy Cox, Designer; Chris Morris, Illustrator; Kelly Frankeny, Art Director; Mignon Khargie, Illustrator; Mark Constantini, Photographer; Bob McLeod, Director of Photography; Jane Kay, Reporter; Joe Shoulak, Illustrator

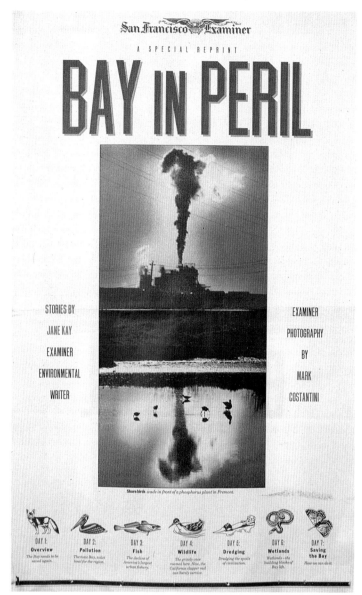

Award of Excellence

Star Tribune
Minneapolis, MN

Bill Dunn, Design Director; Tim Campbell, Graphics Editor; Anders Ramberg, Art Director & Designer; Constance Nelson, Researcher; Marci Scmitt Boettcher, Copy Editor; Jim Dawson, Writer

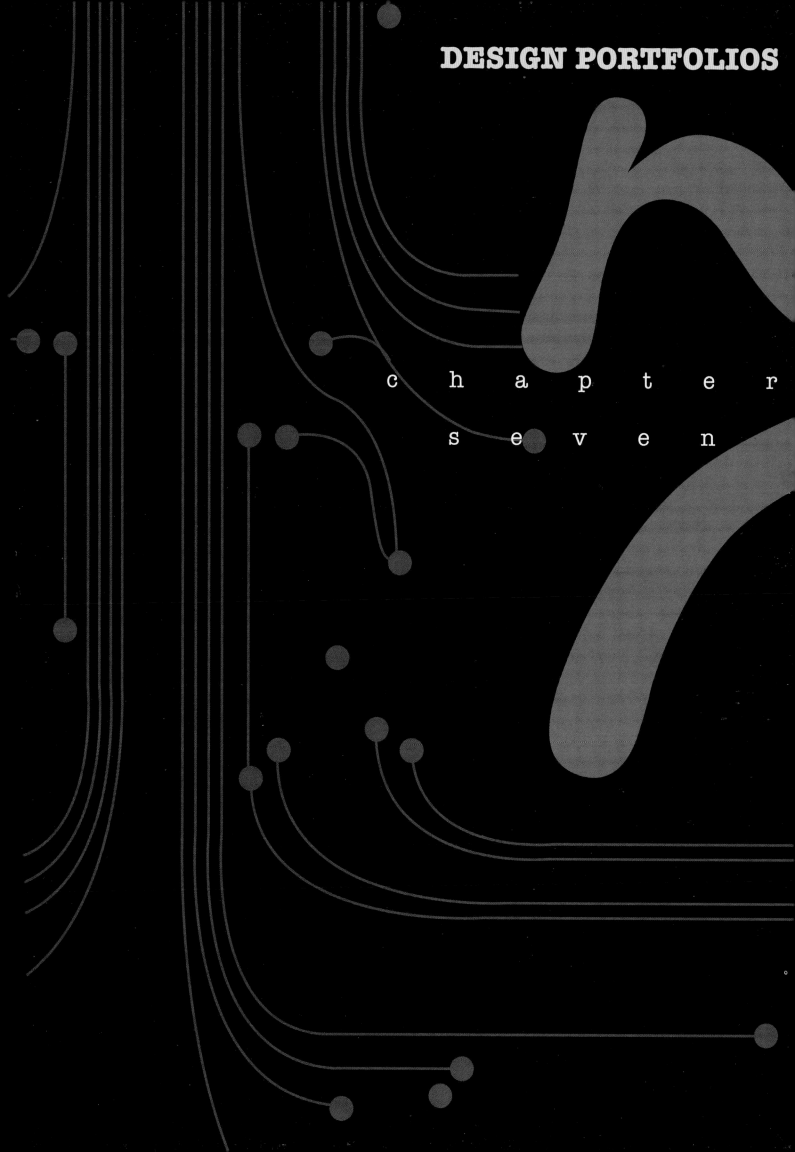

c h a p t e r

s e v e n

Award of Excellence
The Des Moines Register
Des Moines, IA
Mike Pauly, Senior AME; Kathy Richardson, News Editor

Award of Excellence
The Arizona Republic
Phoenix, AZ
Keira Cox, Design Editor

Award of Excellence
The Detroit News
Detroit, MI
Dale Peskin, AME

Award of Excellence
The Globe and Mail
Toronto, Canada
Eric Nelson, Art Director & Designer; David Langford, Editor

Award of Excellence
San Francisco Examiner
San Francisco, CA
Tracy Cox, Designer; Kelly Frankeny, Art Director; Katie Rabin, Business Editor; Dave Ember, Illustrator; Joe Shoulak, Illustrator; Dale Hendersheid, Illustrator

Award of Excellence
Anchorage Daily News
Anchorage, AK
Mike Campbell, AME & Designer

Silver
American Medical News
Chicago, IL
Jef Capaldi, Art Director, Designer & Illustrator; Glynis Sweeny, Illustrator; John Figler, Illustrator; Gwendolyn Wong, Illustrator; Rick Sealock, Illustrator

Bronze (for Illustration)

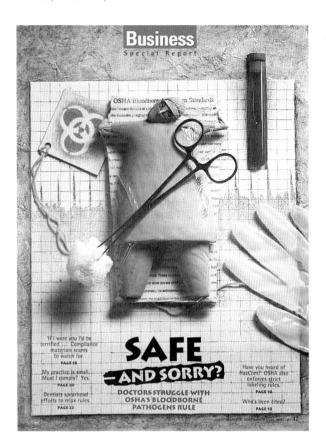

Award of Excellence
The News-Sentinel
Fort Wayne, IN
William Dawson, Designer; M. Daniel Suwyn, Design Editor

Award of Excellence
Tallahassee Democrat
Tallahassee, FL
William Lampkin, Design Director/ News

Award of Excellence
The Post-Standard
Syracuse, NY
Brian Cubbison, A-1 Editor

Silver
The New York Times
New York, NY
Nancy Sterngold, Art Director & Designer

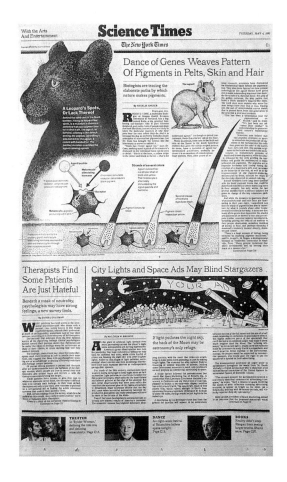

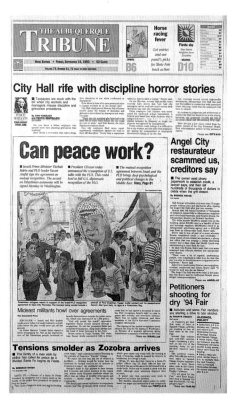

Award of Excellence
The Post-Star
Glens Falls, NY
Scott Goldman, Sunday Sports Editor

Award of Excellence
The Albuquerque Tribune
Albuquerque, NM
Gerald Cox, Designer

Award of Excellence
The Times/Lansing
Lansing, IL
Peter Routman, Display Editor & Staff Writer

Bronze
Goteborgs-Posten
Gothenburg, Sweden
Ulf Johanson, Designer; Gunilla Wernhamn, Staff; Rune Stenberg, Staff; F. Soir Moscara, Photographer; Lars Soderbom, Photographer; Jonny Mattsson, Photographer; Peter Claesson, Photographer

Award of Excellence
The Star-Ledger
Newark, NJ
Lisa Zollinger, Art Director; Jane Hood, Illustrator; Robin Jareaux, Illustrator; Joe Epstein, Photographer; Tom Kitts, Photographer; John O'Boyle, Photographer; Joe Gigli, Photographer; Envision Staff, Photographers; Linda Fowler, Section Editor

Award of Excellence
The Star-Ledger
Newark, NJ
Bernadette Dashiell, Designer; Chris Buckley, Designer & Illustrator; Frank Cecala, Illustrator; Shawn Banner, Illustrator; Pim Van Hemmen, Photographer; Bob Ono, Photographer

Award of Excellence
The Palm Beach Post
West Palm Beach, FL
Lisa M. Griffis, Feature Design Editor

Silver

San Francisco Examiner
San Francisco, CA
Tracy Cox, Illustrator & Designer; Kelly Frankeny, Art Director; Bob McLeod, Director of Photography; David Talbot, Arts & Features Editor; Christine Barnes, Style Editor; Zak Trenholm, Illustrator

Award of Excellence

El Mundo
Madrid, Spain
Carmelo Caderot, Design Director; Manuel De Miguel, Assistant Art Director

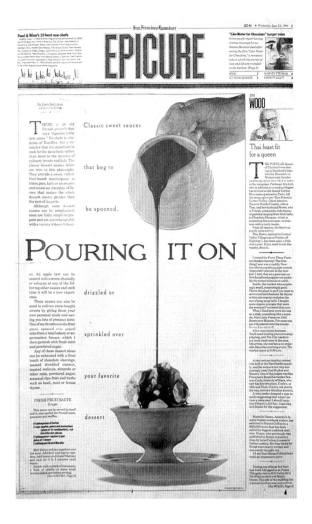

Bronze
San Francisco Examiner
San Francisco, CA
Don McCartney, Designer;
Kelly Frankeny, Art Director;
Bob McLeod, Director of
Photography; Don George,
Travel Editor; Lynn Forbes,
Epicure Editor

Award of Excellence
The Gazette
Montreal, Canada
Gayle Grin, Deputy Art Editor & Designer

Award of Excellence
New Times/Phoenix
Phoenix, AZ
Kim Klein, Art Director; Timothy Archibald, Photographer; Melinda Beck, Illustrator

Bronze
Anchorage Daily News
Anchorage, AK
Dee Boyles, Designer; Galie
Jean-Louis, Design Director;
Lin Mitchell, Photographer

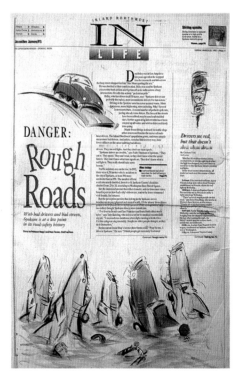

Award of Excellence
San Francisco Examiner
San Francisco, CA
Mignon Khargle, Designer & Illustrator; Kelly Frankeny, Art
Director; Bob McLeod, Director of Photography; Jo Mancuso,
Habitat Editor

Award of Excellence
The Spokesman-Review
Spokane, WA
John Nelson, Art Director & Design Editor

Award of Excellence
The Washington Times
Washington, DC
Joseph Scopin, AME Graphics; Dolores Motichka, Art Director
& Designer

Silver
(for Photojournalism Design Portfoilo)

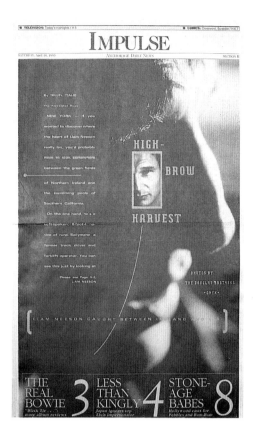

Gold
Anchorage Daily News
Anchorage, AK
Galie Jean-Louis, Illustrator, Designer, Design Director; Frank Ockenfels, Photographer; Amy Guip, Photographer; The Douglas Brothers/Onyx, Photographer; Derek M. Powazek, Photographer

Award of Excellence
(for Illustration)

Silver
The Sunday Tribune
Dublin, Ireland
Stephen Ryan, Design/Photo
Editor; Paul Hopkins, Produc-
tion Editor; Roslyn Dee,
Lifestyles Editor; Ann Marie
Hourihan, Features Editor

Award of Excellence
Anchorage Daily News
Anchorage, AK
Lance Lekander, Designer; Galie Jean-Louis, Design Director;
William Duke, Illustrator

Award of Excellence
Anchorage Daily News
Anchorage, AK
Pamela Dunlap-Shohl, Designer; Galie Jean-Louis, Design Di-
rector; Lin Mitchell, Photographer

Award of Excellence
El Nuevo Herald
Miami, FL
Nuri Ducassi, Art Director & Designer

Bronze
El Nuevo Herald
Miami, FL
Raul Fernandez, Designer; Rosa
Bautista, Editor; Nuri Ducassi, Art Director

Award of Excellence
El Nuevo Herald
Miami, FL
Aurora Arrue, Designer; Nuri Ducassi, Art Director; Rosa
Bautista, Editor; Silvia Licha, Editor

Award of Excellence
The Press Democrat
Santa Rosa, CA
Diane Peterson, Designer; Sharon Roberts, AME Design

Award of Excellence
The Times/Munster
Munster, IN
Channon Seifert, Designer

Bronze

The Phoenix Gazette
Phoenix, AZ
Jennifer Ignaszewski, Designer

Bronze

The Santa Fe New Mexican
Santa Fe, NM
Deborah Ensor, Features Designer

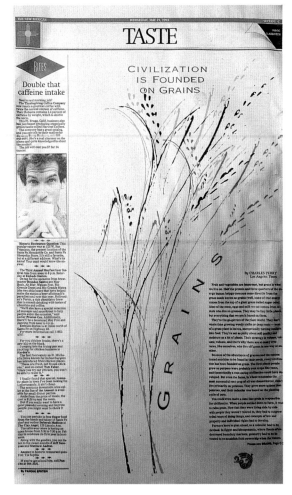

Award of Excellence
El Mundo/El Mundo Magazine
Madrid, Spain
Rodrigo Sanchez, Art Director & Designer; Carmelo Caderot, Design Director

Silver
New Times/Miami
Miami, FL
Brian Stauffer, Art Director & Designer

Award of Excellence
The Davis Enterprise
Davis, CA
Kurt Kland, Illustrator & Designer

Award of Excellence
The Albuquerque Tribune
Albuquerque, NM
Jeff Neumann, Designer

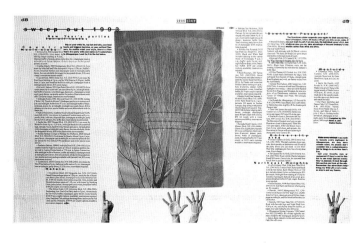

Bronze
The Advocate and Greenwich Time
Stamford, CT
Jacqueline Segal, AME Design &
Photo; Carlo F. Cantavero Jr., De-
signer

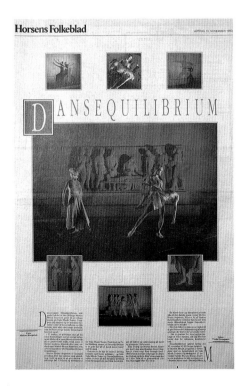

Award of Excellence
Horsens Folkeblad
Horsens, Denmark
Kjeld Torbjorn, Designer

Award of Excellence
Journal and Courier
Lafayette, IN
James Jackson, Graphics Editor; Brenda Buckingham-
Ehrmann, 4 Kidz Only Coordinator

Award of Excellence
The News-Review
Roseburg, OR
Marti Gerdes, Associate Editor

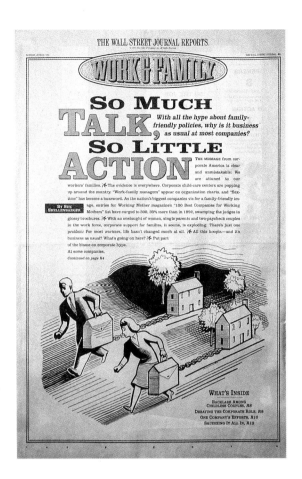

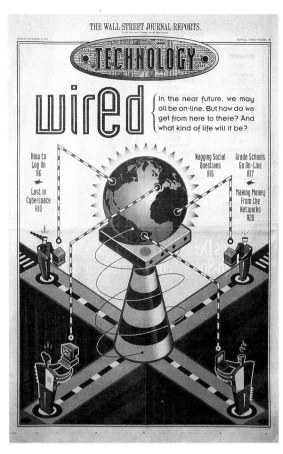

Bronze
The Wall Street Journal
New York, NY
Greg Leeds, Design Director &
Designer; Raul Colon, Illustrator

Award of Excellence
Reporter
Buffalo, NY
Rebecca Farnham, Art Director

Award of Excellence
The Miami Herald
Miami, FL
Dave Hogerty, Designer & Photographer; Candace Barbot,
Photographer

Award of Excellence
The Miami Herald
Miami, FL
Dave Hogerty, Designer & Editor; Brenda Ann Kenneally, Pho-
tographer; Jamie Robinson, Photographer; Patterson Clark,
Illustrator; Phill Flanders, Illustrator

Silver

The Miami Herald

Miami, FL

Dave Hogerty, Designer & Editor; C. W. Griffin, Photographer; Beth A. Keiser, Photographer; Phill Flanders, Illustrator; Ron Coddington, Illustrator; Hiram Henriquez, Graphics Artist; Associated Press, Photographer

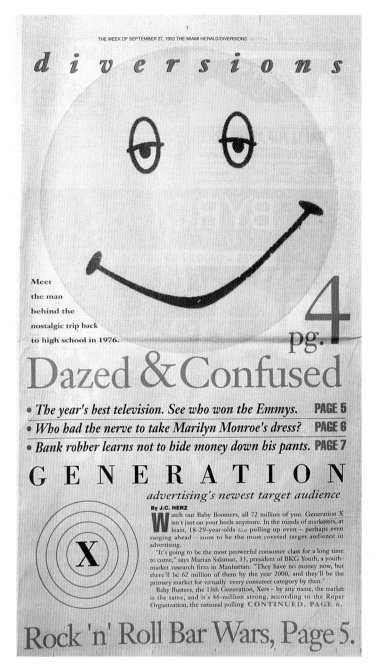

Bronze

The Washington Post Magazine

Washington, DC

Kelly Doe, Art Director, Designer & Illustrator; Lane Smith, Illustrator; Deborah Needleman, Photo Editor; Photographers; Brian Smale, Photographer; Karen Tanaka, Photo Editor; Sylvia Plachy, Photographer; Chris Callas, Photographer; Tom Wolff, Photographer

Bronze
The Washington Post Magazine
Washington, DC
Kelly Doe, Art Director; Sandra Schneider, Deputy Art Director & Designer; Guzman, Photographer

Award of Excellence
The Washington Post
Washington, DC
Marty Barrick, Graphic Designer & Illustrator; Joseph Daniel
Fiedler, Illustrator; Patrick Blackwell, Illustrator; Richard
Thompson, Illustrator; Renee Comet, Photographer

Award of Excellence
The New York Times
New York, NY
Ken McFarlin, Art Director & Designer

Award of Excellence
The Christian Science Monitor
Boston, MA
Karen T. Everbeck, Designer

Silver
The Albuquerque Tribune
Albuquerque, NM
Jeff Neumann, Designer

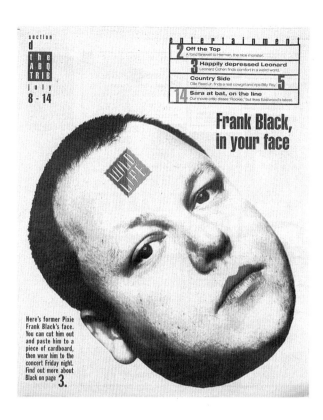

Award of Excellence
The News-Sentinel
Fort Wayne, IN
Denise M. Reagan, Designer & Picture Editor; Steve Linsen-
mayer, Photographer; Keith Hitchens, Photographer; Lisa
Dutton, Photographer

Award of Excellence
The Sun/Lowell
Lowell, MA
Mitchell Hayes, Art Director & Designer; Andrea Wisnewski, Il-
lustrator; Ted Pitts, Illustrator; Tracy Walker, Illustrator; Gregg
Fitzhugh, Illustrator; Debbie Tilley, Illustrator

Silver
Diario 16
Madrid, Spain
Carlos Perez Díaz, Art Director & Designer

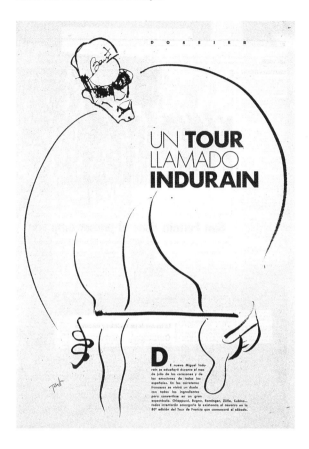

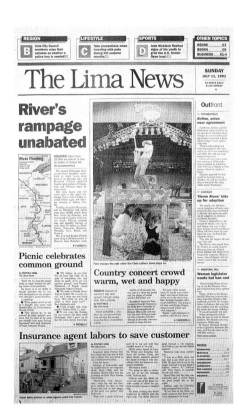

Award of Excellence
The Lima News
Lima, OH
Max Zimmerman, Designer

Award of Excellence
The Village Voice
New York, NY
Robert Newman, Design Director

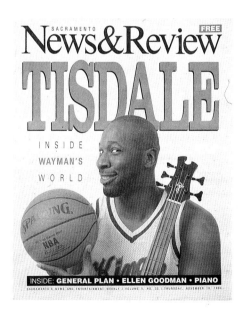

Award of Excellence
Sacramento News and Review
Sacramento, CA
Don Button, Art Director & Designer; Adrian Tomine, Illustrator; Noel Neuburger, Photographer

Bronze
The Emporia Gazette
Emporia, KS
Jill Jess, Features/Design Editor

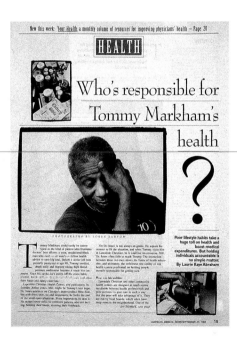

Award of Excellence
American Medical News
Chicago, IL
Jef Capaldi, Art Director & Designer; Loren Santow, Photographer; Meryl Sklut-Lettire, Illustrator; Normand Cousineau, Illustrator; Gwendolyn Wong, Illustrator; Bonnie Timmons, Illustrator; Phil Marden, Illustrator

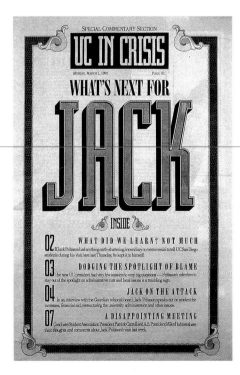

Award of Excellence
The UCSD Guardian
La Jolla, CA
Miguel Buckenmeyer, Design Editor & Senior Editor; Roger Kuo, Graphics Editor & Graphics Artist; Rene Bruckner, Graphics Editor & Graphics Artist; Micha Croft, Graphics Artist; James Collier, Design Consultant

Award of Excellence
The University Daily Kansan
Lawrence, KS
Ezra Wolfe, Features Editor/Designer; Tom Leininger, Photographer; Melissa Lacey, Photographer

PHOTOJOURNALISM

chapter

eight

8

Gold
The Philadelphia Inquirer Magazine
Philadelphia, PA
Bert Fox, Art Director & Designer; Jessica Helfand, Design Director; Carolina Salguero, Photographer

Pursuing peace

PHOTOGRAPHY BY CAROLINA SALGUERO

Silver
The Providence Journal-Bulletin
Providence, RI
James J. Molloy, Photographer; Thea Breite,
Picture Editor & Designer; Bill Ostendorf, Di-
rector of Photography

Bronze
The Detroit News
Detroit, MI
Joe DeVera, Photographer

Bronze
The Globe and Mail
Toronto, ON Canada
Michael Gregg, Designer & Design Director; Richard Emblin, Photographer; Sarah Murdoch, Editor

Bronze
The Times/Munster
Munster, IN
Todd Panagopoulos, Photographer

Everyone was just shocked'

Award of Excellence
Los Angeles Daily News
Woodland Hills, CA
Gus Ruelas, Photographer

Award of Excellence
The Florida Times-Union
Jacksonville, FL
D. Tom Patterson, AME Graphics; Vasin Douglas, Art Director; Bob Mack, Photo Director; Al Vieira, Design Director; Will Dickey, Photographer

A Thanksgiving landing

Award of Excellence
The Holland Sentinel
Holland, MI
Dave Odette, Chief photographer

Playing it by the books

Award of Excellence
The Citizen
Auburn, NY
Kevin Rivoli, Photo Editor

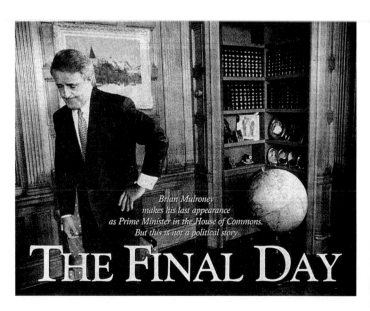

*Brian Mulroney
makes his last appearance
as Prime Minister in the House of Commons.
But this is not a political story*

THE FINAL DAY

Award of Excellence
The Globe and Mail
Toronto, Canada
Michael Gregg, Design Director; Eric Nelson, Designer; Sarah Murdoch, Editor; Pierre Charbonneau, Photographer

Award of Excellence

The Spokesman-Review
Spokane, WA
Anne C. Williams, Photographer; John Sale, Photo Editor;
John Kafentzis, News Editor

Award of Excellence

The San Diego Union-Tribune
San Diego, CA
Robert Gauthier, Photographer

Award of Excellence

The Providence Journal-Bulletin
Providence, RI
Tim Barmann, Photographer; Thea Breite, Picture Editor/Designer; Bill Ostendorf, Director of
Photography

Award of Excellence

The Outlook
Santa Monica, CA
Richard Hartog, Staff Photographer

Award of Excellence
The Times-Picayune
New Orleans, LA
Kathy Anderson, Photographer

Award of Excellence
The Springfield News
Springfield, OR
Rob Romig, Photo Editor

Award of Excellence
The Toronto Star
Toronto, Canada
Paul Watson, Photographer

Award of Excellence
The Times Herald Record
Middletown, NY
Philip Kamrass, Photographer

Award of Excellence
The Springfield News
Springfield, OR
Rob Romig, Photo Editor

Silver
The Spokesman-Review
Spokane, WA
Colin Mulvany, Photographer

Bronze
The San Diego Union-Tribune
San Diego, CA
Michael Franklin, Photographer; Mary Jo Zafis, Photo Editor; Alma Cesena, Designer

"You just can't take these kids and put them on a regular school site and expect them to flourish."
SABRINA TRUMBACH, PARENT

Uncertain future: *Encephalitis victim Guillermo Guerrero, 20, sits in a special walker and listens to music during a Valentine's party at Revere Development Center. His fate will be discussed at a school board meeting Tuesday.*

Disabling a school

Parents fight plan to close center, relocate students

By CLARK BROOKS
Staff Writer

Upset mom: *"It's like we're all parasites, sucking up all their funds," says Karen Napolilli, whose son, Robby, attends Revere.*

Shadows and symbolism transform this scene in a Belfast church.

Surrealistic Portraiture or Reality ?

Bronze
The Christian Science Monitor
Boston, MA
Melanie Stetson Freeman, Photographer

JAZZMEN
The end of the beginning

LIVING LEGACY

A tribute to some of the New Orleans players who learned from the pioneers of jazz

Bronze
The Times-Picayune
New Orleans, LA
John McCusker, Photographer; Doug Parker, Assistant Photo Editor; George Berke, Design Director

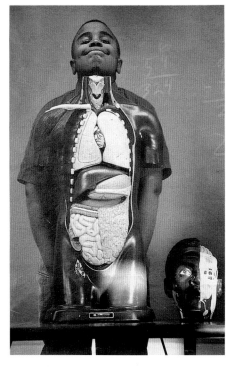

Award of Excellence
The Dallas Morning News
Dallas, TX
Evans Caglage, Photographer

Award of Excellence
The Dallas Morning News
Dallas, TX
Evans Caglage, Photographer

Award of Excellence
Pittsburgh Post-Gazette
Pittsburgh, PA
John Kaplan, Photographer; Anita Dufalla, Art Director; Christopher Pett-Ridge, AME
Graphics; Tracy Collins, Associate Graphics Editor

Award of Excellence
The Florida Times-Union
Jacksonville, FL
D. Tom Patterson, AME Graphics; Vasin Douglas, Art Director; Bob Mack, Photo Di-
rector; Al Vieira, Design Director; Wes Lester, Photographer

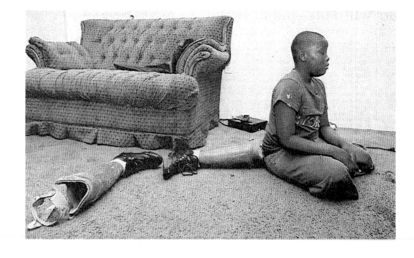

Award of Excellence
The Dallas Morning News
Dallas, TX
Evans Caglage, Photographer

Award of Excellence
The Christian Science Monitor
Boston, MA
Melanie Stetson Freeman, Photographer

Award of Excellence
Goteborgs-Posten
Gothenburg, Sweden
Lars Soderbom, Photographer; Ulf Johansson, Designer; Gunilla Wernhamn, Staff; Rune Stenberg, Staff

Award of Excellence
Goteborgs-Posten
Gothenburg, Sweden
Lars Soderbom, Photographer; Ulf Johanson, Designer; Gunilla Wernhamm, Staff; Rune Stenberg, Staff

Award of Excellence
The Philadelphia Inquirer Magazine
Philadelphia, PA
Bert Fox, Art Director; Jessica Helfand, Design Director & Designer; J. Kyle Keener, Photographer

Award of Excellence
The News & Observer
Raleigh, NC
Roger Winstead, Photographer & Designer; John Hansen, Picture Editor; David Pickel, AME/Art Director

Award of Excellence
Portland Press Herald
Portland, ME
Tina Rosell, Photographer; Rick Wakely, Designer; Andrea
Philbrick, Designer

Award of Excellence
The Press-Enterprise
Riverside, CA
Nick Souza, Photographer

Award of Excellence
The Spokesman-Review
Spokane, WA
Shawn Jacobson, Photographer

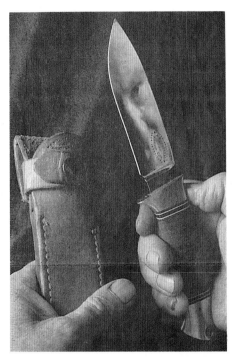

Award of Excellence
(also winner for Feature Photo)
The Spokesman-Review
Spokane, WA
Anne C. Williams, Photographer; John Sale, Photo Editor; Jim Allen, Copy Editor

Award of Excellence
The Providence Journal-Bulletin
Providence, RI
Kris Craig, Photographer

Award of Excellence
The Providence Journal-Bulletin
Providence, RI
Steve Szydlowski, Photographer; Anestis Diakopoulos, Photo Editor; Susan Huntemann, Designer; Bill Ostendorf, Director of Photography

Award of Excellence
The Spokesman-Review
Spokane, WA
Colin Mulvany, Staff Photographer; Scott Sines, AME

Award of Excellence
St. Paul Pioneer Press
St. Paul, MN
Richard Marshall, Photographer

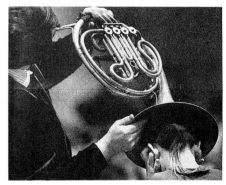

Award of Excellence
The Washington Post Magazine
Washington, D.C.
Kelly Doe, Art Director & Designer; Karen Tanaka, Photo Editor; Tom Wolff, Photographer

Award of Excellence
The Providence Journal-Bulletin
Providence, RI
Glenn Osmundson, Photographer; Anestis Diakopoulos, Picture editor/designer; Bill Ostendorf, Director of photography; Susan Huntemann, Designer & Creative Director

Award of Excellence
Portland Press Herald
Portland, ME
John Ewing, Photographer

Silver
The Providence Journal-Bulletin
Providence, RI
Ruben Perez, Photographer; Thea Breite, Photo Editor & Designer; Bill Ostendorf, Photo Director; Mike Duval, Graphics
Artist

Silver
The Spokesman-Review
Spokane, WA
Colin Mulvany, Photographer; Jim Allen, Copy Editor; Warren Huskey, Graphics Artist; John Sale, Photo Editor; Scott Sines, AME

Bronze
San Jose Mercury News/West Magazine
San Jose, CA
Sandra Eisert, Art Director/Photo Editor/Designer

Springtime and the fashions are easy. From hemlines to shoulder pads, designers are no longer dictators.

Freedom of *Choice*

STORIES BY MARY GOTTSCHALK

PHOTOGRAPHY BY GARY PARKER

Growing Up Too Soon

Born addicted to heroin, abused, neglected, pregnant at 16; Brandy Tricas was caught in the destructive cycle that threatens our society. But she's determined not to be destroyed by the past.

BY CAROLE RAFFERTY
PHOTOGRAPHS BY JOHN M. GOON

Award of Excellence
The Hartford Courant
Hartford, CT
Toni Finch Kellar, Picture Editor; Cecilia Prestamo, Photographer

A world of hurt
One brother walks a tightrope of anger, the other slips

The Well • a short story by Jesus Burgos

Award of Excellence
The Miami Herald
Miami, FL
Candace Barbot, Photographer

Wish Book

'We were afraid. But we just kept thinking about a better future.'
RAFAEL MATINEZ,
on the journey from Cuba

SURVIVORS: Rafael and Hilda Martinez, with their baby Rafael, 11 months, say they were afraid on their journey from Cuba to the United States, but kept on course by thinking of their future. It has been a struggle since their arrival.
CANDACE BARBOT / Miami Herald Staff

Refugee family works hard for very little

WISH LIST NO. 5

'The kids came to me saying, "Grandma, you love us. Can't we stay with you?" I couldn't say no.'
VOYGENE DELVA,
grandmother

DON'T WANT TO GO: Twins Jasmine, left, and Jose Simmons want to live with their grandmother Voygene Delva.
CANDACE BARBOT / Miami Herald Staff

Grandmother raising new generation

By DONNA GEHRKE
Herald Staff Writer

WISH LIST NO. 9

Award of Excellence
The Philadelphia Inquirer Magazine
Philadelphia, PA
Bert Fox, Art Director & Designer; Jessica Helfand, Design Director; April Saul, Photographer

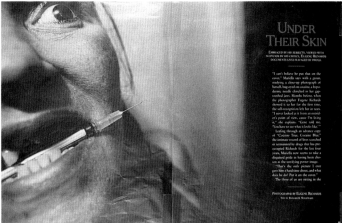

Award of Excellence
The New York Times
New York, NY
Janet Froelich, Art Director; Richard Baker, Designer; Kathy
Ryan, Photo Editor; Eugene Richards, Photographer

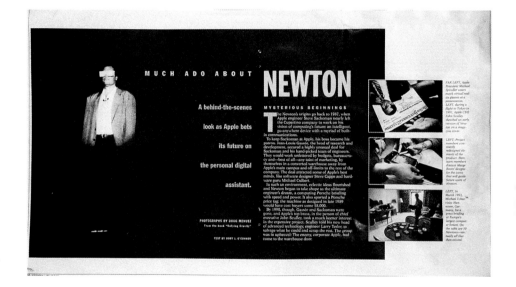

Award of Excellence
San Jose Mercury News/West Magazine
San Jose, CA
Doug Menuez, Freelance Photographer; Sandra Eisert, Art Director & Designer

Bronze
Star Tribune
Minneapolis, MN
Stormi Greener, Photographer; Susie Eaton Hopper, Senior Photo/Graphics Editor

Award of Excellence
The San Diego Union-Tribune
San Diego, CA
Robert Gauthier, Photographer & Writer; Randy Wright, Photo Editor & Designer

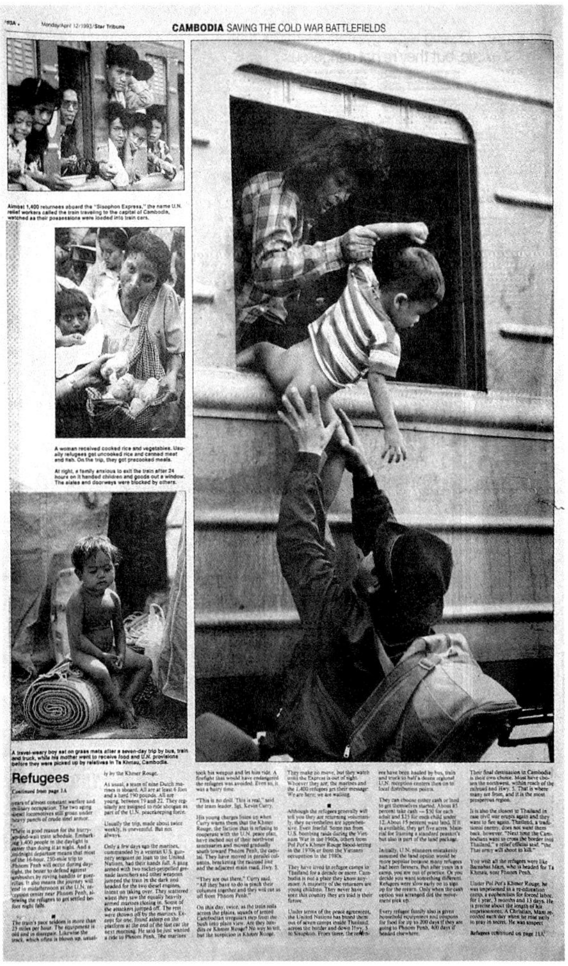

CAMBODIA SAVING THE COLD WAR BATTLEFIELDS

Refugees

Bronze

Star Tribune
Minneapolis, MN
Stormi Greener, Staff Photographer; Mike Healy, Weekend/Special Projects Photo Editor

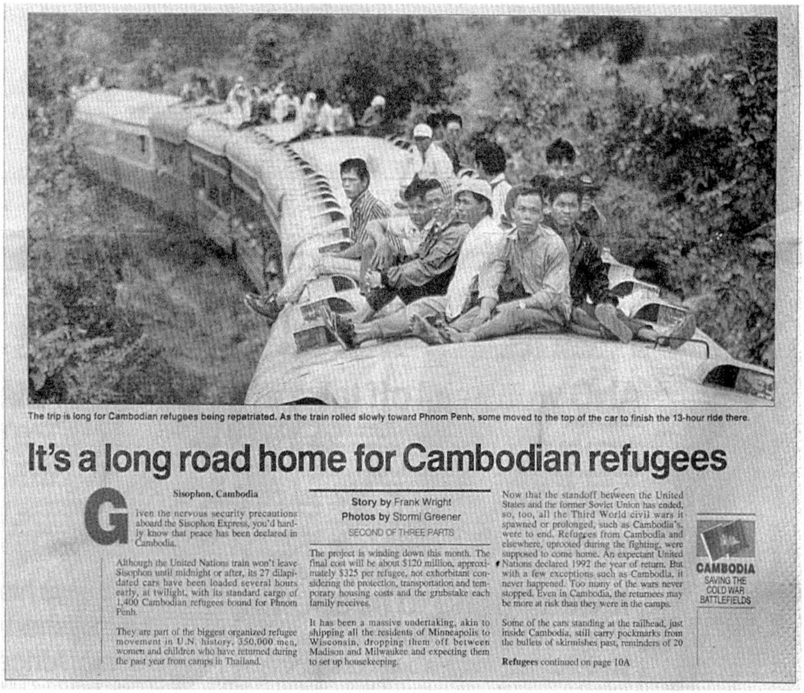

The trip is long for Cambodian refugees being repatriated. As the train rolled slowly toward Phnom Penh, some moved to the top of the car to finish the 13-hour ride there.

It's a long road home for Cambodian refugees

Sisophon, Cambodia

Story by Frank Wright
Photos by Stormi Greener
SECOND OF THREE PARTS

Given the nervous security precautions aboard the Sisophon Express, you'd hardly know that peace has been declared in Cambodia.

Although the United Nations train won't leave Sisophon until midnight or after, its 27 dilapidated cars have been loaded several hours early, at twilight, with its standard cargo of 1,400 Cambodian refugees bound for Phnom Penh.

They are part of the biggest organized refugee movement in U.N. history, 350,000 men, women and children who have returned during the past year from camps in Thailand.

The project is winding down this month. The final cost will be about $120 million, approximately $325 per refugee, not exorbitant considering the protection, transportation and temporary housing costs and the grubstake each family receives.

It has been a massive undertaking, akin to shipping all the residents of Minneapolis to Wisconsin, dropping them off between Madison and Milwaukee and expecting them to set up housekeeping.

Now that the standoff between the United States and the former Soviet Union has ended, so, too, all the Third World civil wars it spawned or prolonged, such as Cambodia's, were to end. Refugees from Cambodia and elsewhere, uprooted during the fighting, were supposed to come home. An expectant United Nations declared 1992 the year of return. But with a few exceptions such as Cambodia, it never happened. Too many of the wars never stopped. Even in Cambodia, the returnees may be more at risk than they were in the camps.

Some of the cars standing at the railhead, just inside Cambodia, still carry pockmarks from the bullets of skirmishes past, reminders of 20

Refugees continued on page 10A

CAMBODIA SAVING THE COLD WAR BATTLEFIELDS

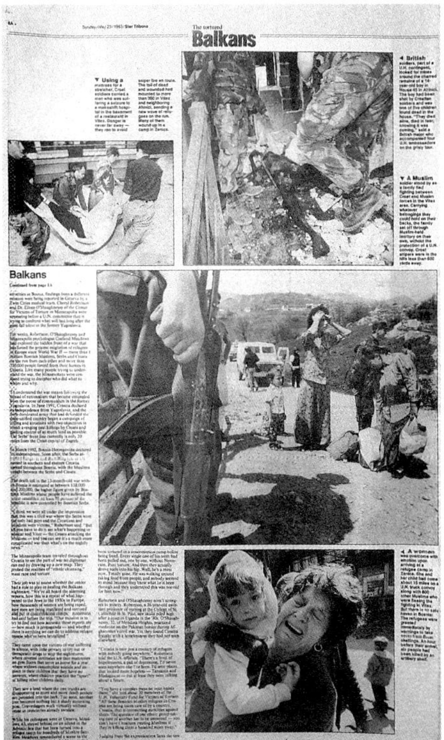

The tortured Balkans

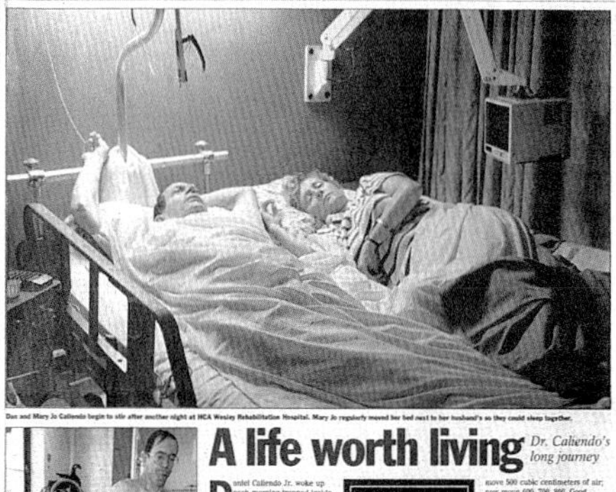

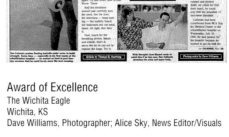

A life worth living

Dr. Caliendo's long journey

Rehabilitation was arduous and painful

Article by Thomas B. Koetting

Photographs by Dave Williams

Award of Excellence

The Wichita Eagle
Wichita, KS
Dave Williams, Photographer; Alice Sky, News Editor/Visuals

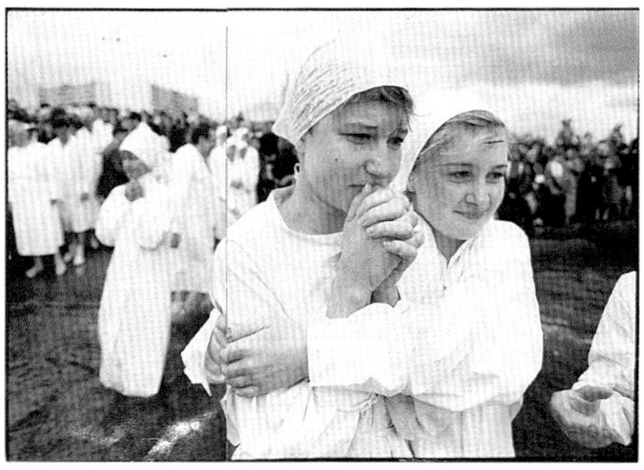

Award of Excellence

The Washington Post Magazine
Washington, DC
Kelly Doe, Art Director & Designer; Lucian Perkins, Photographer; Deborah Needleman, Photo Editor

Award of Excellence

Star Tribune
Minneapolis, MN
Rick Sennott, Photographer; Mike Healy, Weekend/Special Project Photo Editor

Gold
Fort Worth Star-Telegram
Fort Worth, TX
Victor Panichkul, Design Editor; Larry Price, Photographer

Silver
The Philadelphia Inquirer Magazine
Philadelphia, PA
Bert Fox, Art Director/Designer; Sabastiao Salgado, Photographer

Bronze
The Boston Globe Magazine
Boston, MA
Lucy Bartholomay, Art Director & Designer; Stan Grossfield, Photographer

Award of Excellence
The Boston Globe
Boston, MA
John Tlumacki, Photographer;
Jacqueline Berthet, Designer;
Ande Zellman, Focus Editor

Bronze
The Detroit News
Detroit, MI
Dale Peskin, AME & Designer; Donna Terek, Photographer; Julie Heaberlin, AME/Features

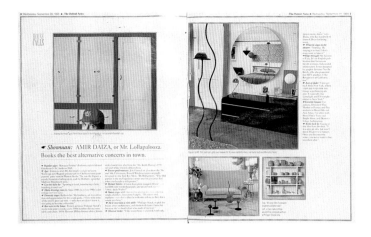

Award of Excellence
Morgenavisen Jyllands-Posten
Aarhus, Denmark
Poul Blak, Photographer; Bodil Krogh, Subeditor

Award of Excellence
The Boston Globe Magazine
Boston, MA
Lucy Bartholomay, Art Director & Designer; Michele McDonald, Photographer

Award of Excellence
New Times/Phoenix
Phoenix, AZ
Kim Klein, Art Director; Timothy Archibald, Photographer

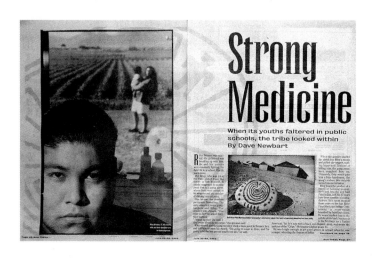

Award of Excellence
Fort Worth Star-Telegram
Fort Worth, TX
Brenda Lefernik, Designer; Ralph Lauer, Photographer

Award of Excellence

The News & Observer
Raleigh, NC
Nan Wintersteller, Designer; Scott Sharpe, Photographer; John Hansen, Picture Editor; David Pickel, AME/Art Director; Fraser Van Asch, Graphics Artist; Melanie Sill, Deputy Metro Editor

Award of Excellence

San Jose Mercury News
San Jose, CA
Murray Koodish, Photo Editor/Designer; Jeff Thomas, News Editor/Designer

Award of Excellence

The Philadelphia Inquirer Magazine
Philadelphia, PA
Bert Fox, Art Director & Designer; Ron Tarver, Photographer

Award of Excellence

The Spokesman-Review
Spokane, WA
Anne C. Williams, Staff Photographer; Scott Sines, AME

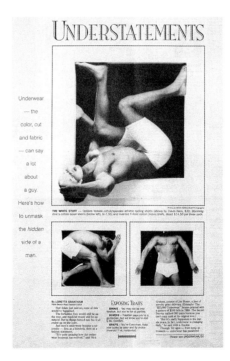

Award of Excellence

The Palm Beach Post
West Palm Beach, FL
Cheney Baltz, Designer; Mark Mirko, Photographer; Mark Edelson, Photo Editor

Award of Excellence

San Jose Mercury News
San Jose, CA
Linda M. Baron, Graphics Editor; Angela Cara Pancrazio, Photographer; Jim Gensheimer, Photographer

Silver
The Spokesman-Review
Spokane, WA
Colin Mulvany, Photographer

Award of Excellence
The Albuquerque Tribune
Albuquerque, NM
KayLynn Deveney, Photographer

Award of Excellence
The Charlotte Observer
Charlotte, NC
Mark Sluder, Photographer

Bronze
The Spokesman-Review
Spokane, WA
Anne C. Williams, Photographer

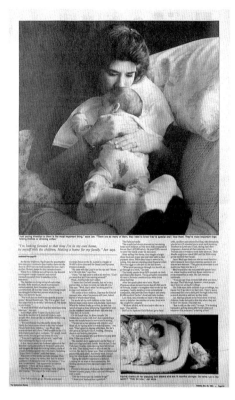

BUSTING THE BIKERS

You're a tattooed giant on a Harley. You're a member of the Dirty Dozen. You're toast.

BY DAVID PASZTOR PHOTOGRAPHS BY TIMOTHY ARCHIBALD

"THEY THINK ABOUT NOTHING BUT CRIME FROM THE TIME THEY GET UP IN THE MORNING UNTIL THEY GO TO BED AT NIGHT," SAYS DPS LIEUTENANT DAVID GONZALES.

Bronze
New Times/Phoenix
Phoenix, AZ
Kim Klein, Art Director; Timothy Archibald, Photographer

Bronze
Baltimore Jewish Times
Baltimore, MD
Craig Terkowitz, Photographer

Award of Excellence

The Christian Science Monitor
Boston, MA
Melanie Stetson Freeman, Photographer

Award of Excellence

The Sacramento Bee
Sacramento, CA
Randy Pench, Photographer

Award of Excellence

The Philadelphia Inquirer Magazine
Philadelphia, PA
Bert Fox, Art Director & Designer; Eric Mencher, Photographer

Award of Excellence

Los Angeles Times/Orange County
Costa Mesa, CA
Gail Fisher, Photographer; Colin Crawford, Photo Editor;
Chuck Nigash, Designer

Award of Excellence

San Jose Mercury News
San Jose, CA
Paul Kitagaki Jr., Photographer

Silver
The Des Moines Register
Des Moines, IA
Harry Baumert, Photographer

Award of Excellence
The Fresno Bee
Fresno, CA
Kurt Hegre, Photographer; Mark Crosse, Photographer; Richard Darby, Photographer; Michael Penn, Photographer; Thom Halls, Director of Photography

Award of Excellence
Sydsvenska Dagbladet
Malmoe, Sweden
Hans Johnsson, Photographer; Daniel Rydén, Reporter

Silver
The Providence Journal-Bulletin
Providence, RI
Bill Ostendorf, Director of Photography; Staff,
Photographer; Stephanie Gay, Picture Editor;
Susan Huntemann, Designer

RISE AND FALL

Photographs
by
Journal-Bulletin
Staff
Photographers

Edited by
Stephanie Gay

THE YEAR IN
PHOTOGRAPHS

Former Rhode Island Chief Justice Thomas F. Fay, below, sits in District Court, Providence, last month after being convicted of ethics violations; photograph by Steve Szydlowski. At left, the opening this month of the $356-million Rhode Island Convention Center, in Providence; photograph by Kris Craig.

THE YEAR OPENED with guarded optimism. Rhode Island, the "State of Disgrace," seemed to have turned a corner. The banking crisis was nearly resolved; the culprits were in jail — so maybe the state was in the clear. But just when it seemed that the ethical climate was finally improving, the cloud of scandal spread to the state Supreme Court. In October, Chief Justice Thomas F. Fay resigned, adding another episode to one of the darkest chapters in the state's history.

Looking back, we can see that 1993 has been a year in which a few notes of levity and joy have been heard above the themes of despair and sorrow. As violent crime flourished, as a parade of scoundrels passed through the courts en route to prison, Rhode Islanders paused at times to express their love of friends, of family, of country. As the economy languished, the Rhode Island Convention Center rose over the Providence skyline, a monument to progress. As 1993 ends, surely we can welcome in the new year — cautiously, but with hope.

THE YEAR
IN PHOTOGRAPHS   UP AND AWAY

In April, Block Island's historic Southeast Light perches on eroding cliffs before being moved, later in the year, 245 feet inland to safety. Photograph by Andy Dickerman.

THE YEAR
IN PHOTOGRAPHS
FAME AND FORTUNE

Campaigning in October for health-care reform, First Lady Hillary Rodham Clinton comes to Rhode Island, where one of her stops (below) is the Kent Nursing Home, in Warwick. Photograph by Kris Craig.

We've Been
Building Bridges
in
Rhode Island

Bronze
The Times-Picayune
New Orleans, LA
Kurt Mutchler, Graphics Editor; George Berke, Design Director; Tyrone Turner, Photographer; Doug Parker, Assistant Photo Editor; Dinah Rogers, Assistant Photo Editor

DEJA BLUE

Late miscue
helps
Heels win
national title
again in
Dean's
Dome

HEALING ZACH

THE MAYOR OF MIGRANTS

Migrants/ Teaching kids about hard work, self reliance

Silver
Star Tribune
Minneapolis, MN
Photo Staff, Photo Editors

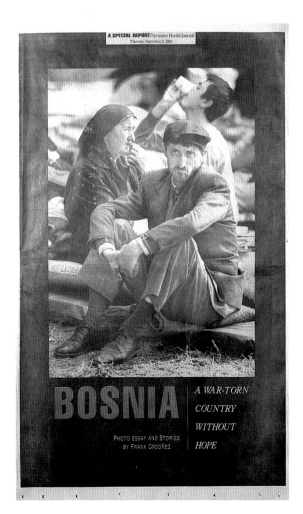

A SPECIAL REPORT/Syracuse Herald-Journal
Thursday, September 2, 1993

BOSNIA
A WAR-TORN
COUNTRY
WITHOUT
HOPE

PHOTO ESSAY AND STORIES
BY FRANK ORDOÑEZ

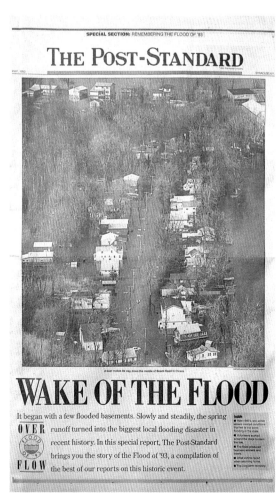

SPECIAL SECTION: REMEMBERING THE FLOOD OF '93

THE POST-STANDARD

WAKE OF THE FLOOD

It began with a few flooded basements. Slowly and steadily, the spring
OVER runoff turned into the biggest local flooding disaster in
recent history. In this special report, The Post-Standard
FLOW brings you the story of the Flood of '93, a compilation of
the best of our reports on this historic event.

Bronze
The Syracuse Newspapers
Syracuse, NY
Renee Byer, Picture Editor & Designer

Award of Excellence
The Miami Herald
Miami, FL
Dave Hogerty, Editor/Designer; Alan Freund, Photographer

Award of Excellence
Los Angeles Times
Los Angeles, CA
Steve Moore, Executive News Editor; Cindy Hively, Photo Editor; Howard Schatz, Photographer

Award of Excellence
Houston Chronicle
Houston, TX
Kellye B. Sanford, Designer

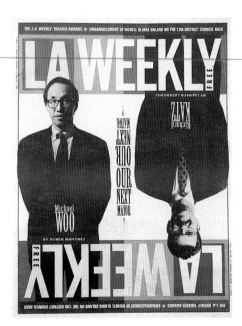

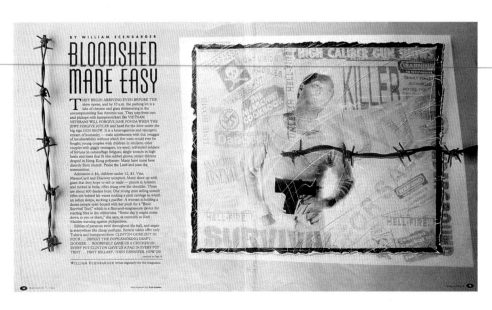

Award of Excellence
LA Weekly
Los Angeles, CA
Scott Ford, Art Director & Designer; Howard Rosenberg, Photographer; Ted Soqui, Photographer

Award of Excellence
The Philadelphia Inquirer Magazine
Philadelphia, PA
Bert Fox, Art Director & Designer; J. Kyle Keener, Photographer; Sebastiao Salgado, Photographer

Award of Excellence

The Spokesman-Review
Spokane, WA
Anne C. Williams, Photographer; Colin Mulvany, Photographer; Shawn Jacobson, Photographer; Chris Anderson, Photographer; Dan Pelle, Photographer; Blair Kooistra, Photographer; John Sale, Photo Editor; Scott Sines, AME

Award of Excellence

The Sacramento Bee
Sacremento, CA
Rick Shaw, Photo Editor/Designer; Carolyn Cole, Photographer

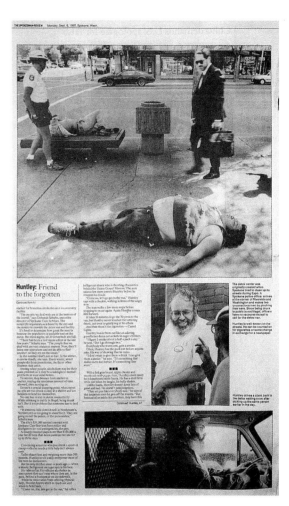

Award of Excellence

The Sacramento Bee
Sacramento, CA
Merrill Oliver, Photo Editor & Designer; Jose Luis Villegas, Photographer

Award of Excellence

The Seattle Times
Seattle, WA
Robin Avni, Art Director & Designer; Gary Settle, Picture Editor; Harley Soltes, Photographer; Benjamin Benschneider, Photographer; Eduardo Calderon, Photographer; Robin Avni, Picture Editor; Photo Staff

Bronze
The Spokesman-Review
Spokane, WA
John Sale, Photo Editor; John Nelson, Design editor; Lisa Cowan, Designer; Scott Sines, AME/Visuals; Vince Grippi, Graphics Editor; John Kafentzis, News Editor

Award of Excellence
The Register-Guard
Eugene, OR
Carl Davaz, Graphics Director; George Millener, Asst. Graphics Director; Andy Nelson, Photographer; Paul Carter, Photographer; Associated Press, Photographer

Award of Excellence
The Palm Beach Post
West Palm Beach, FL
Cheney Baltz, Page Designer; Mark Buzek, Page Designer; Sarah Franquet, Page Designer; Paulette Senior, Page Designer; Jan Tuckwood, Page Designer; Mark Edelson, Photo Editor; Jeff Greene, Photo Editor; John Lopinot, Photo Editor

Award of Excellence
The Spokesman-Review
Spokane, WA
Lisa Cowan, Page Designer; John Kafentzis, News Editor; Scott Sines, AME/Visuals; John Sale, Photo Editor; Vince Grippi, Graphics Editor

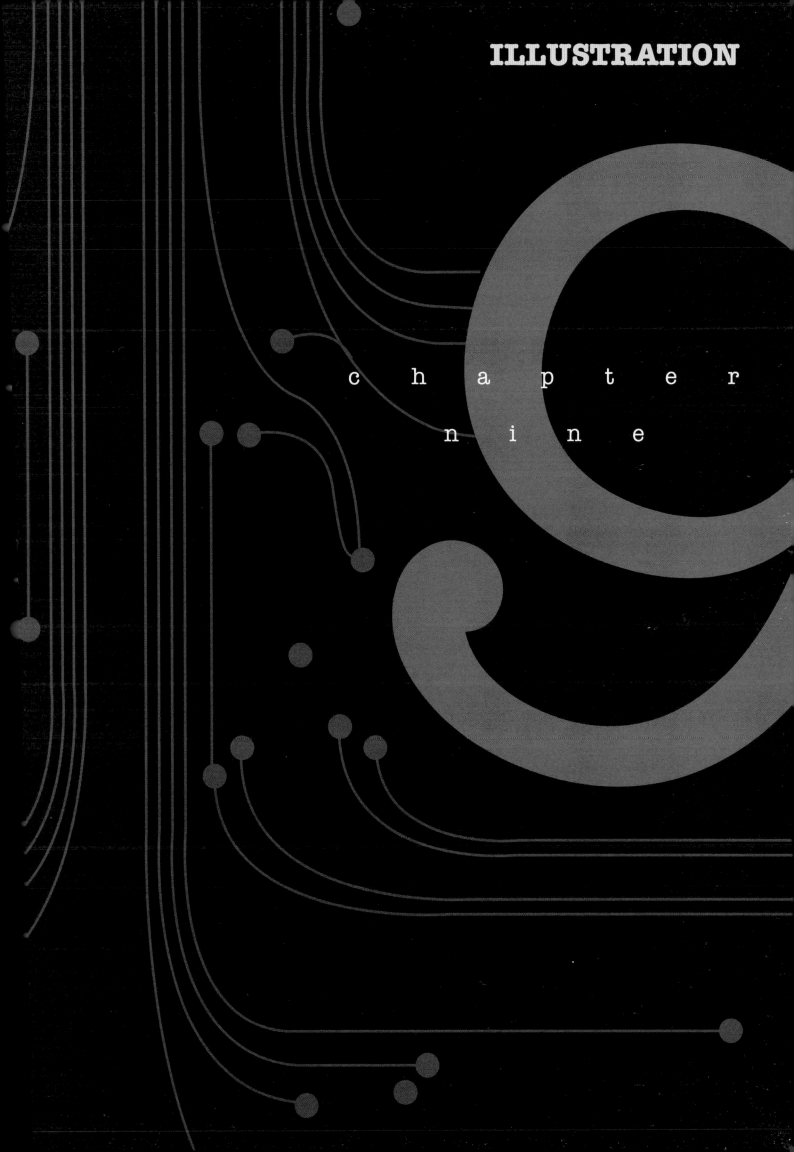

ILLUSTRATION

c h a p t e r

n i n e

Silver
El Mundo
Madrid, Spain
Tono Benavides, Graphics Artist

Silver
San Jose Mercury News
San Jose, CA
Doug Griswold, Illustrator & Designer; Ed Clendaniel, Designer; Molly Swisher, Art Director

Bronze
El Nuevo Dia
San Juan, PR
Jose L. Diaz de Villegas Jr., Illustrator; Jose L. Diaz de Villegas Sr., Art Director & Designer

Bronze
The Detroit News
Detroit, MI
Pat Sedlar, Illustrator & Designer

Bronze
El Nuevo Dia
San Juan, PR
Stanley Coll, Illustrator; Jose L. Diaz de Villegas, Sr., Art Director

Bronze
El Nuevo Dia
San Juan, PR
Walter Gastaldo, Illustrator; Jose L. Diaz de Villegas, Sr., Art Director & Designer

Bronze
The Village Voice
New York, NY
Robert Newman, Design Director; Florian Bachleda, Senior Art Director; Jordin Isip, Illustrator

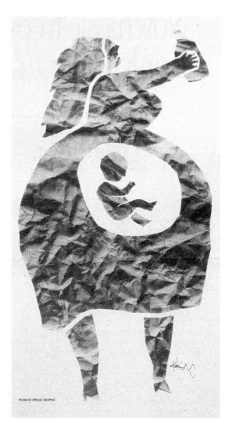

Bronze
San Francisco Examiner
San Francisco, CA
Lynn Forbes, Epicure Editor; Kelly Frankeny, Art Director; Mignon Khargle, Illustrator; Don McCartney, Designer; Bob McLeod, Director of Photography

Bronze
St Paul Pioneer Press
St Paul, MN
Kirk Lyttle, Illustrator

Award of Excellence
Dagens Nyheter
Stockholm, Sweden
Stina Wirsen, Illustrator

Award of Excellence
Anchorage Daily News
Anchorage, AK
Kevin E. Ellis, Illustrator & Designer; Galie Jean-Louis, Design
Director

Award of Excellence
The Miami Herald
Miami, FL
Patterson Clark, Illustrator; Rich Bard, Viewpoint Editor; Randy Stano, Director of Editorial Art & Design

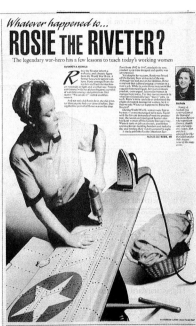

Award of Excellence
The Charlotte Observer
Charlotte, NC
Brenda Pinnell, Graphics Artist; Mike Fisher, Art Director

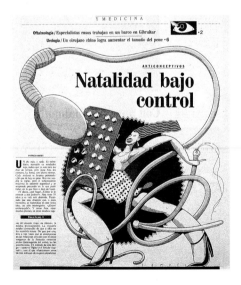

Award of Excellence
Dayton Daily News
Dayton, OH
David Kordalski, Illustrator

Award of Excellence
El Mundo
Madrid, Spain
Samuel Velasco, Graphics Artist

Award of Excellence
El Mundo
Madrid, Spain
Ulises Culebro, Illustration Editor

Award of Excellence
El Nuevo Dia
San Juan, PR
Jose L. Diaz de Villegas, Jr.,
Illustrator; Jose L. Diaz de
Villegas, Sr., Art Director &
Designer

Award of Excellence
El Mundo
Madrid, Spain
Samuel Velasco, Graphics Artist

Award of Excellence
El Pais
Madrid, Spain
Acacio Puig, Graphic Journalist

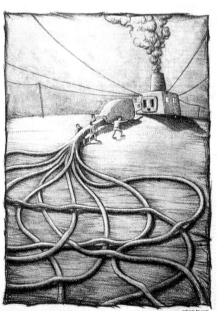

And the answer to Maine's energy needs is . . .

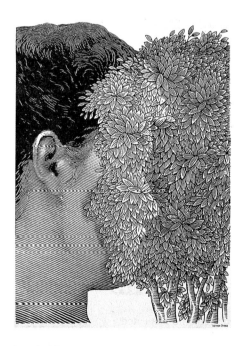

Award of Excellence
Maine Sunday Telegram
Portland, ME
Pete Gorski, Graphic Artist

Award of Excellence
The New York Times
New York, NY
Mirko Ilic, Art Director & Designer; Istvan Orosz, Illustrator

Award of Excellence
Pittsburgh Post-Gazette
Pittsburgh, PA
Ted Crow, Illustrator; Steve Urbanski, Designer; Christopher
Pett-Ridge, AME Graphics; Tracy Collins, Associate
Editor/Graphics; Anita Dufalla, Art Director

Award of Excellence
The New York Times
New York, NY
Jerelle Kraus, Art Director & Designer; Ronald Searle, Illustrator

Award of Excellence
Newsday
Melville, NY
Gary Viskupic, Illustrator

Award of Excellence
St. Paul Pioneer Press
St. Paul, MN
Kirk Lyttle, Graphics Artist; Laura Treston, Designer; Bill Bradley, Editor

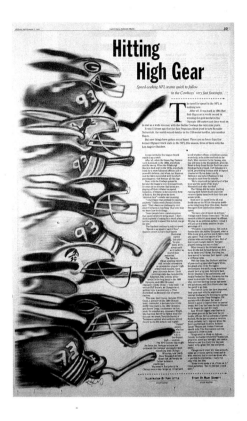

Award of Excellence
The Washington Post Magazine
Washington, DC
Richard Baker, Art Director; Kelly Doe, Deputy Art Director & Designer; Ward Schumaker, Illustrator

Award of Excellence
Pittsburgh Post-Gazette
Pittsburgh, PA
Stacy Innerst, Illustrator; Christopher Pett-Ridge, AME Graphics; Tracy Collins, Associate Editor/Graphics; Anita Dufalla, Art Director

Award of Excellence
The San Francisco Chronicle
San Francisco, CA
Dan Hubig, Illustrator

Award of Excellence
San Francisco Examiner
San Francisco, CA
Mignon Khargle, Designer & Illustrator; Kelly Frankeny, Art Director; Jo Mancuso, Habitat Editor

Award of Excellence
San Jose Mercury News
San Jose, CA
Jenny Anderson, Illustrator & Designer; Molly Swisher, Art Director

Award of Excellence
The Village Voice
New York, NY
Robert Newman, Design Director;
Kate Thompson, Associate Art Director; Jordin Isip, Illustrator

Award of Excellence
San Francisco Examiner
San Francisco, CA
Paul Wilner, AME Features; Joey Rigg, Art Director; Zahid Sardar, Associate Art Director; Zach Trenholm, Illustrator

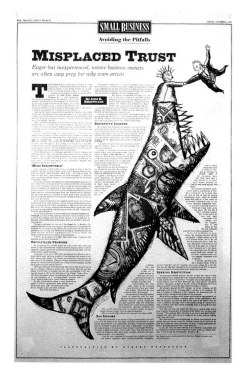

Award of Excellence
The Wall Street Journal
New York, NY
Greg Leeds, Designer & Design Director; Raul Colon, Illustrator

Award of Excellence
The Wall Street Journal Reports
New York, NY
Greg Leeds, Design Director&Designer&Illustrator; Christopher Bing, Illustrator

Award of Excellence
(also winner for Special Section Inside Page)
The Wall Street Journal Reports
New York, NY
Greg Leeds, Design Director & Designer; Robert Neubecker, Illustrator

Gold
The Washington Post Magazine
Washington, DC
Kelly Doe, Art Director & Designer; Owen Smith, Illustrator

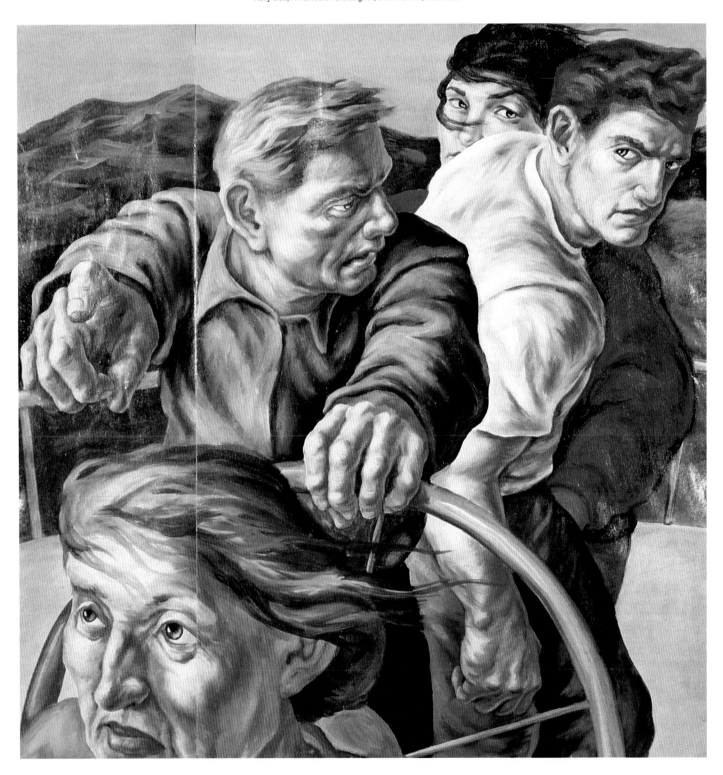

Gold
The Washington Post Magazine
Washington, DC
Kelly Doe, Art Director & Designer; C. F. Payne, Illustrator

Silver
American Medical News
Chicago, IL
Rick Sealock, Illustrator; Jef Capaldi, Art Director

Silver
(also winner of Silver Medal for Combination Portfolio and Award of Excellence for Business Page)
American Medical News
Chicago, IL
Barbara Dow, Art Director & Designer; Eric White, Illustrator

Silver
El Mundo
Madrid, Spain
Tono Benavides, Illustration Editor

Silver
(also winner of Award of Excellence for Illustration Portfolio)
Anchorage Daily News
Anchorage, AK
Dee Boyles, Illustrator & Designer; Galie Jean-Louis, Design Director;
Lin Mitchell, Photographer

Silver
The New York Times
New York, NY
Janet Froelich, Art Director; Kathi Rota, Designer; Anita Kunz, Illustrator

El padre le advirtió «Aléjate del pecado niña, Las bailarinas son abominables ante los ojos de Alá». Quizás presagiaba que su hija acabaría dando función en el mundo de la farándula de El Cairo

Silver
The Kansas City Star
Kansas City, MO
Sue Spade, Designer; Tom Dolphens, Design Director; Rich Bowman, Illustrator

Silver
El Mundo
Madrid, Spain
Ulises Culebro, Illustration Editor

Silver
The New York Times
New York, NY
Janet Froelich, Art Director & Designer; Rayo der Serkissian, Designer; Owen Smith, Illustrator

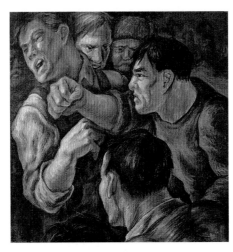

Silver
The Sun/Lowell
Lowell, MA
Mitchell Hayes, Art Director & Designer; Andrea Wisnewski, Illustrator

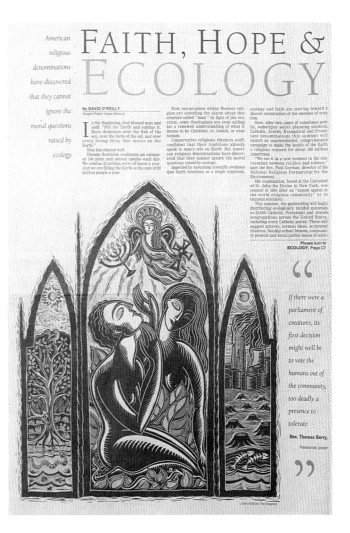

Silver
The Oregonian
Portland, OR
Lydia Hess, Graphics Artist; Shawn Vitt, Art Director; Reed Darmon, Designer

Louise,
terminally ill,
sought a
painless
death.

THERE'S
NO SIMPLE
SUICIDE

To help her,
the Rev.
Ralph Mero
offered
instruction,
not
machinery.

BY LISA BELKIN

ILLUSTRATIONS BY
MAX GINSBURG

Silver
The New York Times
New York, NY
Janet Froelich, Art Director; Gina Davis, Designer; Max
Ginsburg, Illustrator

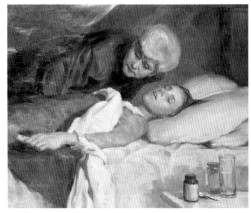

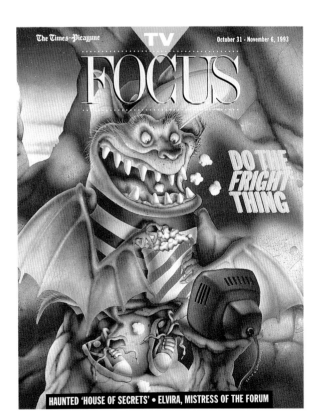

The Times-Picayune   TV   October 31 - November 6, 1993

FOCUS

DO THE FRIGHT THING

HAUNTED 'HOUSE OF SECRETS' • ELVIRA, MISTRESS OF THE FORUM

Silver
The Times-Picayune
New Orleans, LA
Tony O. Champagne, Illustrator & Designer; Jean McIntosh, Art Director

MOTHER
OF HIS
INVENTION

By Véronique Vienne / Illustrations by Sydney Fischer

Silver
San Jose Mercury News/West Magazine
San Jose, CA
Sydney Fischer, Graphics Artist; Sandra Eisert, Art Director & Designer

Bronze

Anchorage Daily News
Anchorage, AK
Jordin Isip, Illustrator; Galie Jean-Louis,
Design Director; Pete Spino, Designer

Bronze

Akron Beacon Journal
Akron, OH
John Backderf, Illustrator & Designer; Dennis Gordon, Designer

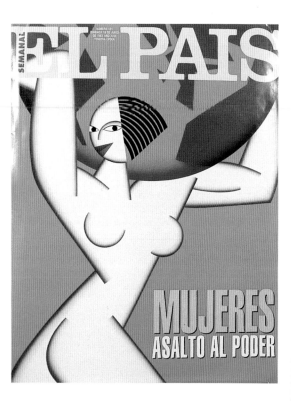

Bronze

Financial Times
London, England
Philip Thompson, Designer; James Ferguson, Illustrator

Bronze

El Pais/El Pais Semanal
Madrid, Spain
Eugenio Gonzalez, Art Director; Gustavo Sanchez, Designer; Isabel Benito,
Designer; Marta Calzada, Designer; Angel de Pedro, Illustrator

Bronze
The Indianapolis Star
Indianapolis, IN
W. Matt Pinkney, Illustrator

Award of Excellence
La Vanguardia
Barcelona, Spain
Carlos Perez de Rozas, Art Director; Rosa Mundet, Art Director; Ferran Grau, Designer; Ajubel, Illustrator

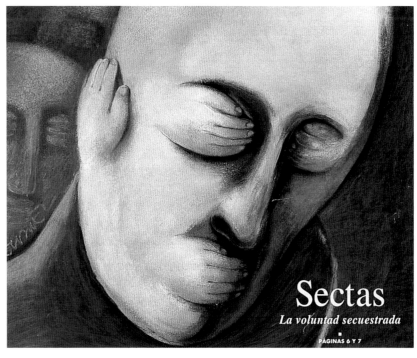

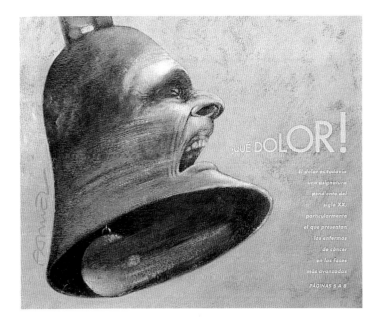

Bronze
La Vanguardia
Barcelona, Spain
Carlos Perez de Rozas, Art Director; Rosa Mundet, Art Director; Ferran Grau, Designer; Joan Corbera, Designer; Ajubel, Illustrator

Bronze
La Vanguardia
Barcelona, Spain
Carlos Perez de Rozas, Art Director; Rosa Mundet, Art Director; Joan Corbera, Designer; Ajubel, Illustrator

Bronze
Pittsburgh Post-Gazette
Pittsburg, PA
Juliette Borda, Illustrator; Anita Dufalla, Art Director; Catherine Tigano, Designer

Bronze
The Washington Post Magazine
Washington, DC
Kelly Doe, Art Director & Designer; Lane Smith, Illustrator

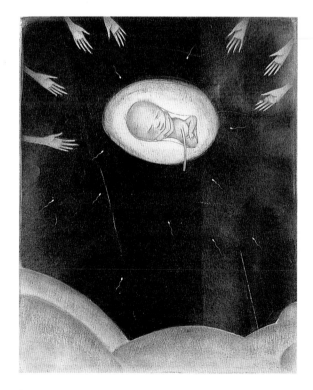

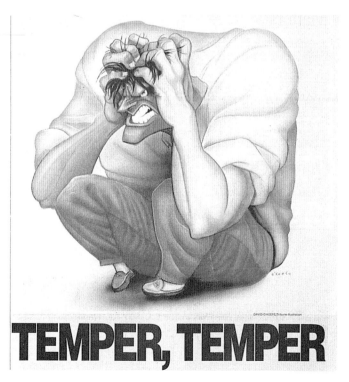

Bronze
San Jose Mercury News/West Magazine
San Jose, CA
Sydney Fischer, Illustrator; Sandra Eisert, Art Director & Designer

Bronze
The Tampa Tribune
Tampa, FL
David O'Keefe, Graphics Artist

Award of Excellence
The Arizona Republic
Phoenix, AZ
Jo Anne Izumi, Graphics Artist; Patti Valdez, Art Director

Bronze
The Tampa Tribune/Friday Extra
Tampa, FL
Greg Williams, Graphics Artist

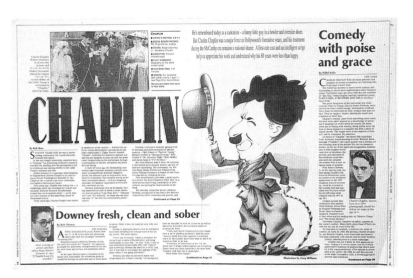

Award of Excellence
Anchorage Daily News
Anchorage, AK
Genevieve Cote, Illustrator; Galie Jean-Louis, Design
Director; Pete Spino, Designer

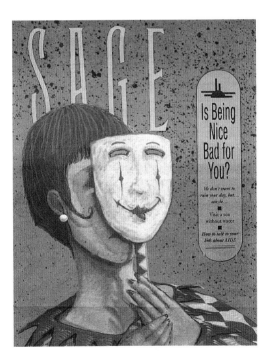

Award of Excellence
Albuquerque Journal
Albuquerque, NM
Russ Ball, Illustrator; Susan Vogle, Designer; Carolyn Flynn, Design
Director

Award of Excellence
(also Award of Excellence for Business Page)
American Medical News
Chicago, IL
Barbara Dow, Art Director & Designer; Eric White, Illustrator

Award of Excellence
The Columbus Dispatch
Columbus, OH
Evangelia Philippidis, Graphics Artist; Scott Minister, Art Director

Award of Excellence
Computer Reseller News
Manhasset, NY
Gene Fedele, Art Director; Marc Taffet, Designer; Joe Fleming, Illustrator

Award of Excellence
Communication Week International
Manhasset, NY
Denise Edkins, Art Director & Designer; Ted Pitts, Illustrator

Award of Excellence
Dayton Daily News
Dayton, OH
Randy Palmer, Illustrator; David Kordalski, Art & Design Director

Award of Excellence
El Nuevo Dia
San Juan, PR
Jose L. Diaz de Villegas, Sr., Illustrator; Jose L. Diaz de Villegas, Jr., Art Director & Designer

Award of Excellence
El Nuevo Dia
San Juan, PR
Nivea Ortiz, Illustrator; Jose L. Diaz de Villgas Jr., Art Director & Designer

Award of Excellence
El Pais/El Pais Semanal
Madrid, Spain
Eugenio Gonzalez, Art Director; Gustavo Sanchez, Designer;
Isabel Benito, Designer; Marta Calzada, Designer; Angel de
Pedro, Illustrator

Award of Excellence
El Nuevo Herald
Miami, FL
Nuri Ducassi, Art Director, Designer & Illustrator; Silvia Licha,
Editor

Award of Excellence
El Nuevo Herald
Miami, FL
Aurora Arrue, Illustrator & Designer; Nuri Ducassi, Art Director

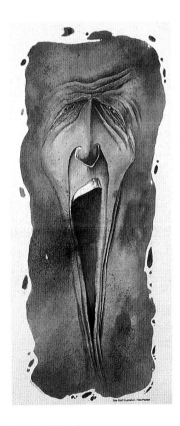

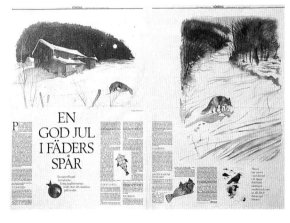

Award of Excellence
Goteborgs-Posten
Gothenburg, Sweden
Goran Dalhov, Illustrator; Ulf Johanson, Designer

Award of Excellence
Financial Times
London, England
Andrew Chappin, Art Editor & Designer; Kevin Hauff,
Illustrator

Award of Excellence
The Indianapolis Star
Indianapolis, IN
Tom Peyton, Illustrator & Designer

Award of Excellence
The Miami Herald
Miami, FL
Philip Brooker, Illustrator; Randy Stano, Director of Editorial Art & Design

Award of Excellence
Los Angeles Daily News
Woodland Hills, CA
Jorge Irribarren, Graphics Artist

Award of Excellence
The Medina County Gazette
Medina, OH
Kathy Hagedorn, Illustrator & Designer; David Giffels, Accent Editor; John Gladden, Associate Accent Editor

Award of Excellence
The Miami Herald
Miami, FL
Phill Flanders, Illustrator; Bill Grant, Sports Design Editor; Tim Burke, Asst Sports Editor; Bonnie Snyder, Sports Design Editor; Woody Vondracek, Graphics Artist; Hiram Henriquez, Graphics Artist; Juan Lopez, Graphics Artist/Intern; Derek Hembd, Graphics Artist/Intern; Randy Stano, Director of Editorial Art & Design

Award of Excellence
La Vanguardia
Barcelona, Spain
Carlos Perez de Rozas, Art Director; Rosa Mundet, Art Director; Rocarols, Illustrator

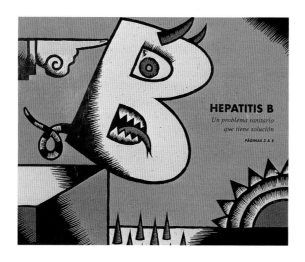

Award of Excellence
The Miami Herald
Miami, FL
Phill Flanders, Illustrator; Rhonda Prast, Design Desk Editor; Randy Stano, Director of Editorial Art & Design

Award of Excellence
The New York Times
New York, NY
Janet Froelich, Art Director; Kathi Rota, Designer; Amy Guip, Illustrator

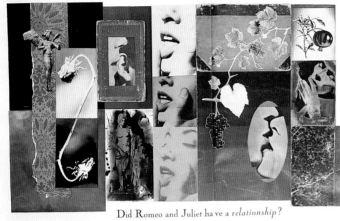

The Death of Eros

Did Romeo and Juliet have a *relationship*?

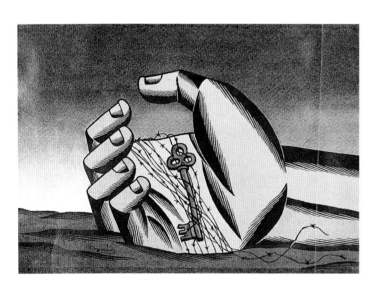

Award of Excellence
The Oregonian
Portland, OR
Dana E. Olsen, Photographer; Shawn Vitt, Art Director; Reed Darmon, Designer

PRECIOUS METALS

With glittery tones and jeweled straps, the season's sandals are just the place to rest your golden arches

The SANDALS of TIME

Award of Excellence
The New York Times
New York, NY
Janet Froelich, Art Director; Gina Davis, Designer; Brian Cronin, Illustrator

Award of Excellence
The Orange County Register
Santa Ana, CA
Gwendolyn Wong, Graphics Artist; Nanette Bisher, AME/Art Director

Award of Excellence
The Palm Beach Post
West Palm Beach, FL
Pat Crowley, Staff Cartoonist

Award of Excellence
The Philadelphia Inquirer Magazine
Philadelphia, PA
Bert Fox, Art Director; Jessica Helfand, Designer & Design Director; Gregory Manchess, Illustrator

show

special report — ARE THE GRAMMYS ARCHAIC? PAGE 4

books — 'MIRACLES OF A BLACK CHURCH' PAGE 22

JOLTIN' JAVA

The BUZZ on the brave new world of pumped-up COFFEE PAGE 6

Award of Excellence
San Jose Mercury News/West Magazine
San Jose, CA
Greg Spalenka, Freelance Artist; Sandra Eisert, Art Director &
Designer

Award of Excellence
San Jose Mercury News/West Magazine
San Jose, CA
David Shannon, Freelance artist

Award of Excellence
The Sunday Tribune
Dublin, Ireland
Jon Berkeley, Illustrator; Stephen Ryan, Design Editor

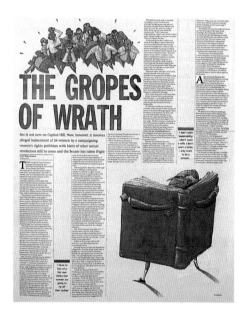

Award of Excellence
St Paul Pioneer Press
St Paul, MN
Kirk Lyttle, Graphics Artist; Larry
May, Designer

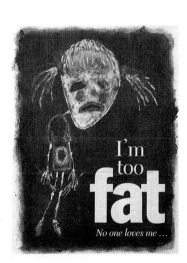

Award of Excellence
The Spokesman-Review
Spokane, WA
Anne Heitner, Graphics Artist; Vince Grippi, Graph-
ics Editor; Scott Sines, AME/Visuals

Award of Excellence
Richmond Times-Dispatch
Richmond, VA
Kenny P. Talbott, Graphics Artist

Award of Excellence
The Tampa Tribune
Tampa, FL
Tim Price, Graphics Artist

Award of Excellence
The Tampa Tribune/Florida Television
Tampa, Fl
Greg Williams, Graphics Artist

Award of Excellence
The Providence Journal-Bulletin
Providence, RI
Bob Selby, Illustrator

Award of Excellence
The Washington Post Magazine
Washington, DC
Richard Baker, Art Director & Designer; Philip
Burke, Illustrator

Award of Excellence
Pittsburgh Post-Gazette
Pittsburgh, PA
Stacy Innerst, Illustrator; Anita
Dufalla, Art Director; Christopher
Pett-Ridge, AME Graphics; Tracy
Collins, Associate editor/graphics

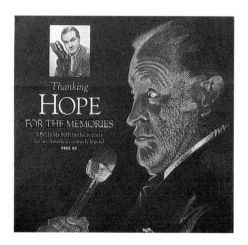

Award of Excellence
The Phoenix Gazette
Phoenix, AZ
Nancy Pendleton, Graphics Artist

Award of Excellence
Rocky Mountain News
Denver, CO
Joseph Wagner, Graphics Artist

Award of Excellence
San Francisco Examiner
San Francisco, CA
Kelly Frankeny, Art Director; Christine Barnes,
Style Editor; David Talbot, Arts & Ideas Editor;
Tracy Cox, Illustrator & Designer

Gold

El Mundo

Madrid, Spain

Ricardo Martinez, Illustration Editor

Gold

(Illustration Black & White)

Ricardo Martinez, Illustration Editor

Gold

(Illustration Black & White)

Ricardo Martinez, Illustration Editor

Gold

(Illustration Black & White)

Ricardo Martinez, Illustration Editor

Silver
(Illustration Black & White)
Ricardo Martinez, Illustration Editor

Silver
(Illustration Black & White)
(also Award of Excellence for Magazine Cover)
Ricardo Martinez, Illustration Editor

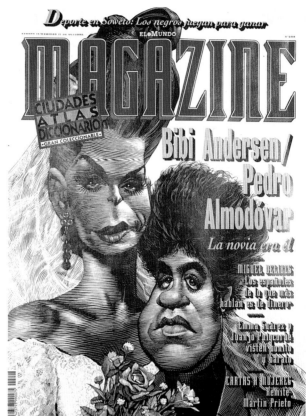

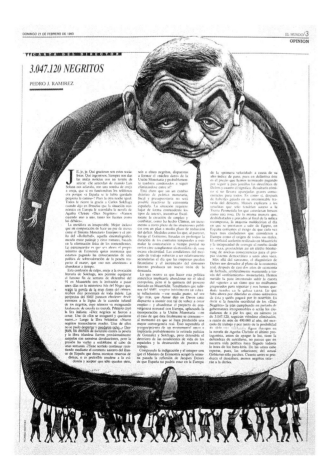

Silver
(Illustration Black & White)
Ricardo Martinez, Illustration Editor

Bronze
(Illustration Black & White)
Ricardo Martinez, Illustration Editor

Silver

Anchorage Daily News
Anchorage, AK
(also a Silver Medal for Illustration)
Lance Lekander, Illustrator; Pam Dunlop-Shohl,
Designer; Galie Jean-Louis, Design Director

Silver

(Illustration Two or More Colors)
Lance Lekander, Illustrator & Designer

Bronze

(Illustration Two or More Colors)
Lance Lekander, Illustrator & Designer

Silver
The Des Moines Register
Des Moines, IA
Mark Marturello, Illustrator

SPEED COOKING

A race through the pages of several new cookbooks discloses recipes and tips for healthful, hassle-free holiday meals.

Silver
(Illustration Two or More Colors)
Mark Marturello, Illustrator

ANGER

Hostile attitudes can raise blood pressure with deadly results

Do you have a hostile personality?

The battle against baldness

A vast array of costly, and even unsafe, options confronts those seeking hair replacement.

By PAT ANSTETT
KNIGHT-RIDDER NEWSPAPERS

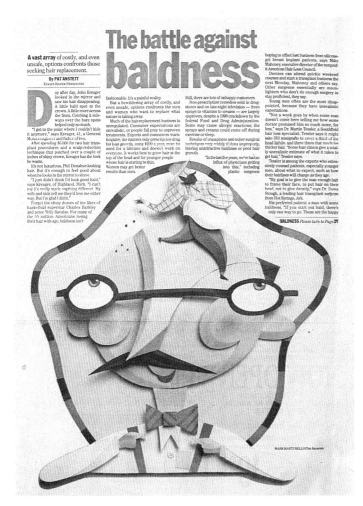

Wired

Caffeine, a cup of controversy

It's a legal drug, but caffeine is not harmless. Still, it's not considered a health threat to most Americans.

By DEBORAH CUSHMAN
REGISTER STAFF WRITER

A primer on caffeine

Award of Excellence
(Illustration Two or More Colors)
Mark Marturello, Illustrator

Award of Excellence
(Illustration Two or More Colors)
Evangelia Phílippidis, Graphics Artist & Designer

Bronze
The Columbus Dispatch
Columbus, OH
Evangelia Philippidis, Graphics Artist & Designer; Scott Minister, Art Director

Bronze
El Mundo
Madrid, Spain
Ulises Culebro, Illustrator

Award of Excellence
(Illustration Black & White)
Ulises Culebro, Graphics Artist

Bronze
El Pais
Madrid, Spain
Jose Belamonte, Illustrator

Bronze
San Francisco Examiner
San Francisco, CA
Mignon Khargie, Illustrator; Kelly Frankeny, Art Director

Bronze
(Illustration Two or More Colors)
Mignon Khargie, Illustrator

Award of Excellence
Anchorage Daily News
Anchorage, AK
Dee Boyles, Illustrator; Galie Jean-Louis, Design Director; Dee Boyles, Designer; Lin Mitchell, Photographer

Award of Excellence
(Illustration Black & White)
Dee Boyles, Illustrator & Designer

Award of Excellence
Detroit Free Press Magazine
Detroit, MI
Deborah Withey, Art Director; Coleen Lancester, Designer;
Jordin Isip, Illustration

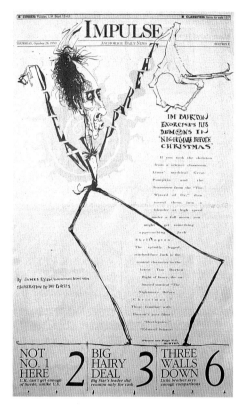

Award of Excellence
The Detroit News
Detroit, MI
Glynnis Sweeny, Illustrator; Wes Bausmith, Designer

Award of Excellence
El Mundo
Madrid, Spain
Samuel Velasco, Graphics Artist

Award of Excellence
The Detroit News
Detroit, MI
Pat Sedlar, Illustrator & Designer

Award of Excellence
The Miami Herald
Miami, FL
Philip Brooker, Illustrator; Randy Stano, Director of Editorial
Art & Design

The Mind of the Stalker
The Terror of the Stalked

Award of Excellence
El Mundo
Madrid, Spain
Tono Benavides, Illustration Editor

Award of Excellence
El Mundo
Madrid, Spain
Raul Arias, Illustrator; Carmelo Caderot, Design Director

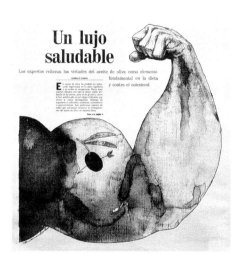

Award of Excellence
The Miami Herald
Miami, FL
Patterson Clark, Illustrator & Designer; Rich Bard, Viewpoint
Editor; Randy Stano, Director of Editorial Art & Design

Award of Excellence
Kauppalehti Optio
Helsinki, Finland
Kristian Lindbohm, Illustrator & Designer

Award of Excellence
Pittsburgh Post-Gazette
Pittsburgh, PA
Daniel Marsula, Illustrator; Christopher Pett-Ridge, AME
Graphics; Tracy Collins, Associate Editor/Graphics; Anita Du-
falla, Art Director

Award of Excellence
The Orange County Register
Santa Ana, CA
Lisa Mertins, Graphics Artist; Tia Lai, News Editor/Graphics;
Nanette Bisher, AME/Art Director

Award of Excellence
The Palm Beach Post
West Palm Beach, FL
Lina Lawson, Art Director

Award of Excellence
Pittsburgh Post-Gazette
Pittsburgh, PA
Dan Marsula, Illustrator; Christopher Pett-Ridge, AME Graph-
ics; Tracy Collins, Associate Editor/graphics; Anita Dufalla, Art
Director

Award of Excellence
San Jose Mercury News
San Jose, CA
Doug Griswold, Illustrator & Designer; Ed Clendaniel, Design-
er; Molly Swisher, Art Director

Award of Excellence
LA Weekly
Los Angeles, CA
Bill Smith, Art Director & Illustrator; Laura Steele, Art Director;
Calef Brown, Illustrator; Barbara Lambase, Illustrator; Paul
Lee, Illustrator; Michiko Stehrenberger, Illustrator

Silver
American Medical News
Chicago, IL
Jem Sullivan, Illustrator; Lane Smith, Illustrator; Elizabeth Lada, Illustrator; Eric White, Illustrator; Gwendolyn Wong, Illustrator; Barbara Dow, Art Director; Jef Capaldi, Assistant Art Director

Silver
American Medical News
Chicago, IL
Eric White, Illustrator; Elizabeth Lada, Illustrator; Gwendolyn Wong, Illustrator; Anthony Russo, Illustrator; Bonnie Timmons, Illustrator; Rick Sealock, Illustrator; Barbara Dow, Art Director; Jef Capaldi, Assisstant Art Director

Award of Excellence

San Francisco Examiner
San Francisco, CA
Mignon Khargie, Illustrator; Zach Trenholm, Illustrator; Dave Ember, Illustrator; Chris Morris, Illustrator; Tracy Cox, Illustrator; Kelly Frankeny, Art Director

Bronze

San Francisco Examiner
San Francisco, CA
Mignon Khargie, Illustrator; Zach Trenholm, Illustrator; Dave Ember, Illustrator; Chris Morris, Illustrator; Kelly Frankeny, Art Director

Award of Excellence

Detroit Free Press
Detroit, MI
Claire C. Innes, Art Director & Designer; James Steinberg, Illustrator

Bronze

The Sun/Lowell
Lowell, MA
Mitchell Hayes, Art Director; Tracy Walker, Illustrator; Andrea Wisnewski, Illustrator; Ted Pitts, Illustrator; Stuart Yetts, Illustrator

Bronze

(Illustration Two or More colors)
Andrea Wisnewski, Illustrator

Award of Excellence

The Press-Enterprise
Riverside, CA
Carolita Feiring, Art Director; Stephen Sedam, Graphics Artist; Don Wood, Graphics Artist

c h a p t e r

t e n

10

Award of Excellence
ABC
Madrid, Spain
Fernando Rubio, Illustrator Director; Antonio Rodriguez, Graphics Artist

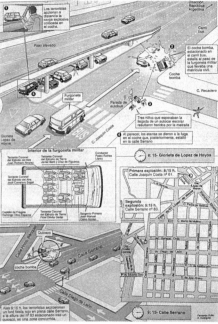

Award of Excellence
Newsday
Melville, NY
Philip Dionisio, Graphic Supervisor & Illustrator; Linda McKenny, Graphics Artist

Bronze
El Mundo
Madrid, Spain
Mario Tascon, Infographics Director; Gorka Sampedro, Graphics Artist; Dina Sanchez, Graphics Artist

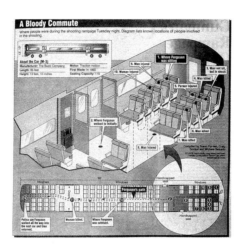

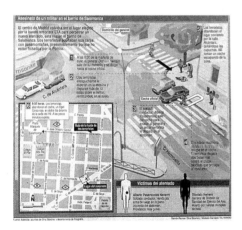

Award of Excellence
El Mundo
Madrid, Spain
Mario Tascon, Infographics Director; Ramon R. Ramos, Graphics Artist; Dina Sanchez, Graphics Artist; Modesto J. Carrasco, Graphics Artist

Award of Excellence
The New York Times
New York, NY
John Papasian, Artist; David Montesino, Graphics Editor

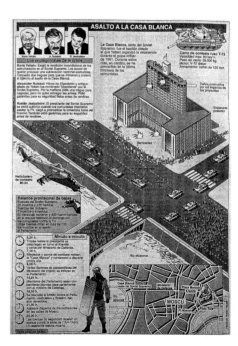

Award of Excellence
ABC
Madrid, Spain
Fernando Rubio, Illustrator Director

Award of Excellence
The Miami Herald
Miami, FL
Tiffany Grantham, Graphics Artist; Dan Clifford, Graphics Artist; Randy Stano, Director of Editorial Art & Design

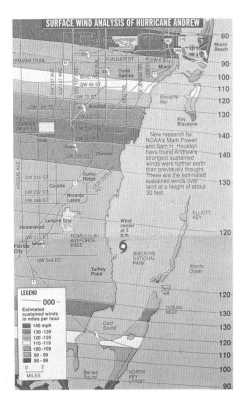

Award of Excellence
The Orange County Register
Santa Ana, CA
Lisa Mertins, Graphic Journalist; Nam Nguyen, Graphic Journalist; Ronald Campbell, Reporter; Danny Sullivan, Graphics Reporter; Michelle Nicolosi, Reporter; Teri Sforza, Reporter; Liz Pulliam, Reporter; Chris Boucly, Reporter

Bronze
Springfield News-Leader
Springfield, MO
Gregory A. Branson, Graphics Artist & Researcher; John L. Dengler, Graphics Editor; George Benge, ME

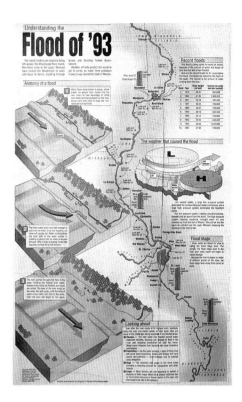

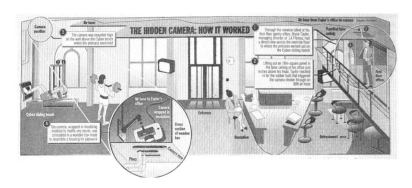

Award of Excellence
The Sunday Times
London, England
Phil Green, Graphic Editor & Graphic Artist

Award of Excellence
The Mobile Press Register
Mobile, AL
Michael Callahan, Illustrator & Designer; John Hart, Staff Designer; David Holloway, research; Michael Arbanas, research

Award of Excellence
Los Angeles Times/Orange County
Costa Mesa, CA
Scott M. Brown, Graphics Artist; Doris Shields, Graphics Artist; David Puckett, Graphics Artist; April Jackson, Researcher; Juan Thomassie, Art Director; Tom Reinken, Deputy Graphics Editor; Lily Dow, Graphics Editor

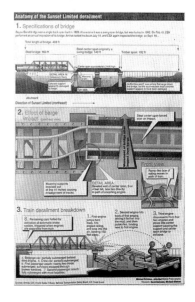

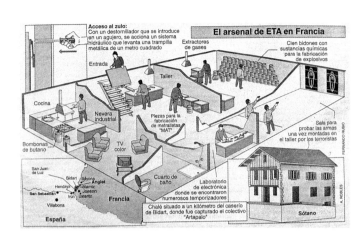

Silver
ABC
Madrid, Spain
Fernando Rubio, Illustrator Director

Muere un legionario al estallar dos granadas croatas en el destacamento de Jablanica

Diecisiete españoles resultaron heridos por el impacto, que se produjo mientras dormían

Defensa no replegará al destacamento, que las Naciones Unidas consideran como vital

Madrid. **Manuel Abizanda** / Alvaro Martinez

El conflicto de los Balcanes se cobró ayer una nueva víctima mortal española, la décima. En esta ocasión, el acuartelamiento español en Jablanica fue blanco de dos granadas de mortero de 120 milímetros que acabaron con la vida del legionario José León Gómez y provocó heridas, graves en seis casos, a otros diecisiete «cascos azules». Las dos granadas procedían de bando croata, según informaron a ABC fuentes de Defensa, aunque mostraron sus dudas ante la posibilidad de que el ataque hubiese sido premeditado, pues en ese momento las milicias del HVO se encontraban bombardeando la carretera que pasa junto al destacamento español.

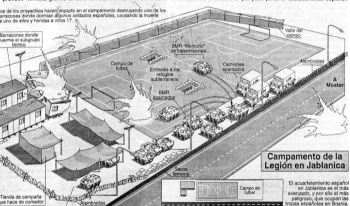

El informe de la ONU revela que un capitán tuvo que abrir fuego para salvar al sargento Fernández

Francotiradores habían disparado contra el oficial que auxiliaba al herido

Madrid. M. Abizanda

Las operaciones que los «cascos azules» de la Agrupación Madrid llevaron a cabo el pasado sábado para proceder a la evacuación del sargento primero Jorge Fernández y el cadáver del capitán Fernando Álvarez se realizaron bajo el fuego de francotiradores que dispararon contra el oficial que procedía a auxiliar a los militares. El capitán se vio obligado a utilizar su arma para repeler los disparos y poder llegar hasta donde se encontraban los «cascos azules» españoles.

Award of Excellence
La Vanguardia
Barcelona, Spain
Carlos Perez de Rozas, Art Director; Rosa Mundet, Art Director; Jordi Paris, Graphics Artist

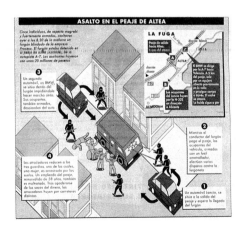

Bronze
El Mundo
Madrid, Spain
Mario Tascon, Infographics Director; Ramon Ramos, Graphics Artist; Gorka Sampedro, Graphics Artist; Dina Sanchez, Graphics Artist; Juan Velasco, Graphics Artist; Modesto Carrasco, Graphics Artist; Samuel Velasco, Graphics Artist

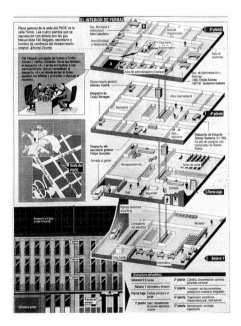

Bronze
El Mundo
Madrid, Spain
Mario Tascon, Infographics Director; Dina Sanchez, Graphics Artist; Chema Matia, Graphics Artist; Juan Velasco, Graphics Artist; Ramon R. Ramos, Graphics Artist; Samuel Velasco, Graphics Artist; Modesto J. Carrasco, Graphics Artist; Gorka Sampedro, Graphics Artist; Ulises Culebro, Graphics Artist

Bronze
El Mundo
Madrid, Spain
Juan Velasco, Graphics Artist; Ramon R. Ramos, Graphics Artist; Ulises Culebro, Graphics Artist; Benito Munoz, Graphics Editor

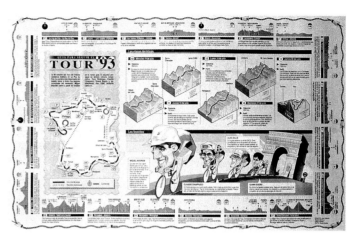

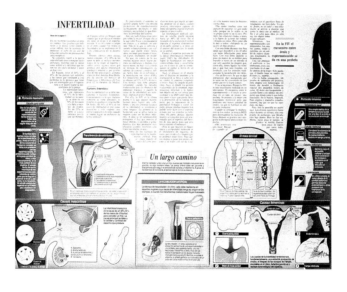

Award of Excellence
El Mundo
Madrid, Spain
Juan Velasco, Graphics Artist;
Jaime de Andres, Graphics Artist

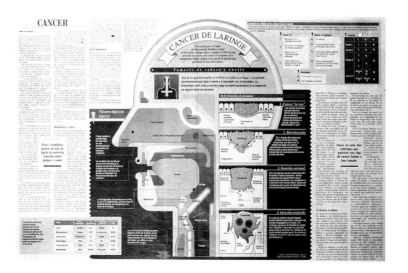

Award of Excellence
El Mundo
Madrid, Spain
Juan Velasco, Graphics Artist;
Samuel Velasco, Graphics Artist;
Modesto J. Carrasco, Graphics Artist

Award of Excellence
El Periodico de Catalunya
Barcelona, Spain
Jaime Serra, Art Director

Award of Excellence
El Periodico de Catalunya
Barcelona, Spain
Jordi Catala, Artist

Award of Excellence
El Pals
Madrid, Spain
Gustavo Hermoso, Graphic Journalist

Award of Excellence
The New York Times
New York, NY
Anne Cronin, Graphics Editor; Hank Iken, Illustrator; Al Granberg, Illustrator;
John Cayea, Art Director

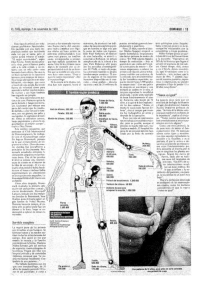

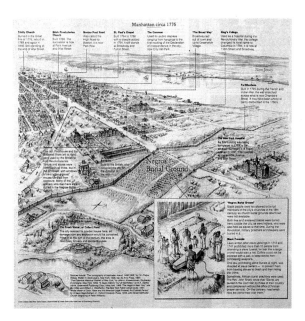

Award of Excellence
The New York Times
New York, NY
Michael Valenti, Art Director; Megan
Jaegerman, Illustrator; Paul Jean, Designer

Award of Excellence
Los Angeles Times/Orange
County
Costa Mesa, CA
Scott M. Brown, Graphics
Artist; Caroline Lemke, Re-
searcher; Juan Thomassie, Art
Director; Tom Reinken, Deputy
Graphics Director; Lily Dow,
Graphics Editor

Award of Excellence
The New York Times
New York, NY
Megan Jaegerman, Researcher, Il-
lustrator & Designer; Michael
Valenti, Art Director

Silver
Los Angeles Times/Orange County
Costa Mesa, CA
David Puckett, Graphics Artist; Janice L. Jones, Researcher; April Jackson, Researcher; Tom Reinken, Deputy Graphics Editor; Juan Thomassie, Art Director; Lily Dow, Graphics Editor

Bronze
Anchorage Daily News
Anchorage, AK
Dee Boyles, Designer & Illustrator; Galie Jean-Louis, Design Director

Silver
Marca
Madrid, Spain
Jose Juan Gamez, Graphics Editor; Pablo Ma Ramirez, Graphics Artist

Silver
The Miami Herald
Miami, FL
Dan Clifford, Graphics Editor/systems; Stephen K. Doig, Research Editor

Bronze
The Boston Globe
Boston, MA
Neil C. Pinchin, Illustrator & Designer

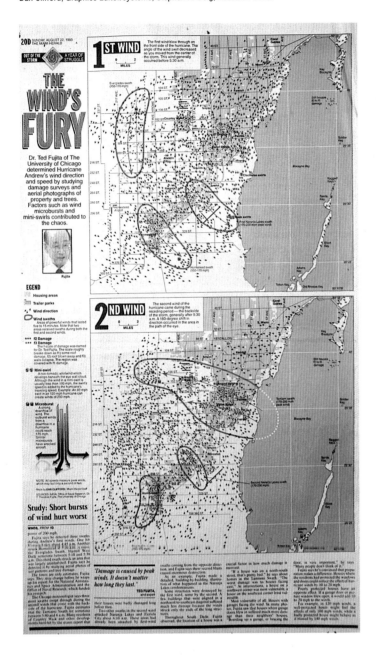

Bronze
Marca
Madrid, Spain
Jose Juan Gamez, Graphics Editor; Pablo Ma Ramírez, Graphics Artist; Miguel Angel Fernández, Graphics Artist; Chus Aycart, Graphics Artist; Mar Domingo, Graphics Artist; Sofía Valgañón, Graphics Artist; Pedro M. Garcia, Graphics Artist; Cesar Galera, Graphics Artist; Belen Vega, Graphics Artist

Bronze
The Oregonian
Portland, OR
Steve Cowden, Artist; Michelle Wise, Art Director;
Mark Wigginton, Art Director

Bronze
The Oregonian
Portland, OR
Kevin Hendrickson, Graphics Artist; Steve Cowden, Graphics Artist; Mark Wigginton, Art Director;
Therese Bottomly, Editor

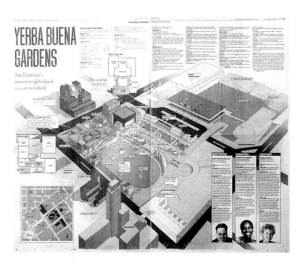

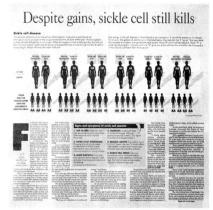

Award of Excellence
The Star-Ledger
Newark, NJ
Lisa Zollinger, Art Director; Frank Cecala, Graphic Designer

Award of Excellence
San Francisco Examiner
San Francisco, CA
Christine Barnes, Style Editor; Kelly Frankeny, Art Director; Chris Morris, Illustrator; Tracy Cox, Designer

Award of Excellence
The Augusta Chronicle/Herald
Augusta, GA
Rick McKee, Chief Artist

Award of Excellence
Florida Today
Melbourne, FL
R. Scott Horner, Graphics Artist

Award of Excellence
Florida Today
Melbourne, FL
R. Scott Horner, Graphics Artist

Award of Excellence
The Boston Globe
Boston, MA
David Butler, Graphics Artist; Richard Sanchez, Graphics Artist;
Scott Allen, Writer

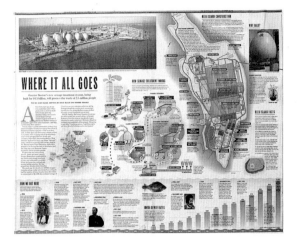

Award of Excellence
Greensboro News & Record
Greensboro, NC
Tim Rickard, Graphics Artist

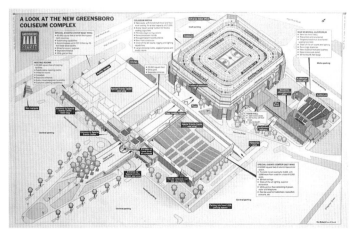

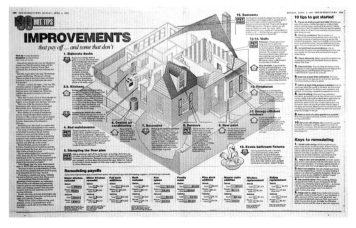

Award of Excellence
The Fresno Bee
Fresno, CA
S. W. Parra, Project Coordinator; Brenda Moore, Project Editor; Perry Huffman, Graphics Artist;
Debbi Soligian, Graphics Artist; Doug Hansen, Graphics Artist; Rob Veneski, Librarian

Award of Excellence
The Detroit News
Detroit, MI
David Pierce, Graphics Editor; Felix Grabowski, Art Director; Nolan Finley, Section Editor; Mark
Lett, AME; Noreen Seebacher, Reporter

Award of Excellence
Los Angeles Times
Los Angeles, CA
James Owens, Editorial Artist

Award of Excellence
Los Angeles Times
Los Angeles, CA
Anders Ramberg, Designer; Victoria McCargar, Art Director;
Richard Barnes, Real Estate Editor; Maria Rock, Writer

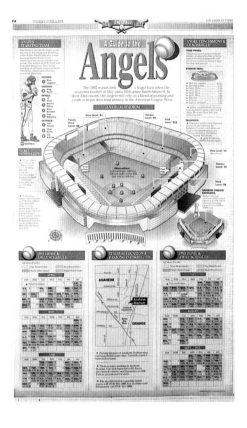

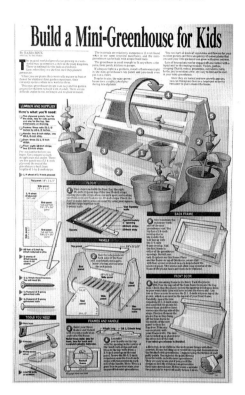

Award of Excellence
The Miami Herald
Miami, FL
Reginald Myers, Graphics Artist; Lynn Medford, Living Editor;
Rhonda Prast, Design Desk Editor; Randy Stano, Director of
Editorial Art & Design

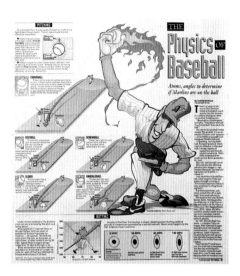

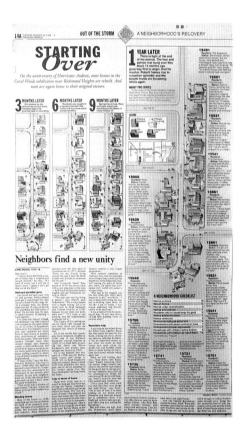

Award of Excellence
The Miami Herald
Miami, FL
Reginald Myers, Graphics Artist & Illustrator; Patrick May,
Reporter; Rick Hirsch, City Desk Editor; Randy Stano, Director
of Editorial Art & Design

Award of Excellence
The Oregonian
Portland, OR
Rene Eisenbart, Graphics Artist; Michelle Wise, Art Director;
Mark Wigginton, Art Director

Award of Excellence
The Oregonian
Portland, OR
Steve Cowden, Graphics Artist; Michelle Wise,
Art Director; Mark Wigginton, Art Director

Award of Excellence
San Gabriel Valley Newspapers
West Covina, CA
Todd Trumbull, Graphics Artist

Award of Excellence
Star Tribune
Minneapolis, MN
Sidney Jablonski, Infographic Artist & Researcher; Arnie Robbins, AME Features; Liz McConnell, Features Editor; Gordon Slovut, Writer

Award of Excellence
The Palm Beach Post
West Palm Beach, FL
Steve Madden, Graphics Artist; Eliot Kleinberg, Reporter

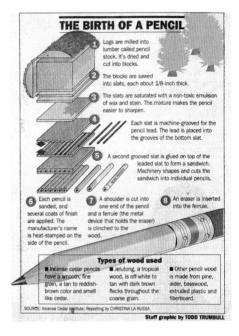

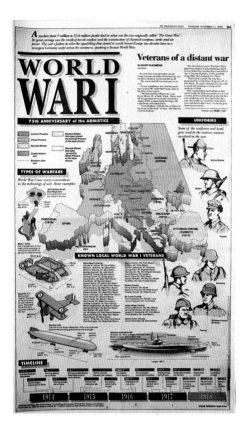

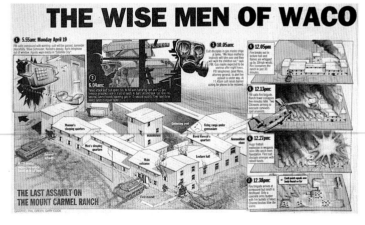

Award of Excellence
The Sunday Times
London, England
Phil Green, Graphics Editor; Gary Cook, Deputy Graphics Editor

Award of Excellence
Richmond Times-Dispatch
Richmond, VA
Stephen Rountree, Graphics Artist; Tom Roberts, Graphics Artist; Martin Rhodes, Graphics Artist; John G. Ownby, Graphics Artist

Award of Excellence

The St. Petersburg Times
St. Petersburg, FL
Don Morris, News artist; Nelda Barrow, News artist; Anne Hand, News artist; Earl Towery, News artist

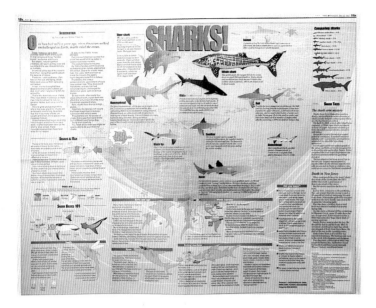

Award of Excellence

Star Tribune
Minneapolis, MN
Dilly Steve Clayton, Graphic Designer; Constance Nelson, Graphic Reporter

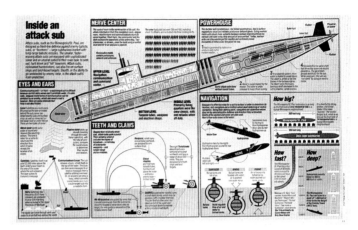

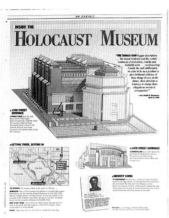

Award of Excellence

The Washington Post
Washington, DC
John Anderson Jr., Graphics Artist; Jackson Dykman, Art Director

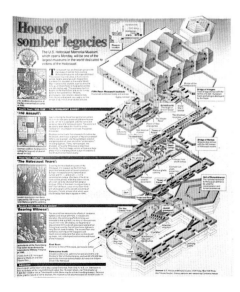

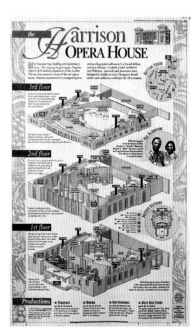

Award of Excellence

Star Tribune
Minneapolis, MN
Sidney Jablonski, Infographic Artist; Tim Campbell, Graphics Director; Constance Nelson, Researcher

Award of Excellence

The Press-Enterprise
Riverside, CA
Stephen Sedam, Graphics Artist

Award of Excellence

The Virginian-Pilot
Norfolk, VA
Bob Voros, Infographic Specialist; Jeff Glick, Art Director

Bronze

El Mundo
Madrid, Spain
Juan Velasco, Graphics Artist; Samuel Velasco, Graphics Editor; Modesto J. Carrasco, Graphics Editor;
Ramon Rodriguez, Researcher

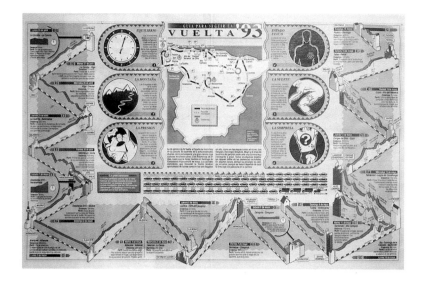

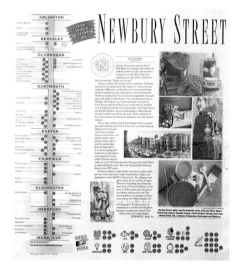

Award of Excellence

The Boston Globe
Boston, MA
Neil C. Pinchin, Graphics Artist

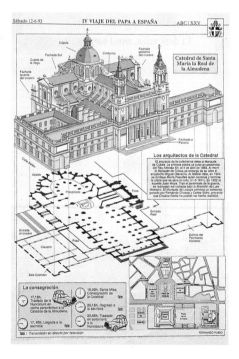

Award of Excellence

ABC
Madrid, Spain
Fernando Rubio, Illustrator Director

Award of Excellence

Los Angeles Times
Los Angeles, CA
James Owens, Graphics Artist

Award of Excellence

Los Angeles Times/Orange County
Costa Mesa, CA
Scott M. Brown, Graphics Artist; April Jackson, Researcher; Juan Thomassie, Art Director;
Tom Reinken, Deputy Graphics Editor; Lily Dow, Graphics Editor

Award of Excellence

The Orange County Register
Santa Ana, CA
Paul Carbo, Graphics Artist; Tia Lai, News Editor & Graphics; Nanette Bisher, AME
& Art Director

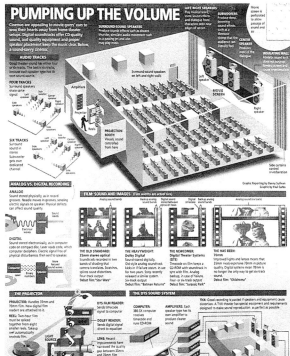

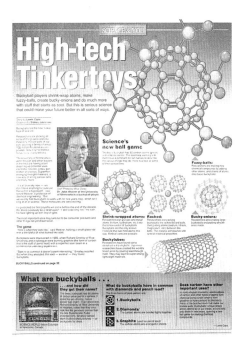

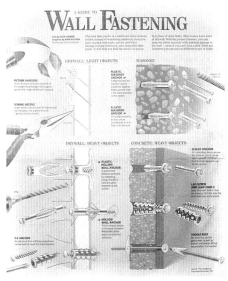

Award of Excellence

Marca
Madrid, Spain
Jose Juan Gámez, Graphics Editor; Pablo Ma Ramírez, Graphics Artist; Mar Domingo, Graphics Artist; Sofía Valgañón, Graphics Artist; Miguel Angel Fernández, Graphics Artist; Martina Gil, Graphics Artist; César Galera, Graphics Artist; Belén Vega, Graphics Artist; Chus Aycart, Graphics Artist

Award of Excellence

Star Tribune
Minneapolis, MN
Sidney Jablonski, Infographic Artist & Researcher

Award of Excellence

The Orange County Register
Santa Ana, CA
Nam Nguyen, Graphics Artist; Danny Sullivan, Graphic Reporter; Ricky Young, Graphic Reporter; Susan Peterson, Graphic Reporter; Nick Harder, Graphic Reporter; Mary Ann Milbourn, Graphic Reporter

Silver & JSR
(for comprehensive Tour de France graphics)
Marca
Madrid, Spain
Jose Juan Gámez, Graphics Editor; Pablo Ma Ramírez, Graphics Artist; Mar Domingo, Graphics Artist; Sofía Valgañón, Graphics Artist; Miguel Angel Fernández, Graphics Artist; Martina Gil, Graphics Artist; César Galera, Graphics Artist; Belén Vega, Graphics Artist; Chus Aycart, Graphics Artist

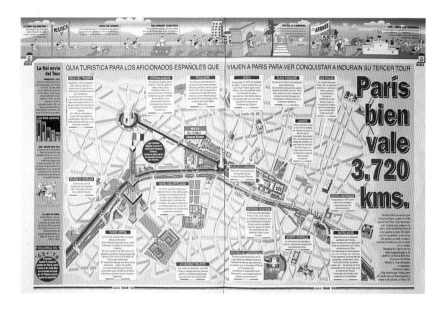

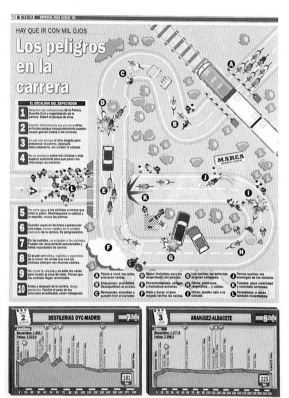

Award of Excellence
Marca
Madrid, Spain
Jose Juan Gamez, Graphics Editor; Pablo Ma Ramirez, Graphics Artist; Chus Aycart, Graphics Artist

Award of Excellence
Marca
Madrid, Spain
Jose Juan Gámez, Graphics Editor;
Pablo Ma Ramírez, Graphics Artist

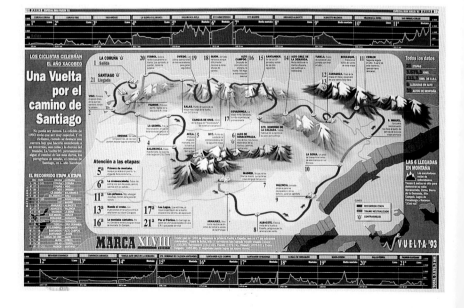

chapter

eleven

Award of Excellence
Ft. Pierce Tribune
Ft. Pierce, FL
Paul Carbo, Graphics Artist

Award of Excellence
The Hartford Courant
Hartford, CT
Patricia Cousins, Illustrator/Designer/Typography; Cheryl Magazine, Art Director; Tony Bacewicz, Photographer

Award of Excellence
El Mundo
Madrid, Spain
Rodrigo Sanchez, Art Director & Designer; Carmelo Caderot, Design Director; Popa Gomez, Designer

Award of Excellence
El Mundo
Madrid, Spain
Rodrigo Sanchez, Art Director & Designer; Carmelo Caderot, Design Director; Popa Gomez, Designer

Award of Excellence
Diario de Noticias
Funchal - Madeira, Portugal
Jose da Camara, Editor; Lurdes Gomes, Art Director; Mario
Garcia, Designer; Jeff Goertzen, Informational Graphics Concept

Before

After

Before

After

Award of Excellence
Die Furche
Vienna, Austria
Bernhard Sassmann, Publisher; Hannes Schopf, Editor; Raco
Jevtovic, Art Director; Mario Garcia, Design Consultant

Award of Excellence
The Seattle Times
Seattle, WA
David Miller, Art Director & Designer; Marian Wachter, Designer; Celeste Ericsson, Designer; Rob Kemp, Designer

Before

After

Award of Excellence
Aberdeen American News
Aberdeen, SD
Deborah Withey, Art Director & Designer; Shannon Imbery, Designer; Cindy Eikamp, Executive Editor

Before

Bronze
El Norte
Monterrey, Mexico
Lourdes de la Rosa, Designer

Before

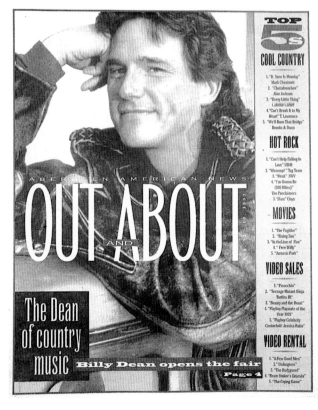

After

After

Award of Excellence

Albuquerque Journal
Albuquerque, NM
Carolyn Flynn, Design Director; Tim Coder; Journal North Editor; Bill Gerhold, Graphics Artist; Carol Cooperrider, Graphics Artist; Derek Nolen, Designer

Before

Before

After

Award of Excellence

The Albuquerque Tribune
Albuquerque, NM
Jeff Neumann, Graphics Artist & Designer; Randall K. Roberts, AME Graphics; Kevin Hellyer, Features Editor; Scott Gullett, Wild Life Editor

Award of Excellence

The Chicago Tribune
Chicago, IL
Nancy Canfield, Art Director; Troy Thomas, Illustrator

Before

After

After

Award of Excellence
The Detroit News
Detroit, MI
Felix Grabowski, Art Director & Designer; Nolan Finley, Section Editor; Mark Lett, AME; Don Asmussen, Graphics Artist; Robert Graham, Graphics Artist

Before

After

Before

After

Award of Excellence
The Ledger
Lakeland, FL
Mark Friesen, Design Editor; Daniela Dornic, Assistant Life Editor

Award of Excellence
Newsday
Melville, NY
Miriam Smith, Art Director

Before

After

Award of Excellence

The Seattle Times
Seattle, WA
David Miller, Art Director & Designer; Celeste Ericsson, Designer; Marian Wachter, Designer

Before

Before

Award of Excellence

The Seattle Times
Seattle, WA
David Miller, Art Director & Designer; Celeste Ericsson, Designer; Marian Wachter, Designer; Rob Kemp, Designer

Before

After

After

Award of Excellence

The Seattle Times
Seattle, WA
David Miller, Art Director; Celeste Ericsons, Designer; Marian Wachter, Designer; David Miller, Designer; Rob Kemp, Designer

After

Award of Excellence
The Seattle Times
Seattle, WA
David Miller, Art Director & Designer; Marian Wachter, Designer; Celeste Ericsson, Designer

Before

Before

Award of Excellence
Albuquerque Journal
Albuquerque, NM
Juliette Torrez, Designer; Paula Summar, YES Editor; Tom Harmon, Trends Editor; Frankie McCarty, Managing Editor; Paul Bearce, Photo Editor; Carolyn Flynn, Design Director

Before

After

After

Award of Excellence
The Spokesman-Review
Spokane, WA
John Nelson, Design Editor; Neal Pattison, Former AME

After

Before

After

Silver

The Orange County Register
Santa Ana, CA
Paul Carbo, Graphics Artist; Nanette
Bisher, AME/Art Director

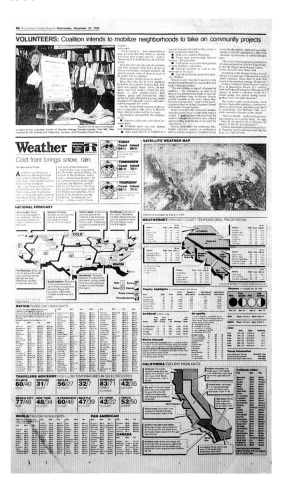

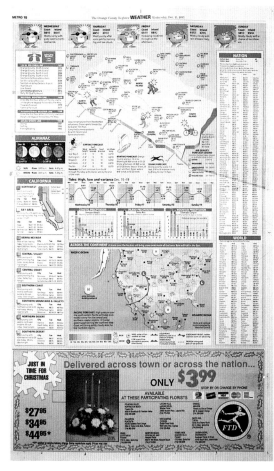

Silver

American Medical News
Chicago, IL
Barbara Dow, Art Director; Jef Capaldi, Assistant Art Director

Business

Groups grapple with income issues

Finding the right compensation plan is tough

Formula 'hopefully will keep everyone happy'
The surgery group of Bruce Steffes, MD, based each physician's revenue on individual production.

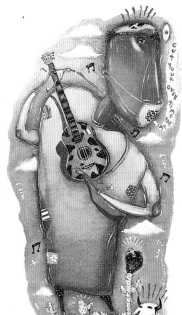

Bronze
American Medical News
Chicago, IL
Barbara Dow, Art Director; Jef Capaldi, Assistant Art Director

Before

Award of Excellence
Asahi Evening News
Tokyo, Japan
John MacLeod, Design Consultant

Before

Before

After

Award of Excellence
The Seattle Times
Seattle, WA
Marian Wachter, Designer; Celeste Ericsson, Designer; David
Miller, Art Director & Designer

After

After

Award of Excellence

The Charlotte Observer
Charlotte, NC
Barry Kolar, Business Graphics Editor; Al Phillips, Graphics Artist; Cliff Glickman, Assistant Business Editor; Brian Melton, Executive Business Editor; Tom Palmer, News Editor

Before

After

Before

After

Award of Excellence

Lexington Herald-Leader
Lexington, KY
Jim Jennings, AME Graphics; Randy Medema, Designer; Cheryl Truman, Business Editor; Chris Ware, Graphics Artist; Charles Bertram, Photographer; Debbie Cockrell, Designer

Award of Excellence

The Indianapolis Star
Indianapolis, IN
Jay Small, Art Director; Ted Daniels, AME; Curt Wellman, News Editor

Before

After

Before

Award of Excellence
The Orange County Register
Santa Ana, CA
Nanette Bisher, AME/Art Director; Helayne Perry, Assistant
News Editor/Design; Robert Beamesderfer, Copy Editor; Lisa
M. Ginther, Copy Editor; Rich Kershner, Copy Editor; Lynn
Meersman, Copy Editor

Before

Award of Excellence
Ragged Right
Toronto, Canada
Tony Sutton, Editor & Designer; Brian Gable, Illustrator;
Michael Custode, Illustrator; Alex Groen, Illustrator

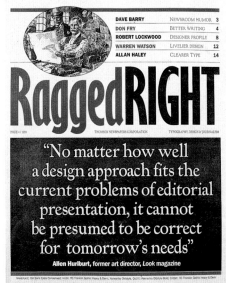

After

Award of Excellence
GeoFacts/GeoDatos- National Geographic Society
Bridgeport, WV
Bill Pitzer, Illustrator & Designer, Pitzo Graphics; Steve
Raymer, Director of the News Service; Joy Aschenbach,
Writer & Editor; John Brewer, New York Times News Service
and Syndicate

After

Award of Excellence
The Toronto Star
Toronto, Canada
Keith Branscombe, AME Director of Design; Wayne Bruan,
Editor; Karen Stephenson, Assistant Systems Editor; Lou
Clancy, ME; Roger Black, Consultant

JONAS DAGSON

Visual reporter & graphics editor, Sweden Today, Götenborg, Sweden

Jonas pioneered graphics in 1988 working as the sole artist at that paper for three years. Before graphics, he worked as an editor and page designer at the sports and news desks. He works also as a consultant and is syndicated in Scandinavia and northern Europe.

JONAS DAGSON

Reportero Visual y Editor de Gráficos, Sweden Today, Gotenborg, Suecia.

Jonas fue pionero en gráficos en 1988 trabajando por tres años como único artista en ese periódico. Antes de la gráfica, trabajó como editor y diseñador de página para las mesas de deportes y noticias. Trabaja también como consultor y es sindicalizado en Escandinavia y el norte de Europa.

TODD DUNCAN

AME/Graphics, The Charlotte Observer, NC

Todd came to the paper from Newsday in 1989 where he was picture editor. Before Newsday, he owned advertising photography studios in Milwaukee and Dallas. He also worked for the Milwaukee Journal and Ebony Magazine.

TODD DUNCAN

Gráfica/AME, The Charlotte Observer, NC.

Todd viene al periódico procedente de Newsday en 1989 donde era editor de visuales. Antes de Newsday, era dueño de estudios de fotografía publicitaria en Milwaukee y Dallas. También trabajó para el Milwaukee Journal y la Revista Ebony.

GEORGE BENGE

Executive editor, Daily Phoenix & Times-Democrat, Muskogee, OK

George is SND's president for 1994. He previously worked for The Springfield (MO) News-Leader, The Fort Lauderdale Sun-Sentinel, The Dallas Morning News, The Miami Herald and The Detroit News. He is also a member of the NAMME board of directors.

GEORGE BENGE

Editor Ejecutivo, Daily Phoenix & Times-Democrat, Muskogee, OK.

George es el presidente de SND para 1994. Previamente trabajó para The Springfield (MO) News-Leader, The Fort Lauderdale Sun-Sentinel, The Dallas Morning News, The Miami Herald y The Detroit News. Es también miembro de la junta de directores de NAMME.

JOSÉ L. DÍAZ DE VILLEGAS, JR.

Art director and illustrator of Revista Domingo, the Sunday magazine of El Nuevo Dia, San Juan, Puerto Rico

José previously has worked as a commercial animator. He now runs a design and illustration studio which services advertising and book publishing clients.

JOSÉ L. DÍAZ DE VILLEGAS, JR.

Director de Arte e Ilustrador de la Revista Domingo, revista dominical de El Nuevo Día, San Juan, Puerto Rico.

José trabajó previamente como animador comercial. Ahora maneja un estudio de diseño e ilustración que sirve a clientes en el área de publicidad y publicaciones de libros.

SUSAN MANGO CURTIS

AME/graphics, Akron Beacon Journal

Susan joined the paper in 1990 and is responsible for overseeing the paper's design. She previously worked at other papers including The Washington Post. She is chair of the Visual Task Force for the NABJ and a member of NAMME.

SUSAN MANGO CURTIS

Gráfica, AME, Akron Beacon Journal

Susan se unió al periódico y es responsable por la supervisión del diseño del periódico. Previamente trabajó en otros periódicos incluyendo The Washington Post. Es presidenta de Visual Task Force para el NABJ y miembro de NAMMB.

TIM GALLAGHER

Editor, The Albuquerque Tribune

Before 1987 Tim worked for the El Paso Herald-Post and the New Mexico Daily Lobo. While editor at The Tribune the staff has won numerous awards including the Pulitzer Prize, the Roy Howard Award for Public Service Journalism and the NPPA award for local photography and design.

TIM GALLAGHER

Editor, The Albuquerque Tribune

Antes de 1987, Tim trabajó para El Paso Herald-Post y el New Mexico Daily Lobo. Durante su estadía como editor en The Tribune, los redactores ganaron numerosos premios incluyendo el Premio Pulitzer, el Royal Howard Award por periodismo de servicio público y el premio NPPA por fotografía local y diseño.

ANA LENSE-LARRAURI
Graphic artist/designer, The Miami Herald
Ana has worked at The Herald 11 years. She has won numerous awards including the Pulitzer Prize for her work in design, illustration and graphics. She has helped to set the personality for The Herald's daily, Sunday and weekly tabloid sections.

ANA LENSE-LARRAURI
Diseñador/Artista Gráfico, The Miami Herald
Ana ha trabajado en The Herald por 11 años. Ha ganado numerosos premios incluyendo el Premio Pulitzer por su trabajo de diseño, ilustración y gráficas. Ha contribuido a establecer la personalidad de la edición diaria y dominical de The Miami Herald y de sus secciones semanales tabloide.

KURT MUTCHLER
Photo and graphics editor, The Times-Picayune
Kurt is responsible for the visual presentation of the news. He is in charge of the photo, graphics and illustration departments at the newspaper. He has won numerous awards for photography, page design and graphics editing.

KURT MUTCHLER
Editor gráfico y de fotografías, The Times-Picayune.
Kurt es responsable por la presentación visual de las noticias. Está encargado del departamento de fotografía, gráficos e ilustraciones en el periódico. Ha ganado numerosos premios de fotografía, diseño de páginas y edición gráfica.

CAROL PORTER
Art director/graphic designer of The Washington Post
Carol began her work 11 years ago art directing the Sunday feature sections, the Sunday business section and the health and food sections. She is a freelance designer in Washington, DC and has experience in commercial television.

CAROL PORTER
Director de Arte/Diseñador Gráfico de The Washington Post.
Carol empezó su trabajo hace 11 años como el director de arte de las secciones dominicales de artículos prominentes, la sección dominical de negocios y las secciones de salud y comida. También es un diseñador a destajo en Washington, DC y tiene experiencia en televisión comercial.

DALE PESKIN
AME/news and graphics, The Detroit News
Dale has earned the paper over 80 SND awards in six years. Before The News he worked in New York and Ohio. He has served as a consultant to more than a dozen newspapers. In 1993, he founded the Detroit Design Conference for Minority Journalists.

DALE PESKIN
AME/ Noticias y gráficos, The Detroit News
Dale a ganado para el periódico más de 80 premios SND en 6 años. Antes de trabajar en The News trabajó en New York y Ohio. Ha servido como consultor a más de una docena de periódicos. En 1993, fundó la Conferencia de Diseño de Detroit para Periodistas de Minorías.

VIKKI PORTER
Executive editor, The Olympian, Olympia, WA
She joined Gannett after being a professional-in-residence at the School of Journalism at the University of Kansas. She earned a Masters in Studies of Law at Yale Law School. She was a member of a Pulitzer Prize winning team at The Denver Post.

VIKKI PORTER
Editor Ejecutivo, The Olympian, Olympia, WA.
Se unió a Gannett después de ser un profesional residente en la Escuela de Periodismo en la Universidad de Kansas. Obtuvo el Master en Leyes en la Escuela de Leyes de Yale. Fue miembro del equipo ganador del Premio Pulitzer de The Denver Post.

PHILLIP RITZENBERG

Newspaper design consultant, Woodmere, NY

Phil has more than 35 years in journalism. At The New York Daily News, he was among the first to hold a senior editorial position with specific responsibility for design. He was editor and publisher of The Jewish Week in New York and a founding member of SND.

PHILLIP RITZENBERG

Consultor de Diseño de Periódicos, Woodmere, NY

Phill tiene más de 35 años en el periodismo. En The New York Daily News, estuvo entre los primeros en tener una posición editorial superior, con responsabilidad específica por el diseño. Fue editor y publicó de The Jewish Week en Nueva York y fue miembro fundador de SND.

SHARON ROBERTS

AME/design, The Press Democrat, Santa Rosa, CA

Sharon is responsible for the photo and graphics departments. She worked at The Palm Beach Post, FL, The Austin American-Statesman and The Dallas Morning News.

SHARON ROBERTS

AME. Diseño, The Press Democrat, Santa Rosa, CA.

Sharon es responsable de los departamentos de fotografía y gráfica. Trabajó en The Palm Beach Post, FL., The Austin American-Statesman y The Dallas Morning News.

MARILYN WEAVER

Professor, Department of Journalism, Ball State University, Muncie, IN

As well as teaching duties, Marilyn assisted in creating a new curriculum for the Department's graphics sequence. She is working on the development of a CD-ROM based instructional unit on crisis reporting for graphic journalists.

MARILYN WEAVER

Profesor en el Departamento de Periodismo de Ball State University, Muncle, IN.

Al igual que sus obligaciones de enseñanza, Marilyn participó en la creación de un nuevo programa de estudios para la secuencia gráfica del departamento. Está trabajando en el desarrollo de una unidad de instrucción basada en CD-ROM sobre reportes de crisis para los periodistas gráficos.

SCOTT SINES

AME, Spokesman-Review, Spokane, WA

Scott manages the photography, art, graphics, design departments, and the technology and editorial sections of the newspaper. He has been a photojournalist and editor for the past 14 years at newspapers in San Antonio, TX, and Providence, RI.

SCOTT SINES

AME, Spokesman-Review, Spokane, WA.

Scott gerencia los departamentos de fotografía, arte, gráfica y diseño y las secciones editorial y de tecnología del periódico. Ha sido reportero gráfico y editor en los últimos 14 años en periódicos de San Antonio, TX y Providence, RI.

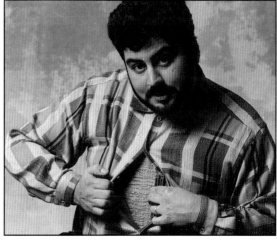

JUAN THOMASSIE

Art director, The Los Angeles Times/Orange County Edition, Costa Mesa, CA

Juan began at that newspaper in 1990 as a senior artist and in 1992 was promoted to art director of the county edition. Before joining The Times he worked for USA TODAY, The Times-Picayune, and the State-Times, Baton Rouge, LA.

JUAN THOMASSIE

Director de Arte, The Los Angeles Times/Edición del Condado Orange, Costa Mesa, CA.

Juan empezó en el periódico en 1990 como artista ya experimentado y en 1992 fue promovido a director de arte de la edición del condado. Antes de unirse a The Times trabajó para USA TODAY, The Times-Picayune y The State-Times, Baton Rouge, LA.

index of winners

by name

Adee, Bill, 44
Afanador, Ruven, 111
Aguillard, Beth, 2, 88
Aguirre, Sergio, 82
Ahrenkiel, Mogens, 94
Ailor, John, 99
Alberto Garza, Ramon, 42
Aldrich, Catherine, 120, 132
Allen, Jim, 184, 186
Allen, Scott, 246
Allen, Terry, 79, 92
Alstetter, Rob, 58
Alvarez, Emili, 117
Anderson, Chris, 201
Anderson, Daniel A., 38
Anderson, Jenny, 66, 209
Anderson, Kathy, 180
Anderson, Steve, 138
Anderson Jr., John, 52, 249
Anger, Paul, 146
Arbanas, Michael, 239
Archibald, Timothy, 75, 161, 192, 195
Arias, Raul, 150, 233
Arnam, Arn, 33, 35
Aronoff, Mark, 144
Arrue, Aurora, 75, 165, 221
Aschenbach, Joy, 264
Asmussen, Don, 26, 33, 110, 258
Astor, Joseph, 128
Aubin, Benoît, 14
Austin, Steven, 31, 41
Avni, Robin, 131, 201
Aycart, Chus, 244, 251-252

Bacewicz, Tony, 254
Bachleda, Florian, 205
Backderf, John, 216
Badovich, Theresa, 30
Baker, Richard, 120, 188, 208, 225
Ball, Russ, 219
Baltasar, Angel, 125
Baltz, Cheney, 193, 202
Bandy, Lee Ann, 87-88
Banks, Steven, 118, 125, 128
Banner, Shawn, 159
Barber, Susan, 135
Barbey, Jacques, 142
Barbot, Candace, 169, 187
Bard, Rich, 71, 206, 233
Barker, Jesse, 151
Barmann, Tim, 135, 179
Barnes, Christine, 73, 76, 160, 225, 245
Barnes, Richard, 130, 247
Baron, Linda M., 193
Barrick, Marty, 171
Barrow, Nelda, 249

Bartholomay, Lucy, 110, 112, 114, 191-192
Baumert, Harry, 197
Bausmith, Wes, 26, 232
Bautista, Rosa, 165
Beahm, Terry, 45
Beamesderfer, Robert, 264
Bean, David, 32
Bearce, Paul, 74, 260
Beaulieau, Pierre, 7
Beauregard, Claude, 14
Beck, Melinda, 100, 161
Becker, Lesley, 114
Becom, Jeffrey, 93
Behne, Mary, 146
Belamonte, Jose, 231
Belil, Ana, 100
Belil, Quique, 150
Benavides, Tono, 204, 212, 233
Benge, George, 2, 6, 46, 239, 265
Benito, Isabel, 105, 117, 126-128, 216, 221
Bennett, Richard, 51
Benny, Mike, 115
Benschneider, Benjamin, 131, 201
Benzkofer, Stephan, 42, 155
Berke, George, 38-39, 55, 62, 135, 181, 198
Berkeley, Jon, 224
Bernal, Nohemi, 79
Berthet, Jacqueline, 92, 191
Bertram, Charles, 263
Belair, Michel, 6, 11-12, 14-15
Binder, Ellen, 130
Bing, Christopher, 149, 209
Birchman, Fred, 27, 66
Bisher, Nanette, 31-32, 34, 84, 142, 223, 234, 251, 261, 264
Bissett, Tom, 31
Bissonnette, Lise, 6, 8
Black, Roger, 42, 264
Blackwell, Mark, 151
Blackwell, Patrick, 171
Blak, Poul, 192
Blasutta, Mary Lynn, 83
Blaydon, Sarah, 90
Bliss, Alan, 47
Blow, Charles, 63, 97, 139
Bodkin, Tom, 55, 63
Boone, Lyle, 59
Borda, Juliette, 218
Borgman, Tom, 151
Borowski, Nadia, 34
Bosler, Clif, 134
Bottomly, Therese, 245
Bowman, Rich, 213
Boyles, Dee, 81-82, 85-86, 162, 213, 232, 243
Bradford, Christy, 30
Bradley, Bill, 208
Branscombe, Keith, 264

Branson, Gregory A., 151, 239
Breite, Thea, 135, 176, 179, 186
Brewer, John, 264
Brewer, Linda, 79, 115
Brooker, Philip, 222, 233
Brothers, The Douglas, 163
Brown, Calef, 234
Brown, Scott M., 239, 242, 251
Brown, Tom, 134
Bruan, Wayne, 264
Bruckner, Rene, 72, 174
Brusic, Ken, 64
Bryant, Jay, 142
Bryant, Michael, 84
Buckenmeyer, Miguel, 72, 174
Buckingham-Ehrmann, Brenda, 168
Buckley, Chris, 74, 159
Buechel, Jon, 138
Burgess, John, 144
Burke, Philip, 118, 225
Burke, Tim, 146, 222
Burzynski, Sue, 30
Bustos, Tony, 119, 151
Butler, David, 246
Button, Don, 173
Buzek, Mark, 149, 202
Byer, Renee, 199
Bynum, Chris, 88
Byrne, Kevin, 31, 34, 38, 64, 84

Caderot, Carmelo, 104, 110, 114-116, 121-122, 125-127, 132, 134, 150, 160, 167, 233, 254
Cafone, Pete, 45
Caglage, Evans, 182
Calderon, Eduardo, 201
Calderon Hayes, Luisa, 31, 41, 57
Callahan, Michael, 239
Callas, Chris, 170
Calzada, Marta, 105, 117, 126-128, 216, 221
Camara, Jose da, 255
Campbell, Mike, 39, 48, 154
Campbell, Ronald, 239
Campbell, Tim, 62, 152, 249
Canfield, Nancy, 257
Cantavero Jr., Carlo F., 81, 168
Capaldi, Jef, 50, 95, 157, 174, 212, 235, 261-262
Capobianco, Pat, 78
Carbo, Paul, 34, 142, 251, 254, 261
Cardon, Michele, 68
Carignan, Roland-Yves, 6, 10-12, 15
Carlin, Joan, 39, 77
Carlos, John, 22

Carlson, Chris, 32, 53
Carne, Vernon, 44
Carney, Kim, 138
Carrasco, Modesto, 238, 240-241, 250
Carrion, Ignacio, 127
Carter, Paul, 202
Casey, Olivia, 26, 30, 54, 56
Catala, Jordi, 242
Catalano, Amy, 78
Cayea, John, 242
Cecala, Frank, 159, 245
Ceron, Juan Jose, 82-83
Cesena, Alma L., 96
Chamberlin, Charles, 79
Chambers, Bruce, 38
Champagne, Tony O., 215
Chappin, Andrew, 221
Charbonneau, Pierre, 178
Charlton, Aldona, 78, 107
Chelist, Sandra, 71
Cheverton, Richard, 142
Christ, Kirk, 49
Chwast, Seymour, 111, 118
Ciscar, Jesus, 127
Claesson, Peter, 159
Clancy, Lou, 264
Clark, Patterson, 71, 84, 169, 206, 233
Clayton, Billy Steve, 249
Clendaniel, Ed, 66, 204, 234
Clifford, Dan, 239, 244
Clifton, Denise, 66
Close, Tom, 138
Cloud, Marla, 135
Cochran, Mick, 131
Cockrell, Debbie, 263
Cocks Hamilton, Alison, 150
Coddington, Ron, 170
Coder, Tim, 257
Coe, Sue, 129
Cole, Carolyn, 201
Coll, Stanley, 205
Collier, James, 68, 84, 174
Collins, Tracy, 182, 207-208, 225, 234
Collison, Cathy, 138
Colon, Raul, 169, 209
Comet, Renee, 171
Compton, Paul, 53
Condon, James, 51
Cone, Marla, 43
Constantini, Mark, 152
Cook, Gary, 248
Cook, Steve, 152
Cooperrider, Carol, 257
Copeland, Dennis, 38, 146
Corbera, Joan, 141-142, 147, 217
Cote, Genevieve, 219
Coulson, Cotton, 120
Countryman, Andy, 136
Cousineau, Normand, 174

Cousins, Patricia, 254
Cowan, Lisa, 202
Cowden, Steve, 245, 247
Cox, Christine, 27
Cox, Gerald, 158
Cox, Keira, 154
Cox, Tracy, 45, 50-51, 73, 76, 152, 154, 160, 225, 236, 245
Cozart, Peggy, 35
Cote, Roch, 6-7, 14
Craig, Kris, 184
Crawford, Colin, 196
Croft, Micha, 174
Cronin, Anne, 242
Cronin, Bob, 136
Cronin, Brian, 223
Crosse, Mark, 197
Crow, Ted, 207
Crowe, Kathleen P., 78
Crowe, Tracy, 83
Crowley, Pat, 75, 223
Cubbison, Brian, 157
Culebro, Ulises, 206, 213, 230, 241
Curtis, Susan Mango, 37, 265
Custode, Michael, 101, 264
Cutting, Robert F., 107
Cvengros, Stephen, 33, 35

D'Avignon, Yves, 6, 12
Dalhov, Goran, 221
Dallaire, Aime, 6, 12
Dalziel, Kim, 86
Dandy, Steve, 33
Daniel Fiedler, Joseph, 171
Daniels, Cynthia, 96-97
Daniels, Ted, 263
Danilo, Eduardo, 42
Dao, Tuan, 111
Darby, Richard, 197
Darmon, Reed, 214, 223
Dashiell, Bernadette, 74, 76, 85, 159
Davaz, Carl, 202
Davis, Gina, 109, 111, 115, 123, 130, 215, 223
Davison, Pat, 134
Dawson, Jim, 152
Dawson, Susan, 83
Dawson, William, 32, 53, 157
de Andres, Jaime, 241
de la Rosa, Lourdes, 102, 256
de Miguel, Manuel, 114, 116, 134, 150, 160
de Pedro, Angel, 216, 221
Dean, Michael, 149
Dee, Roslyn, 22, 164
DeFeria, Tony, 35, 44
Deheza, Emilio, 42
DeMarzo, Camille, 147
DeMuesy, Scott, 55
Dengler, John L., 46, 151, 239
Denk, James, 24-25

Denney, Monica, 32
der Serkissian, Kayo, 130
Descoteaux, Bernard, 6-10, 12
Deveney, KayLynn, 194
DeVera, Joe, 177
Devlin, Paula, 61
Diakopoulos, Anestis, 131, 185
Diaz de Villegas Jr., Jose L., 116, 204, 207, 220
Diaz de Villegas Sr., Jose L., 204-205, 207, 220
Dickerson, Jeff, 35
Dickey, Will, 178
Dionisio, Philip, 238
Do, Ahn, 53
Doe, Kelly, 119, 170-171, 185, 189, 208, 210-211, 218
Doig, Stephen K., 244
Dolan, Mark, 48
Dolphens, Tom, 213
Domingo, Mar, 244, 251-252
Donovan, Carrie, 111
Dornic, Daniela, 258
Doughtie, Dan, 148
Douglas, Vasin, 150, 178, 182
Dow, Barbara, 49-50, 74, 95, 212, 219, 235, 261-262
Dow, Lily, 43, 139, 239, 242-243, 251
Drawson, Blair, 119
Ducassi, Nuri, 75, 164-165, 221
Duckworth, Nancy, 112, 118, 125, 128-129
Dufalla, Anita, 182, 207-208, 218, 225, 234
Duffy, Sean Patrick, 48
Dugdale, John, 115
Duke, William, 164
Dungan, Ron, 94
Dunlap-Shohl, Pamela, 91, 112, 164
Dunleavy, Chrissy, 84
Dunn, Bill, 62, 152
Dutton, Lisa, 57, 172
Duval, Mike, 135, 186
Dykman, Jackson, 249

Eames, Dave, 151
Eaton Hopper, Susie, 188
Edelson, Mark, 193, 202
Edge, Lara, 76-77, 156
Edkins, Denise, 220
Edwards, Craig, 30
Eikamp, Cindy, 86, 256
Eisenbart, Rene, 247
Eisert, Sandra, 119, 187-188, 215, 218, 224
Ekstrom-Frisk, Eleonor, 70
Ellis, Kevin E., 206
Ember, Dave, 154, 236
Emblin, Richard, 177
Endenburg, Kees, 75
Engelke, Gale, 66
Engstrom, Ron, 39

Enocson, Olle, 99
Enos, Randall, 145
Ensor, Deborah, 166
Epstein, Joe, 159
Ericsson, Celeste, 255, 259-260, 262
Escobedo, Carmen, 82-83
Everbeck, Karen T., 134, 171
Everhart-Hill, Angela, 143
Ewing, John, 185

Fabris, John, 38, 64
Farmer, Greg, 43
Farnham, Rebecca, 169
Fasolino, Teresa, 111
Fecht, Michele, 139-140
Fedele, Gene, 147, 220
Feiring, Carolita, 236
Ferguson, James, 71, 216
Fernandez, Raul, 165
Fernandez, Miguel Angel, 244, 251-252
Feyder, Susan, 51
Figler, John, 157
Finch Kellar, Toni, 139, 187
Finley, Bernadette, 31, 64
Finley, Nolan, 33, 110, 246, 258
Fischer, Martin, 134
Fischer, Sydney, 215, 218
Fisher, Gail, 196
Fisher, Mike, 206
Fitzgerald, Barry, 149
Fitzhugh, Gregg, 172
Flanders, Phill, 38, 169-170, 222
Fleming, Joe, 220
Flynn, Carolyn, 74, 219, 257, 260
Fogel, John Paul, 43
Forbes, Lynn, 84-85, 161, 205
Ford, Scott, 200
Forst, Don, 38
Foster, Phil, 52
Fowler, Linda, 159
Fox, Bert, 16, 112, 132, 176, 183, 188, 191, 193, 196, 200, 223
Fox, Randee S., 27
Fracassa, Hawkc, 33
Franklin, Michael, 84, 181
Franquet, Sarah, 75, 202
Freeman, Melanie Stetson, 181-182, 196
Frempong, Lee, 55
Fresty, Paul, 149
Freund, Alan, 200
Friedman, Jane, 62
Friesen, Mark, 258
Frishman, Mel, 38, 146
Froelich, Janet, 109, 111, 113, 115-116, 119, 123-124, 129-130, 188, 213-215, 223

Gaber, Mi-ai, 51
Gable, Brian, 264

Gabor, Tim, 125
Gabrenya, Mark, 82
Galera, Cesar, 251-252
Gallo, Aldino, 47
Gamez, Jose Juan, 243-244, 252
Gannon, James P., 139
Garcia, Mario, 255
Garcia, Pedro M., 244
Garner-Mitchell, Mary, 68, 99
Garrison, Ben, 138, 141
Gaspard, Bill, 149
Gastaldo, Walter, 205
Gatti, Jim, 30
Gauthier, Robert, 179, 188
Gay, Stephanie, 198
Gensheimer, Jim, 193
George, Don, 69, 93-94, 161
Gerdes, Marti, 168
Gerhold, Bill, 257
Giacobetti, Francis, 126
Giffels, David, 222
Gigli, Joe, 159
Gil, Martina, 251-252
Gillespie, Scott, 51
Ging, Michael, 138
Ginsburg, Max, 215
Ginther, Lisa M., 264
Gladden, John, 222
Gladstone, Penni, 106, 112, 119, 130-131
Glaser, Marilyn, 134
Glaser, Milton, 118
Glick, Jeff, 249
Glickman, Cliff, 263
Gludnason, Torkil, 119
Godson, Rory, 22
Goecke, John, 120
Goertzen, Jeff, 255
Goldman, Scott, 33, 48, 158
Gomes, Lurdes, 255
Gomez, Popa, 104, 110, 121-122, 125-127, 132, 254
Gonzalez, Eugenio, 105, 117, 126-128, 216, 221
Gordon, Dennis, 216
Gorski, Pete, 207
Goulait, Bert V., 53
Grabowski, Felix, 26, 33, 62-63, 97, 110, 139-140, 246, 258
Grace, Keith, 50
Graham, Robert, 26, 33, 63, 110, 139-140, 258
Graman, Kevin, 61
Granberg, Al, 242
Grant, Bill, 222
Grantham, Tiffany, 239
Grau, Ferran, 100, 141-142, 147, 217
Gray, Dave, 141
Green, Phil, 239, 248
Greenberg, Steve, 138, 141
Greene, Jeff, 202
Greener, Stormi, 62, 188-189
Greenfield, Lois, 109
Gregg, Michael, 177-178
Gregory, Tom, 58

Grenier, Jacques, 6, 14
Gressette, Felicia, 84
Grewe, David, 78
Griffin, C. W., 170
Griffis, Lisa M., 159
Griffone, Betts, 36
Grimes, Melissa, 90
Grin, Gayle, 87, 161
Grippi, Vincc, 61, 202, 224
Griswold, Doug, 66, 204, 234
Groen, Alex, 264
Grossfield, Stan, 191
Groth, Chuck, 88, 91
Grow, Jason M., 119
Gruau, Rene, 87
Gubern, Roman, 126
Gudnason, Torkil, 120
Guerrero, Claudia, 68
Guip, Amy, 81, 163, 223
Gullett, Scott, 68, 257
Gutierrez, Fernando, 106, 151

Hagedorn, Kathy, 222
Hales-Tooke, Hugh, 111, 115
Halls, Thom, 197
Hamersly, Kendall, 145
Hamilton, Polly, 123-124
Hancock, John, 144
Hand, Anne, 249
Hannon, Jeff, 33
Hansen, Doug, 246
Hansen, John, 183, 193
Harder, Joe, 43
Harder, Nick, 251
Harmon, Tom, 260
Harper, Jeff, 46
Harris, Nancy, 119
Harris, Peter A., 53
Harris, Roderick, 86
Hart, John, 239
Hartog, Richard, 179
Hass, Mark, 26, 140
Hatcher, Brent, 63
Hauff, Kevin, 221
Hayes, Luisa Calderon, 31, 41, 57
Hayes, Mitchell, 47, 172, 214, 236
Heaberlin, Julie, 192
Healy, Mike, 62, 189
Hegre, Kurt, 197
Heitner, Anne, 76, 224
Helfand, Jessica, 112, 132, 176, 183, 188, 223
Heller, Steven, 70, 101
Hellyer, Kevin, 68, 257
Hembd, Derek, 146, 222
Henderscheid, Dale, 51
Henderson, Felecia, 33
Hendrickson, Kevin, 245
Henle, Mark, 138
Henriquez, Hiram, 89, 146, 170, 222
Henry, Sharon, 148
Herde, Tom, 110, 112
Hermoso, Gustavo, 242
Heron, W. Kim, 136
Herrera, Marco, 51

Hess, Lydia, 214
Higgins, James V., 140
Hill, Erik, 48
Hirsch, Rick, 247
Hirschfeld, Al, 79
Hitchens, Keith, 41, 57, 172
Hively, Cindy, 200
Hodges, Jill, 51
Hoffman, Cynthia, 90
Hoffmann, Duane, 138, 141
Hogerty, Dave, 89, 169-170, 200
Holloway, David, 239
Holm, Eigil, 94
Hood, Jane, 85, 159
Hopkins, Paul, 22-23, 164
Hornbeck, Mark, 140
Horner, R. Scott, 246
Horsey, David, 138
Horsey, Kim, 141
Hourihan, Ann, 164
Howard, Bob, 30, 38
Howard, Rupert, 90
Huba, John, 111
Hubig, Dan, 208
Huffman, Perry, 246
Hulshizer, Jennifer A., 76
Humenik, John, 40, 42, 61, 155
Hundley, Kara, 42
Hunt, Douglas, 41
Huntemann, Susan, 131, 185, 198
Huskey, Warren, 186
Hutchinson, Joseph, 120

Ignaszewski, Jennifer, 119, 142, 166
Iken, Hank, 242
Ilic, Mirko, 71, 207
Imbery, Shannon, 256
Infante, Emmanual, 79
Innerst, Stacy, 208, 225
Innes, Claire C., 115, 236
Irribarren, Jorge, 222
Isip, Jordin, 205, 209, 216, 232
Izumi, Jo Anne, 219

Jablonski, Sidney, 248-249, 251
Jackson, April, 239, 243, 251
Jackson, James, 168
Jacobson, Shawn, 184, 201
Jaegerman, Megan, 242
Jaffe, Rick, 44
Jager, Jim, 48
Jantze, Michael, 2-4, 58, 61, 143
Jareaux, Robin, 159
Jarque, Fietta, 128
Jean, Paul, 242
Jean-Louis, Galie, 77, 80-82, 85-86, 91, 112, 162-164, 206, 213, 216, 219, 228, 232, 243
Jennings, Jim, 2, 263

Jensen, Gregers, 98
Jensen, John, 71
Jeskey, Ray, 110
Jess, Jill, 174
Jevtovic, Raco, 255
Jimenez, Arturo, 75
Johanson, Ulf, 70, 88, 102, 159, 183, 221
Johansson, Karin, 70, 102
Johnsson, Hans, 197
Johnston, Robin, 33, 35
Jones, Janice L., 243
Jones, Latane, 43
Jones-Hulfachor, Cindy, 31, 41, 57, 77
Jose Ceron, Juan, 82-83

Kadoch, Ariane, 88
Kafentzis, John, 61, 179, 202
Kalish, Nicki, 69, 91-93, 111, 118
Kamidoi, Wayne, 45
Kamrass, Philip, 180
Kan Lee, Jeff, 144
Kannberg, Daryl, 38, 146
Kaplan, John, 182
Kappler, Brian, 87
Kascht, John, 28, 50, 66
Kaskovich, Steve, 62-63, 139
Katz, Robyn, 112
Katz, Tonnie, 64
Kaufman, Carol, 117
Kausler, Don, 48
Kay, Jane, 152
Keating, Michael, 28
Keener, J. Kyle, 183, 200
Keiser, Beth A., 170
Keith, Luther, 33
Keller, Germaine, 51
Kelso, Karen, 34, 64
Kemp, Rob, 255, 259
Kempin, Bill, 151
Kenneally, Brenda Ann, 169
Kennedy, Tony, 51
Kenner, Herschel, 38, 146
Kerr, Tom, 78
Kershner, Rich, 264
Kessler, Meda, 156
Kettlewell, Vicky, 62
Khargie, Mignon, 85, 90, 94, 152, 231, 236
Kitagaki, Paul, 45, 196
Kitts, Tom, 159
Kland, Kurt, 167
Klein, Kim, 75, 161, 192, 195
Klein, Nick, 145
Kleinberg, Eliot, 248
Knupp, Justin, 43
Kolar, Barry, 263
Kolb, George, 46
Kolyer, Diane, 89
Koodish, Murray, 39, 53, 55, 193
Kooistra, Blair, 201
Koon, Nick, 84
Kordalski, David, 50, 144, 206, 220

Kothari, Sanjay, 112
Krasner, Carin, 129
Kraus, Jerelle, 208
Krogh, Bodil, 192
Krummel, Art, 37
Kunz, Anita, 213
Kuo, Roger, 72, 174
Kuper, Peter, 101
Kurtz, Karen, 53

Lacava, Lucie, 6-12, 14-15
Lacey, Melissa, 174
Lada, Elizabeth, 74, 95, 235
Lai, Tai, 30, 38, 142, 234, 251
Lambase, Barbara, 234
Lampkin, William, 157
Lanchester, Colleen, 98
Landis, Joan, 118
Langford, David, 154
Lanuza, Joan, 41
Larkin, Michael, 107
Lauer, Ralph, 148, 192
Lawson, Lina, 234
Layton, Steve, 50
Leclerc, Andre, 8
Lee, Craig, 90
Lee, Paul, 234
Lee, Richard, 38
Leeds, Greg, 145, 149, 169, 209
Leferink, Brenda, 148
Legault, Jean-Pierre, 6, 10
Leininger, Tom, 43, 174
Lekander, Lance, 48, 77, 164, 228
Lemke, Caroline, 43, 242
Lense-Larrauri, Ana, 146, 266
Lentini, Joan K., 48
Lessard, Marie, 12
Lester, Wes, 182
Lett, Mark, 33, 62-63, 110, 139, 246, 258
Lewis, Mike, 48
Levesque, Claude, 6, 10
Licha, Silvia, 75, 165, 221
Lima, Maria Jose, 147
Lindbohm, Kristian, 233
Linden, Bill, 44
Lins, Rico, 97
Linsenmayer, Steve, 41, 53, 57, 78, 86, 172
Londen, Ron, 31, 38, 64, 141
Loop, Paul, 32
Lopez, Juan, 38, 222
Lopinot, John, 202
Lovely, Randy, 149
Lowe, Dennis, 43
Lu, Lily, 76
Lund, Rick, 46
Lyons, Steve, 119
Lyttle, Kirk, 205, 208, 224

Mack, Bob, 150, 178, 182
MacLeod, John, 262
Madden, Steve, 248
Madueno, Pedro, 117

Magan, Luis, 106, 127, 151

Magazine, Cheryl, 254

Magerl, Chris, 45

Mahurin, Matt, 118

Molloy, James J., 176

Monahan, Iona, 87

Mones, Jim, 55

Monroe, Bryan, 39, 55, 66

Monroe, Linda, 144

Montesino, David, 55, 63, 238

Montesino Rutter, Jean, 55

Montgomery, Robb, 33, 35

Moore, Brenda, 246

Moore, Steve, 200

Morris, Chris, 45, 85, 152, 236, 245

Morris, Don, 85, 97, 249

Morris, Ron, 46

Morson, Mark, 76

Moscara, F. Soir, 159

Motichka, Dolores, 162

Moxam, Jean, 151

Mudgett, Allen, 47

Muina, Nuria, 106

Mulvany, Colin, 181, 185-186, 194, 201

Mundet, Rosa, 100, 141-142, 147, 217, 222, 240

Munoz, Benito, 241

Munoz, Reuben, 138

Murdoch, Sarah, 177-178

Mutchler, Kurt, 2, 38-39, 58, 61-62, 135, 198, 266

Myers, Reginald, 247

Nadeau, Jacques, 6, 10, 14

Nakagawa, Carol, 66

Needleman, Deborah, 170, 189

Nelson, Andy, 202

Nelson, Connie, 62

Nelson, Constance, 152, 249

Nelson, Eric, 149, 154, 178

Nelson, John, 76, 162, 202, 260

Nelson, Patti, 116-117

Neubecker, Robert, 209

Neuburger, Noel, 173

Neumann, Jeff, 68, 82, 167, 172, 257

Newhouse, Nancy, 111

Newman, Robert, 52, 173, 205, 209

Nguyen, Nam, 239, 251

Nicolosi, Michelle, 239

Nigash, Chuck, 139, 196

Nolen, Derek, 43, 257

Norgaard, Fred, 45

Norton, Thomas, 78

Nurre, Marc, 31

O'Boyle, John, 159

O'Brien, Michael, 116

O'Connor, Margaret, 55, 63

O'Keefe, David, 218

O'Midheach, Con, 22

O'Sullivan, Tim, 117

Ockenfels, Frank, 82, 163

Odette, Dave, 178

Ogami, Nancy, 128

Oliver, Merrill, 201

Oliver, Tim, 136

Olsen, Dana E., 223

Olsen, Patrick, 31, 36

Ono, Bob, 74, 159

Ontanon, Francisco, 127

Orosz, Istvan, 207

Oroza, Ilena, 146

Ortiz, Nivea, 220

Osmundson, Glenn, 185

Ostendorf, Bill, 135, 176, 179, 185-186, 198

Osterberg, Gayle, 43

Owens, James, 247, 250

Ownby, John G., 248

Palma, Eric, 52

Palmer, Ally, 67

Palmer, Randy, 220

Palmer, Tom, 263

Panagopoulos, Todd, 177

Pancrazio, Angela Cara, 193

Panichkul, Victor, 68, 190

Pantages, Marty, 146, 222

Papasian, John, 63, 238

Papendick, John, 86

Paris, Jordi, 240

Parker, Doug, 135, 181, 198

Parker, Sue, 60

Parra, S. W., 246

Parry, Nigel, 81

Parsons, Donald, 55

Patterson, D. Tom, 150, 178, 182

Pattison, Neal, 2, 260

Pauly, Miko, 50, 151

Payne, C. F., 211

Pea, John, 40, 44

Peebles, Douglas, 93

Pelle, Dan, 201

Pench, Randy, 196

Pendleton, Nancy, 225

Penn, Michael, 197

Perez, Ruben, 186

Perez de Albeniz, Javier, 127

Perez de Rozas, Carlos, 100, 117, 141-142, 147, 217, 222, 240

Perez Diaz, Carlos, 126, 147

Perkins, Lucian, 189

Perry, Helayne, 264

Persinger, Michael, 148

Peskin, Dale, 6, 26, 30, 33, 38, 54, 56, 58-59, 62-63, 140, 148, 154, 192, 266

Peterson, Diane, 165

Pett-Ridge, Christopher, 182, 207-208, 225, 234

Peyton, Tom, 73, 221

Philbrick, Andrea, 184

Philippidis, Evangelia, 220, 230

Phillips, Al, 263

Piccirillo, Gary, 40-41, 60-61

Pickel, David, 183, 193

Pierce, David, 97, 246

Pinchin, Neil C., 90, 93, 96, 244, 250

Pine, D. W., 35

Pinkney, W. Matt, 217

Pinnell, Brenda, 206

Pinson, Ginger, 76

Pires, Jose, 147

Pitts, Ted, 144, 172, 220, 236

Pitzer, Bill, 264

Plachy, Sylvia, 170

Player, Jonathan, 93

Poon, Albert, 45

Porcella, Philip, 120

Porter, Kent, 144

Porter, Tracy, 42-43, 48, 66, 72

Powazek, Derek M., 163

Powers, Guy, 85

Prast, Rhonda, 84, 145, 222, 247

Prendimano, Andrew, 78

Prestamo, Cecilia, 139, 187

Preston, Jim, 135

Precourt, Diane, 6, 14

Price, Larry, 190

Price, Tim, 224

Prisching, Jim, 134

Prouse, Marcia, 136

Puckett, David, 139, 239, 243

Puig, Acacio, 207

Pulliam, Liz, 239

Putrimas, Peter, 55

Quirk, Mari, 120

Rabin, Katie, 51, 154

Raddatz, Katy, 85

Ramborg, Anders, 51, 62, 152, 247

Ramirez, Pablo Ma, 244, 251-252

Ramos, Ramon, 238, 240-241

Ravenscraft, Stephen, 134

Ravgiala, Gail, 107

Raymer, Steve, 264

Reagan, Denise M., 31, 57, 77, 86, 172

Reese, Tom, 27

Reichman, Amy, 85

Reinken, Tom, 43, 239, 242-243, 251

Renfroe, Don, 28

Resendes, Mario, 147

Rhodes, Martin, 99, 248

Ribeironho, Jose Maria, 147

Rice, Jim, 32

Rice, Marge, 152

Rice, Steve, 38, 146

Richards, Bob, 140

Richards, Eugene, 188

Richards, Robert, 26

Richardson, Kathy, 154

Richer, Barbara, 79

Rickard, Tim, 246

Riddick, Cathy, 149

Riddick, Ken, 149

Riechi, Ruth, 83

Rigg, Joey, 106, 112, 119, 130-131, 209

Rikken, Freddy, 72

Riley, Kevin, 50

Rivlin, Hornick, 132

Rivoli, Kevin, 53, 77-78, 178

Robbins, Arnie, 248

Roberts, Charmaine, 66

Roberts, Lisa, 140

Roberts, Max, 89

Roberts, Randall K., 46, 68, 257

Roberts, Sharon, 120, 144, 165, 267

Roberts, Tom, 99, 248

Robinson, Jamie, 169

Roche, Louise, 132

Rock, Maria, 247

Rodriguez, Antonio, 238

Rodriguez, Ramon, 250

Rogers, Dinah, 198

Rollins, Ron, 144

Romig, Rob, 180

Ronald, Steve, 62

Ronay, Vivian, 53

Rondinelli, Lori, 52

Rondou, Michael, 45

Roschuni, Gil, 28

Rosell, Tina, 184

Rosenberg, Howard, 200

Rota, Kathi, 116, 129, 213, 223

Roth, Bill, 39, 91

Rountree, Stephen, 99, 248

Routman, Peter, 158

Ruberstein, Hal, 109, 111, 115

Rubio, Fernando, 238, 240, 250

Rubio, Ignacio, 106

Ruclas, Gus, 178

Russo, Anthony, 95, 235

Rutter, Jean, 63

Ryan, Greg, 50

Ryan, Kathy, 113, 116, 130, 188

Ryan, Mark, 86

Ryan, Stephen, 22-23, 164, 224

Ryden, Daniel, 197

Sage, Nickie, 97

Saget, Bedel, 36

Sale, John, 61, 179, 184, 186, 201-202

Salgado, Sabastiao, 191

Salguero, Carolina, 176

Sampedro, Gorka, 114, 238, 240-241

Samuelsson, Karin, 70, 100

Sanchez, Dina, 238, 240-241

Sanchez, Gustavo, 105, 117, 126-128, 216, 221

Sanchez, Richard, 96, 110, 246

Sanchez, Rodrigo, 104, 110, 115, 121-122, 125-127, 132, 167, 254

Sandford, Gerry, 22

Sandor, Patrick, 120

Sanford, Kellye B., 200

Santelices, Janet, 84, 145

Santow, Loren, 174

Saphino, Jose, 147

Sardar, Zahid, 106, 112, 119, 130-131, 209

Sassmann, Bernhard, 255

Saul, April, 16, 188

Schatz, Howard, 200

Schleifstein, Mark, 143

Schneider, Sandra, 101, 171

Schopf, Hannes, 255

Schumaker, Ward, 208

Schwartz, Glenn, 45

Scmitt Boettcher, Marci, 152

Scopin, Joseph, 28, 53, 66, 162

Sealock, Rick, 157, 212, 235

Searle, Ronald, 208

Sedam, Stephen, 76, 236, 249

Sedlar, Pat, 204, 232

Seebacher, Noreen, 246

Segal, Jacqueline, 81, 168

Seifert, Channon, 165

Selby, Bob, 225

Senior, Paulette, 202

Sennott, Rick, 189

Serra, Jaime, 241

Settle, Gary, 131, 201

Severson, John, 149

Sevick, Joe, 55

Sforza, Teri, 239

Shanklin, Pat, 90

Shannon, David, 71, 224

Shantic, Diana, 98, 138

Shapiro, Marilyn, 84

Sharpe, Scott, 193

Shaver, Julie, 55, 63

Shaw, Rick, 201

Shea, Dan, 61

Shepherd, Jan, 78

Sherlock, John, 155

Shields, Doris, 239

Shimabukuro, Betty, 34, 53, 141-142

Shoaff, Susan, 143

Shoulak, Joe, 152, 154

Shoun, Brenda, 34, 53, 64, 68, 141-142

Siegel, Harris, 98

Sievers, Anette, 99

Siggins, Ger, 22

Sill, Melanie, 193

Silvertsson, Elisabeth, 70

Simon, Jane, 99

Simon, Meri, 148

Sines, Scott, 2, 61, 185-186, 193, 201-202, 224, 267

Siu, Peter, 147

Sklut-Lettire, Meryl, 174

Sky, Alice, 189

Slovut, Gordon, 248

Sluder, Mark, 194

Smale, Brian, 170

Small, Jay, 263

Smith, Bill, 234

Smith, Lane, 170, 218, 235

Smith, Mike, 136

Smith, Miriam, 258

Smith, Owen, 130, 210, 214

Snyder, Bonnie, 146, 222

Soderbom, Lars, 159, 183

Sokolow, Rena, 79, 120

Soligian, Debbi, 246

Soltes, Harley, 201

Soqui, Ted, 200

Souza, Nick, 184

Spade, Sue, 213

Spalenka, Greg, 224

Spino, Pete, 216, 219

Stackelberg, Ewa, 99

Stamm, Alan, 62-63, 139

Stano, Randy, 3, 38, 71, 84, 89, 145-146, 206, 222, 233, 239, 247

Starr, Charles, 96

Stauffer, Brian, 72, 167

Steele, Laura, 234

Stegel, Mark, 149

Stehrenberger, Michiko, 234

Steinberg, James, 236

Stenberg, Rune, 70, 102, 159, 183

Stephenson, Karen, 264

Sterngold, Nancy, 158

Stevens, Carol, 139

Stewart, Tony, 39

Stickland, Billy, 22

Stirnkorb, Amy, 84, 97

Stricklin, Walt, 35

Strong, Bruce, 34, 53, 141

Stubbe, Glen, 28

Sullivan, Danny, 239, 251

Sullivan, Jem, 49, 95, 235

Summar, Paula, 74, 260

Summers, Mark, 101

Summers, Tim, 155

Surmick, Chad, 144

Sutton, Tony, 101, 264

Suwyn, M. Daniel, 31-32, 41, 53, 57, 78, 157

Sveningson, Ulf, 88, 99

Sweat, Stacy, 134

Sweeny, Glynis, 157

Sweeny, Glynnis, 232

Swisher, Molly, 39, 55, 204, 209, 234

Szerlag, Hank, 138

Szydlowski, Steve, 185

Taffet, Marc, 220

Talbot, David, 73, 76, 160, 225

Talbott, Kenny P., 224

Tanaka, Karen, 170, 185
Tarver, Ron, 193
Tascon, Mario, 238, 240-241
Teghammar-Arell, Karin, 70
Tepps, David, 45
Terek, Donna, 192
Terkowitz, Craig, 195
Thain, Alastair, 128
Thatcher, Lisa, 134
Thayer, Bob, 131
Thomas, Cathy, 84
Thomas, Jeff, 39, 55, 193
Thomas, Lance, 151
Thomas, Troy, 257
Thomassie, Juan, 43, 239, 242-243, 251, 267
Thompson, Kate, 209
Thompson, Philip, 71, 216
Thompson, Rachel G., 43
Thompson, Richard, 116, 171
Thomson, John, 50, 144
Tigano, Catherine, 218
Tilley, Debbie, 172
Timmons, Bonnie, 174, 235
Tlumacki, John, 191
Tobin, David, 77
Tomaro, Dave, 40, 44
Tomaszewski, Mark, 32
Tombaugh, Brian, 57
Tomine, Adrian, 173
Tompor, Susan, 139
Torbjorn, Kjeld, 94, 168
Torrez, Juliette, 74, 260
Towery, Earl, 249
Trauer, K. C., 43
Tremblay, Odile, 10, 15
Trenholm, Zach, 209, 236
Trenholm, Zak, 73, 76, 160
Treston, Laura, 208
Trevarthen, Susan, 32
Trowsdale, Frances, 86
Truman, Cheryl, 263
Trumbull, Todd, 248
Tucker, Eric, 118
Tuckwood, Jan, 202
Tuma, Rick, 134
Turner, Billy, 33
Turner, Tyrone, 62, 135, 198
Turnley, David, 136
Turnley, David C., 136
Tuttle, Jean, 91
Tyska, Jane, 82

Uram, Laura, 116
Urbanski, Steve, 207
Utley, Joanne S., 38

Valdez, Patti, 219
Valenti, Michael, 111, 118, 242
Valganon, Sofía, 244, 251-252
Vallbona, Nuri, 135
Van Asch, Fraser, 193
Van Hemmen, Pim, 159
Van Pelt, John, 134

Van Slambrouck, Paul, 39, 55
Van Tassel, Debbie, 37
Vanderwarker, Peter, 114
Vavasour, Tom, 22
Vega, Belen, 251-252
Vegella, Patricia, 97
Velasco, Juan, 240-241, 250
Velasco, Samuel, 206-207, 232, 240-241, 250
Veneski, Rob, 246
Vieira, Al, 150, 178, 182
Vincent, Kathleen, 150
Viskupic, Gary, 208
Vitt, Shawn, 214, 223
Vogle, Susan, 219
Vondracek, Woody, 222
Vorela, Juan, 110
Voros, Bob, 249
Voss, Ellen, 35

Wachter, Marian, 255, 259-260, 262
Wagner, Joseph, 225
Wakano, Carol, 128
Wakely, Rick, 184
Walker, Richard, 67
Walker, Tracy, 172, 236
Ware, Chris, 263
Wark, John, 97
Warner, Wendi, 33, 35
Watson, Paul, 180
Watts, Paul, 66
Webb, Keith A., 24-25, 87
Weeks, John, 36
Wei, Paiching, 51
Weideman, Rob, 151
Wellman, Curt, 263
Wells, Annie, 144
Wernhamm, Gunilla, 183
Wesselhoeft, Conrad, 31, 36
West, Vic, 32
White, Eric, 212, 219, 235
White, Tim, 82
Whitt, Alan, 58
Whitton, Dennis, 47
Widebrant, Mats, 70, 99
Wigginton, Mark, 245, 247
Williams, Anne C., 179, 184, 193, 195, 201
Williams, Dave, 189
Williams, Eric, 35
Williams, Everhard, 114
Williams, Genevieve, 90
Williams, Greg, 219, 225
Williams, Jill, 78
Williamson, Ted, 138
Willis, Chris, 26, 33
Wilner, Paul, 106, 112, 119, 130-131, 209
Wilson, John, 50
Winstead, Roger, 183
Winter, Vic, 151
Winters, Dan, 112
Wintersteller, Nan, 193
Wirsen, Stina, 205
Wirtz, Michael S., 132

Wise, Michelle, 245, 247
Wisnewski, Andrea, 172, 214, 236
Withey, Deborah, 2, 24-25, 37, 60, 86, 136, 138, 232, 256
Wolfe, Art, 112
Wolfe, Ezra, 43, 174
Wolff, Tom, 170, 185
Wolfson, Stan, 38
Wong, Gwendolyn, 157, 174, 223, 235
Wood, Don, 236
Wright, Randy, 188
Wyatt, Don, 55

Yamanaka, Cindy, 114
Yarnold, David, 39, 55
Yarosh, Lee, 37, 60
Yetts, Stuart, 236
Yonzon, Ben, 35
Young, Lisa, 150
Young, Ricky, 251

Zafis, Mary Jo, 96, 181
Zajakowski, Michael, 40
Zakarov, Christopher, 115
Zedek, Dan, 100
Zeff, Joe, 25, 37, 55, 58, 60
Zellman, Ande, 191
Zent, Sherman, 149
Zerby, Mike, 62
Zimmerman, Max, 173
Zisk, James, 38
Zollinger, Lisa, 85, 159, 245

index
by publication

ABC, 238, 240, 250
Aberdeen American News, 86, 256
Advocate and Greenwich Time, The, 81, 168
Akron Beacon Journal, 37, 216, 265
Albuquerque Journal, 74, 219, 257, 260
Albuquerque Tribune, The, 39, 46, 68, 76-77, 82, 156, 158, 167, 172, 194, 257, 265
American Medical News, 49-50, 74, 95, 157, 174, 212, 219, 235, 261-262
Anchorage Daily News, 39, 48, 77, 80-82, 85-86, 91, 112, 154, 162-164, 206, 213, 216, 219, 228, 232, 243
Ann Arbor News, 47
Arizona Republic, The, 138, 154, 219
Asahi Evening News, 262
Asbury Park Press, The, 78, 98
Atlanta Journal-Constitution,The, 35, 44
Augusta Chronicle, The, 148, 245

Baltimore Jewish Times, 112, 195
Baltimore Sun, The, 120
Berlingski Tidende, 98
Birmingham Post-Herald, 48
Boston Globe Magazine, The, 107, 110, 112, 114, 120, 132, 191-192
Boston Globe, The, 78-79, 83, 90, 92-93, 96-97, 99, 244, 246, 250

Charlotte Observer, The, 90, 148, 194, 206, 263, 265
Chicago Reader, The, 97
Chicago Sun-Times, 44
Chicago Tribune, 33, 35, 134, 257
Christian Science Monitor, The, 30, 71, 134, 171, 181-182, 196
Citizen, The, 40-41, 53, 60-61, 77-78, 178
Communication Week International, 220
Computer Reseller News, 147, 220
Contra Costa Times, 148

Dagens Nyheter, 55, 99, 205
Daily Camera, 52

Dallas Morning News, The, 87-88, 134, 150, 182, 265, 267
Dallas Morning News/Dallas Life, 114
Dallas Observer, 156
Davis Enterprise, The, 167
Dayton Daily News, 50, 144, 206, 220
Des Moines Register, The, 59, 63, 154, 197, 229
Detroit Free Press Magazine, 115, 232
Detroit Free Press, 2, 24-25, 37, 45, 55, 58, 60, 87, 136, 138, 236
Detroit News, The, 26, 30, 33, 38, 54, 56, 58-59, 62-63, 97, 110, 139-140, 148, 154, 177, 192, 204, 232, 246, 258, 265-266
Diario 16, 126, 147, 173
Diario de Noticias, 147, 255
Die Furche, 255

Eastside Week, 101
El Mundo Deportivo, 41, 150
El Mundo, 104, 110, 114-116, 121-122, 125-127, 132, 134, 160, 167, 204, 206-207, 212-213, 226, 230, 232-233, 238, 240-241, 250, 254
El Norte, 73, 75, 79, 82-83, 102, 256
El Nuevo Dia, 116, 204-205, 207, 220, 265
El Nuevo Herald, 75, 164-165, 221
El Pais, 63, 105-106, 117, 126-128, 151, 207, 216, 221, 231, 242
El Periodico de Catalunya, 110, 241-242
Emporia Gazette, The, 174

Financial Times, 71, 86, 216, 221
Florida Times-Union, The, 150, 178, 182
Florida Today, 246
Fort Worth Star-Telegram, 68, 148, 190, 192
Fresno Bee, The, 197, 246
Ft. Pierce Tribune, 254

Gazette, The, 87, 161
Globe and Mail, The, 149, 154, 177-178
Goteborgs-Posten, 70, 88, 99-100, 102, 159, 183, 221
Greensboro News & Record, 180, 246

Hartford Courant, The, 116-117, 139, 187, 254
Holland Sentinel, The, 178
Home News, The, 78
Horsens Folkeblad, 94, 168
Houston Chronicle, 149, 200
Houston Post, The, 135

Indianapolis Star, The, 73, 217, 221, 263

Journal and Courier, 168
Journal Review, 40, 44

Kansas City Star, The, 151, 213
Kauppalehti Optio, 233

LA Weekly, 200, 234
La Vanguardia Magazine, 117
La Vanguardia, 100, 141-142, 147, 217, 222, 240
Le Devoir, 3-15
Ledger, 258
Lexington Herald-Leader, 263
Lima News, The, 173
Los Angeles Daily News, 178, 222
Los Angeles Times Magazine, 108, 110, 112, 118, 125, 128-129
Los Angeles Times, 43, 71, 83, 98, 128-129, 139, 196, 200, 239, 242-243, 247, 250-251, 267

Maine Sunday Telegram, 33, 207
Marca, 243-244, 251-252
Medina County Gazette, The, 222
Mesa Tribune, 94
Miami Herald, The, 38, 71, 84, 89, 145-146, 169-170, 187, 200, 206, 222, 233, 239, 244, 247, 265-266
Middlesex News, The, 78
Mobile Press Register, The, 239
Morgenavisen Jyllands-Posten, 192

National Law Journal, The, 41
New York Newsday, 38
New York Times Magazine, The, 109, 111, 113, 115-116, 118-119, 123-124, 129-130
New York Times, The, 36, 45, 50, 55, 63, 69-71, 79, 90-93, 101, 158, 171, 188, 207-208, 213-215, 223, 238, 242

News & Observer, The, 156, 183, 193-194, 206, 263-266
News-Press, 149
News-Review, The, 168
News-Sentinel, The, 31-32, 41, 53, 57, 77-78, 86, 157, 172
Newsday, 208, 238, 258, 265
NRC Handelsblad, 72, 75

Olympian, The, 53, 266
Orange County Register, The, 31-32, 34, 38, 53, 64, 68, 84, 141-142, 223, 234, 239, 251, 261, 264
Oregonian, The, 214, 223, 245, 247
Outlook, 179

Palm Beach Post, The, 75, 149, 159, 193, 202, 223, 234, 248, 267
Philadelphia Daily News, The, 155
Philadelphia Inquirer Magazine, The, 3, 16-20, 112, 132, 176, 183, 188, 191, 193, 196, 200, 223
Philadelphia Inquirer, The, 79, 84
Phoenix Gazette, The, 45, 119, 142, 151, 166, 225
Pittsburgh Post-Gazette, 182, 207-208, 218, 225, 234
Portland Press Herald, 184-185
Post-Standard, The, 157
Post-Star, The, 33, 48, 158
Press Democrat, The, 144, 165, 267
Press-Enterprise, The, 76, 184, 236, 249
Providence Journal-Bulletin, The, 135, 176, 179, 184-186, 198, 225

Ragged Right, 101, 264
Reforma, 42
Register-Guard, 202
Reporter, 53, 68, 77, 139-140, 143, 152, 169, 197, 239, 246-249, 251, 265
Rhode Islander Magazine, The, 131
Richmond Times-Dispatch, 68, 99, 224, 248
Rockford Register Star, 50
Rocky Mountain News, 225

Sacramento Bee, The, 140, 196, 201
Sacramento News and Review, 173

San Bernadino County Sun, The, 31, 36
San Diego Union-Tribune, The, 49, 84, 96-97, 149, 179, 181, 188
San Francisco Chronicle, The, 208
San Francisco Examiner, 45, 51, 69, 73, 76, 84-85, 90, 93-94, 106, 112, 119, 130-131, 152, 154, 160-162, 205, 208-209, 225, 231, 236, 245
San Gabriel Valley Newspapers, 248
San Jose Mercury News, 39, 45, 53, 55, 66, 119, 187-188, 193, 196, 204, 209, 215, 218, 224, 234
Santa Fe New Mexican, The, 166
Scotland on Sunday, 67
Seattle Post-Intelligencer, 138, 141
Seattle Times, The, 27, 46, 66, 131, 201, 255, 259-260, 262
Seattle Weekly, 100
Spokesman-Review, The, 61, 76, 162, 179, 181, 184-186, 193-195, 201-202, 224, 260

Springfield News, The, 180
Springfield News-Leader, 46, 151, 239
St. Louis Post-Dispatch, 88, 91, 151
St. Paul Pioneer Press, 55, 76, 185, 205, 208, 224
St. Petersburg Times, The, 97, 249
Star Tribune, 51, 62, 152, 188-189, 199, 248-249, 251
Star-Ledger, The, 74, 76, 85, 159, 245
Sun, The, 42, 43, 47-48, 66, 72, 214, 236
Sunday Times, The, 239, 248
Sunday Tribune, The, 22-23, 164, 224
Sydsvenska Dagbladet, 197
Syracuse Newspapers, The, 199

Tallahassee Democrat, 31, 46, 157
Tampa Tribune, The, 218-219, 224-225
Times Herald Record, The, 180
Times, The, 40, 42, 47, 61, 166, 168, 177

Times-Picayune, The, 33, 38-39, 55, 58, 61-62, 88, 135, 143, 180-181, 198, 215, 266-267
Toronto Star, The, 180, 264

UCSD Guardian, The, 72, 174
University Daily Kansan, The, 43, 174

Village Voice, The, 52, 173, 205, 209
Virginian-Pilot, The, 43, 51, 249

Wall Street Journal Reports, The, 145, 149, 209
Wall Street Journal, The, 169
Washington Post Magazine, The, 119-120, 170-171, 185, 189, 208, 210-211, 218, 225
Washington Post, The, 52, 249, 265-266
Washington Times, The, 28, 31, 46, 53, 66, 162
Watertown Press, 82
Wichita Eagle, The, 189

Special Thanks:

The following people assisted during the judging at The S.I. Newhouse School of Public Communications.

Professional Assistants:
G.W. Babb, design director, *American-Statesman,* Austin, TX; Jef Capaldi, assistant art director, *The American Medical News,* Chicago, IL; Neil Chase, president, *Chase Publications,* Washington, DC; Ray Chattman, executive director, *Society of Newspaper Design;* Carolyn Flynn, design director, *The Albuquerque Journal;* Kelly Frankeny, art director, *San Francisco Examiner;* Juan Giner, professor, *University de Navarra,* Pamplona, Spain; Scott Goldman, sports editor, *The Record,* Troy, NY; Michael Jantze, assistant graphics editor, *The Times-Picayune,* New Orleans, LA; Lucie Lacava, art director, *Le Devoir,* Montreal; Bob Malish, Coppell, TX; Marshall Matlock, associate professor, *The S.I. Newhouse School of Public Communications,* Syracuse University; Bob Shields, copy editor, *The Daily Star,* Oneonta, NY; Harris Siegel, AME/design, *Asbury Park Press,* Neptune, NJ; Janis Sih, design editor, *The Arizona Republic,* Phoenix; Randy Stano, director of editorial art & design, *The Miami Herald;* Shamus Walker, Syracuse

Student Assistants:
Marc Bailes, Jeffrey Capellini, David DeVito, Steve Dorsey, Thomas Dowd, Julio Gernandez, Colette Guadagnino, David Josselyn, David Kraus, Titus Mbuya, Danielle Parks, Alana Schneider, Juris Tihonovs

Taking time out: Kelly Frankeny, Janis Sih, G.W. Babb, Harris Siegel, Lucie Lacava, Michael Jantze, Jef Capaldi, Scott Goldman